"The phrase 'health of the environment' is not a literary convention. It has real biological meaning, because the surface of the earth is truly a living organism. Without the countless and immensely varied forms of life that the earth harbors, our planet would be just another fragment of the universe with a surface as drab as that of the moon and an atmosphere inhospitable to man."

—René Dubos, from the chapter *Limits of Adaptability*

IS OUR ENVIRONMENT TO BE DEALT WITH IN THESE TERMS, OR IS IT TO BE HANDED OVER TO CEASELESS, UNTHINKING DEVELOPMENT BY THOSE WHO THINK ONLY OF WHAT IT COULD YIELD TO THEM TODAY?

There is a generation of Americans who are demanding better answers to this question, and to many more about our environment. They speak out in this book with an urgency born of the realization that time is running out. They are joined by those who have long warned that our reckless devotion to headlong development will threaten our very existence. At most we have a decade to deal with some of the problems. In many cases we have already damaged the environment beyond repair.

The Teach-Ins to be held on April 22nd are a hopeful turning point in the battle to save what is left and rebuild what we can. The real turning point is at hand for each of us in our own community and the information and suggestions found in THE ENVIRONMENTAL HANDBOOK can become the source for our efforts. Read it and look around. There's a planet that needs your help . . .

THE
ENVIRONMENTAL
HANDBOOK

PREPARED FOR THE FIRST NATIONAL
ENVIRONMENTAL TEACH-IN

EDITED BY GARRETT DE BELL

A BALLANTINE/FRIENDS OF THE EARTH BOOK

Ballantine Books, Inc. is an
INTEXT Publisher
NEW YORK

FRIENDS OF THE EARTH, founded in 1969 by David Brower, is a non-profit membership organization streamlined for aggressive political and legislative activity aimed at restoring the environment misused by man and at preserving remaining wilderness where the life force continues to flow freely.

FRIENDS OF THE EARTH is neither tax-deductible nor tax-exempt in order to fight without restrictions and invites your participation.

Addresses:

FRIENDS OF THE EARTH

30 East 42nd Street
New York, N.Y. 10017

451 Pacific Avenue
San Francisco, California 94133

323 Maryland Avenue, N.E.
Washington, D.C. 20006

1372 Kapiolani Blvd.
Honolulu, Hawaii 96814

P.O. Box 1977
Anchorage, Alaska 99501

Hardcover edition SBN 345-01892-3-595
Trade paperbound edition SBN 345-01893-1-195
Paperbound edition SBN 345-01894-X-095

"archie and mehitabel," from *the life and times of archie and mehitabel* by Don Marquis, copyright © 1935 by Doubleday & Co., published by Doubleday & Co.

Excerpted remarks by John W. Gardner from speech delivered to The National Press Club, Washington, December 9, 1969.

"A Time for Sarsaparilla," by David Brower, from Foreword to *Summer Island: Penobscot Country*, by Eliot Porter, copyright © 1966 by the Sierra Club, published by the Sierra Club; paperbound edition by Ballantine Books, Inc.

"The Historical Roots of Our Ecologic Crisis," by Lynn White, Jr., from *Science*, Vol. 155, pp. 1203-1207, 10 March, 1967. Copyright © 1967 by American Association for the Advancement of Science.

"The Tragedy of the Commons," by Garrett Hardin, from *Science*, Vol. 162, pp. 1243-1248, 13 December, 1968. Copyright © 1968 by American Association for the Advancement of Science.

First Printing: January, 1970
Second Printing: February, 1970
Third Printing: March, 1970

Printed in the United States of America

BALLANTINE BOOKS, INC.
101 Fifth Avenue, New York, N.Y. 10003

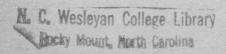

from The Life and Times of Archy and Mehitabel

Don Marquis

"dear boss i was talking with an ant the other day and he handed me a lot of gossip which ants the world around are chewing among themselves

"i pass it on to you in the hope that you may relay it to other human beings and hurt their feelings with it

"no insect likes human beings and if you think you can see why the only reason i tolerate you is because you seem less human to me than most of them

"here is what they are saying

"it wont be long now it wont be long man is making deserts on the earth it wont be long now before man will have used it up so that nothing but ants and centipedes and scorpions can find a living on it

"man has oppressed us for a million years but he goes on steadily cutting the ground from under his own feet making deserts deserts deserts

"we ants remember and have it all recorded in our tribal lore when gobi was a paradise swarming with men and rich in human prosperity it is a desert now and the home of scorpions ants and centipedes

"what man calls civilization always results in deserts man is never on the square he uses up the fat and greenery of the earth each generation wastes a little more of the future with greed and lust for riches.

"north africa was once a garden spot and then came carthage and rome and despoiled the storehouse and now you have sahara sahara ants and centipedes "toltecs and aztecs had a mighty civilization on this continent but they robbed the soil and wasted nature and now you have deserts scorpions ants and centipedes and the deserts of the near east followed egypt and babylon and assyria and persia and rome and the turk the ant is the inheritor of tamerlane and the scorpion succeeds the caesars

"america was once a paradise of timberland and stream but it is dying because of the greed and money lust of a thousand little kings who slashed the timber all to hell and would not be controlled and changed the climate and stole the rainfall from posterity and it wont be long now it wont be long till everything is a desert from the alleghenies to the rockies the deserts are coming the deserts are spreading the springs and streams are drying up one day the mississippi itself will be a bed of sand ants and scorpions and centipedes shall inherit the earth

"men talk of money and industry of hard times and recoveries of finance and economics but the ants wait and the scorpions wait for while men talk they are making deserts all the time getting the world ready for the conquering ant drought and erosion and desert because men cannot learn

"rainfall passing off in flood and freshet and carrying good soil with it because there are no longer forests to withhold the water in the billion meticulations of the roots

"it wont be long now it wont be long till earth is barren as the moon and sapless as a mumbled bone

"dear boss I relay this information without any fear that humanity will take warning and reform signed archy."

Contents

Acknowledgments

I would like to acknowledge the assistance of the many people whose help made this book possible. David Brower of Friends of the Earth suggested the idea of the book to me and arranged for its publication. Donald Aitken, a director of Friends of the Earth, arranged for my initial meetings with potential contributors from the Eastern U.S. Al Robins of the Berkeley Ecology Switchboard helped arrange meetings in the Berkeley area. Kenneth Brower and Larry Luce gave invaluable assistance with writing and editing. I would like to give special thanks to my father, Daryl, and my wife, Suzy, for their help and encouragement, and to my mother for unfailing enthusiasm for my ecological career.

Foreword

In 1969 the United States woke up to the fact that the richest country in the world is in the middle of an environmental crisis. We said good-bye to pelicans, realized that the ubiquitous automobile was the cause of smog and of the Santa Barbara oil slick, and meditated on the fact that our burgeoning multiciplicity of air conditioners, clothes dryers and other aids to gracious living meant another ugly power plant. Mother's milk, we were told, wasn't fit to drink.

We were told that starvation was in store for the "underdeveloped" countries, more cancer in store for the affluent. We learned the meaning of scientific doubletalk. We learned that when scientists said "We have no evidence that DDT is harmful to humans" they meant that the study was still in progress, and *we* were the experimental animals. In fact, many experiments were being conducted on us simultaneously on the greatest conglomeration of guinea pigs ever—smog, tranquilizers, calcium cyclamate, monosodium glutamate, hairspray, deodorants, lead, strontium-90, noise—to name only a few. Statisticians had a peculiar worry: they wouldn't be able to tell exactly how much of the increased cancer, emphysema, mental illness, deafness, and other disease to attribute to any particular environmental insult.

Toward the end of the year the media and the politicians picked up on ecology. We had Governor Reagan's conference at Los Angeles on California's changing environment and the Department of State's U.S. National Commission for UNESCO meeting in San Francisco. At both of these conferences there was a feeling of unreality among the younger participants. We heard statements from many sources. Reagan, denying that he had ever said "If you've seen one redwood tree, you've seen 'em all," was now seeking conservation credentials. The business, water and other vested interests talked much of "practicality, contractual agreements, projected demand, political realities," and about where the money would come from. The ecologists said the world was going under.

Many proposals, both good and bad, were made. But we were uneasy. There was no real feeling of urgency on the part of most participants, even with all the talk about the issue being survival. This was just one of a lifetime of conferences and conventions. There was no indication of any real change in priorities. On our part we were still left with the feeling that when you've attended one conference, you've been to them all.

Only the young seemed to feel any sense of urgency —for inaction now means they will watch this world being destroyed. The California media made it quite clear that these conferences would have been just further sessions of endless talk if it hadn't been for the youth who advanced specific proposals for action.

After the UNESCO conference ended on November 25, David Brower asked me to put together a book for Friends of the Earth (FOE) to serve as a source of ideas and tactics for the April 22 first annual teach-in on the environmental crisis. We thought that the one-month deadline for the writing was impossible, that we could easily spend a year on it. *But a year is about one-fifth of the time we have left if we are going to preserve any kind of quality in our world.*

The material presented in the following pages is varied. The intention of most of the writers, it will be evident, is not to praise the country's present industrial arrogance, but to put a stop to it. Selections include articles written by students and recently self-exiled non-students; suggestions toward an ecological platform; a number of reprinted essays by authorities on economic, ecological, cultural and political change; suggestions and tactics for change; a bibliography of books; and a bibliography of films.

We expect many ideas to be refined as they are put into practice. We hope that much critical discussion, followed by action, will take place as a result of this year's teach-in.

I view this year's teach-in as an attempt to come to grips with the problems of our deteriorating environment at the level of the individual private citizen. The conditions and the media have made people aware of the problems. Now we must propose workable alternatives to our present patterns of living. The ideas in this book represent the thinking of a number of people who have been aware of the ecological crisis for many years. Yet all the answers are not in. Many of our suggestions are for further research in definite directions.

At the end of the book are a number of tear sheets for your responses. We hope that you will respond with any specific criticisms or suggestions that you may have for improving the quality of our environment. Any solutions, projects, or tactics that you have found effective should be sent to: Friends of the Earth, 30 East 42nd Street, New York, New York 10017.

We would like to include examples of successful or unsuccessful action in next year's edition to serve as background for other communities. If you want to do a chapter on any topic for next year, send an inquiry to FOE.

There are also membership applications for some of the groups that are lobbying in Washington and at the state level for a better environment. Contributions to these groups are not tax-deductible but they do depend on a large number of contributors to finance their operations. We urge you to support them as well as the more established conservation groups listed in the section on groups. Some people are cynical about the effectiveness of electoral politics, lobbyists, and so forth. But the vested interests spend millions to maintain their Washington offices. They certainly feel it is worthwhile to have their voices heard frequently on Capitol Hill. Can we afford to do less?

GARRETT DE BELL

The Meaning of Ecology

Five Views

Smokey the Bear Sutra

Once in the Jurassic, about 150 million years ago,
the Great Sun Buddha in this corner of the Infinite
Void gave a great Discourse to all the assembled elements
and energies: to the standing beings, the walking beings,
the flying beings, and the sitting beings—even grasses,
to the number of thirteen billion, each one born from a
seed, were assembled there: a Discourse concerning
Enlightenment on the planet Earth.

"In some future time, there will be a continent called
America. It will have great centers of power called
such as Pyramid Lake, Walden Pond, Mt. Rainier, Big Sur,
Everglades, and so forth; and powerful nerves and channels
such as Columbia River, Mississippi River, and Grand
Canyon. The human race in that era will get into troubles all
over its head, and practically wreck everything in spite of
its own intelligent Buddha nature."

"The twisting strata of the great mountains and the pulsings
of great volcanoes are my love burning deep in the earth.
My obstinate compassion is schist and basalt and granite,
to be mountains, to bring down the rain. In that future
American Era I shall enter a new form: to cure the
world of loveless knowledge that seeks with blind hunger;
and mindless rage eating food that will not fill it."

And he showed himself in his true form of

SMOKEY THE BEAR.

A handsome smokey-colored brown bear standing on his hind legs, showing that he is aroused and watchful.

Bearing in his right paw the Shovel that digs to the truth beneath appearances; cuts the roots of useless attachments, and flings damp sand on the fires of greed and war;

His left paw in the Mudra of Comradely Display—indicating that all creatures have the full right to live to their limits and that deer, rabbits, chipmunks, snakes, dandelions, and lizards all grow in the realm of the Dharma;

Wearing the blue work overalls symbolic of slaves and laborers, the countless men oppressed by civilization that claims to save but only destroys;

Wearing the broad-brimmed hat of the West, symbolic of the forces that guard the Wilderness, which is the Natural State of the Dharma and the True Path of man on earth; all true paths lead through mountains—

With a halo of smoke and flame behind, the forest fires of the kali-yuga fires caused by the stupidity of those who think things can be gained and lost whereas in truth all is contained vast and free in the Blue Sky and Green Earth of One Mind;

Round-bellied to show his kind nature and that the great earth has food enough for everyone who loves and trusts her;

Trampling underfoot wasteful freeways and needless suburbs; smashing the worms of capitalism and totalitarianism;

Indicating the Task: his followers, becoming free of cars, houses, canned food, universities, and shoes, master the Three Mysteries of their own Body, Speech, and Mind; and fearlessly chop down the rotten trees and prune out the sick limbs of this country America and then burn the leftover trash.

Wrathful but Calm, Austere but Comic, Smokey the Bear will Illuminate those who would help him; but for those who would hinder or slander him,

HE WILL PUT THEM OUT.

Thus his great Mantra:

Namah samanta vajranam chanda maharoshana
Sphataya hum traka ham mam

"I DEDICATE MYSELF TO THE UNIVERSAL DIAMOND BE THIS RAGING FURY DESTROYED"

And he will protect those who love woods and rivers, Gods and animals, hobos and madmen, prisoners and sick people, musicians, playful women, and hopeful children;

And if anyone is threatened by advertising, air pollution, or the police, they should chant
SMOKEY THE BEAR'S SPELL:

DROWN THEIR BUTTS
CRUSH THEIR BUTTS
DROWN THEIR BUTTS
CRUSH THEIR BUTTS

And SMOKEY THE BEAR will surely appear to put the enemy out with his vajra-shovel.

Now those who recite this Sutra and then try to put it in
practice will accumulate merit as countless as the
sands of Arizona and Nevada,
Will help save the planet Earth from total oil slick,
Will enter the age of harmony of man and nature,
Will win the tender love and caresses of men, women,
and beasts
Will always have ripe blackberries to eat and a sunny spot
under a pine tree to sit at,

AND IN THE END WILL WIN
HIGHEST PERFECT ENLIGHTENMENT.
thus have we heard.

Excerpted Remarks by John W. Gardner, as Delivered to the National Press Club, December 9, 1969

As we enter the 1970's there are many curious aspects of our situation, but none more strange than our state of mind. We are anxious but immobilized. We know what our problems are, but seem incapable of summoning our will and resources to act.

We see the brooding threat of nuclear warfare. We know our lakes are dying, our rivers growing filthier daily, our atmosphere increasingly polluted. We are aware of racial tensions that could tear the nation apart. We understand that oppressive poverty in the midst of affluence is intolerable. We see that our cities are sliding toward disaster.

And these are not problems that stop at our borders. The problems of nuclear warfare, of population, of the environment, are impending planetary disasters. We are in trouble as a species.

But we are seized by a kind of paralysis of the will. It is like a waking nightmare.

I propose that as we enter the new decade we make a heroic effort to alter both our mood and our state of inactivity. Let 1970 be a year of renewal, and during that year let us give our institutions and ourselves a jolting reappraisal and overhaul.

The place to begin is with our national leadership in both the executive branch and the Congress. With a few notable exceptions, there has been a failure of leadership. More than any other factor, it is the missing ingredient in our situation today.

We have had failures of leadership before. But rarely before have we had the widespread distrust of our own institutions that we see today. And that distrust is not limited to radicals. Ask shopkeepers, housewives, young executives or insurance salesmen what concerns them. If you travel around the country as I do more or less continuously, you will find that there is a deep and pervasive feeling among all segments of the populace that "things aren't working"—and Washington is given a major share of the blame. When the great majority of Americans share that uneasiness, when a growing number are losing all confidence in our society, when the problems themselves are terrifyingly real, then it is immoral for our national leaders—in the Congress and the executive branch—to temporize. It is indecent for them to let us imagine that we can solve our problems without money or that we cannot afford to tackle them. It is criminal for either Republicans or Democrats to put politics before the nation's future. . . .

. . . [one] thing the citizen can do is to throw the weight of public opinion against those in the private sector who are unwilling to work toward the solution of our common problems. He should find out what major firms in his area are equal-opportunity employers. Which firms are shirking on that front? Let those firms know that their failure is recognized. What firms are contributing most to pollution? Let them feel the weight of public disapproval. . . .

. . . an important thing to understand about any institution or social system, whether it is a nation or a city, a corporation or a federal agency: it doesn't move unless you give it a solid push. Not a mild push—a solid jolt. If the push is not administered by vigorous and purposeful leaders, it will be administered eventually by an aroused citizenry or by a crisis. Systemic inertia is characteristic of every human institution, but overwhelmingly true of this nation as a whole. Our system of checks and balances dilutes the thrust of positive action. The competition of interests inherent in our pluralism acts as a brake on concerted action. The system grinds to a halt between crises. . . .

Earth Read-out

Keith Lampe

from Earth Read-out, Nov. 27-Dec. 5, 1969

A year ago hardly anybody in the U.S. knew what ecology meant.

Today almost everybody has at least a sense of it—and most overground media now are providing the kinds of information ERO did when it began last spring. The psychic changes have occurred with surprising rapidity.

Recent conferences sponsored by old-time politicians

(e.g., Reagan's, the State Department's via the U.S. National Commission for UNESCO) indicate the decision already has been taken to initiate massive, superficial programs to "clean up" the environment.

Almost certainly we soon will see the slapdash formation of an eco-peace corps operating both domestically and internationally and created partly to drain off enough youthful energies to avoid a civil war.

It now seems, in fact, that the old-timers—liberals, moderates, right-wingers, left-wingers—are sufficiently aroused to make possible in a few years the phasing out of the internal combustion engine plus short-term patchwork clean-up of certain rivers and lakes plus bans on the more persistent insecticides and on the SST.

All of which provides ERO with an opportunity to take new paths, to begin to define a more specifically radical ("root") approach to the emergency.

For openers, let's look at a few "root" mistakes the old-timers are about to make in the context of their new eco-concern. I use "old-timer" not as a pejorative but to indicate anybody—regardless of age—whose frames of reference are products of the OLD TIME, i.e., the industrial revolution phase of history.

1. They are about to initiate massive programs within the old frames of centralized authority of the nation. Nations are such an artificial construct from an ecological point of view that any further energies poured into them are almost certain to do more long-term harm than good. Nations (including even the projected New Nation, I think) must be phased out as quickly as possible and replaced with tribal or regional autonomous economies rational in root terms of planet topo/climate/watershed/etc. Boycott the words "nation" and "international."

2. They are about to initiate massive programs within the old frames of a competitive society even though this will prove decisively contradictory in terms of our recent root insight into interdependence-of-species. Interdependence of course can be sustained only in a context of cooperation, so competition (capitalism) must be

phased out and replaced with cooperative economic models.

3. They are about to initiate massive programs within the old frames of profit (and recognition, e.g., your photo on the cover of *Time*) even though our natural resources already have dwindled and exploded populations make continued use of those concepts imminently disastrous. Capitalism, phased out, cannot be replaced with socialism or communism because those forms, too, are growth-and-progress oriented. We have very little recent politico-economic inheritance to work from.

4. They are about to initiate massive programs within the old frames of faith-in-infinite-technology even though crucial limitations of planetary energy—energy as root sun *e*—mean the technology, no matter how brilliantly transformed, cannot prevent massive homo-sapiens diebacks and extinctions of thousands of other species. This sort of realism is difficult—yet overwhelmingly important—to reach: when we dropped out of the religions (e.g., Christianity, Judaism) we were originally trained to accept, we unconsciously transferred our sense-of-an-infinite into science and technology. Even some of the activists who recently have shifted into crime as a life style trustingly assume that the techno-system will continue to produce goods worth stealing. We shall have to use a transformed technology to salvage what we can—but technology at its best cannot save the whole scene.

5. They are about to initiate massive programs within the old frames of anthropocentricity even though inter-dependence-of-species means you have to care equally about all earth creatures. Humanism, despite its sweet surfaces, has been enormously unfortunate. Even worse than contemporary graduate-school humanism is the recent (1890) cookbook which says: "Three days before the turkey is slaughtered it should have an English walnut forced down its throat three times a day and a glass of sherry once a day. The meat will be deliciously tender, and have a fine nutty flavor." Practical considerations of survival force us past humanism as fast as we can make it. . . .

The Environmental Teach-In

René Dubos

The world is too much with us. We know this intuitively. But our social and economic institutions seem unable to come to grips with this awareness. The most they do is to appoint blue-ribbon committees and organize symposia which endlessly restate what everybody knows in a turgid prose that nobody reads and that leads to no action.

I do not believe that the environmental teach-in will provide new insight or factual knowledge, but I do hope that it will help alert public opinion to the immediacy of the ecologic crisis. The teach-in should point to action programs that can be developed *now* in each particular community. It should try also to define the areas of concern where knowledge is inadequate for effective action, but could be obtained by pointed research. I know that many scientists and technologists would welcome a form of public pressure that would provide them with the opportunity to work on problems of social importance.

The colossal inertia and rigidity—if not indifference —of social and academic institutions makes it unlikely that they will develop effective programs of action or research focused on environmental problems. Two kinds of events, however, may catalyze and accelerate the process. One is some ecological catastrophe that will alarm the public and thus bring pressure on the social, economic, and academic establishments. Another more attractive possibility is the emergence of a grassroots movement, powered by romantic emotion as much as by factual knowledge, that will give form and strength to the latent public concern with environmental quality. Because students are vigorous, informed, and still uncommitted to vested interests, they constitute one of the few groups in our society that can act as spearheads of this grassroots movement. I wish I were young enough to be a really effective participant in the Environmental Teach-In and to proclaim in action rather than in words my faith that GNP and technological efficiency are far less important than the quality of the organic world and the suitability of the environment for a truly human life.

A Time for Sarsaparilla

David Brower

from Summer Island

There was world enough then, and more time than there is now. Neither had to go and both can return. Not the times and the people whom Eliot Porter remembers here, for their time was a special one, a golden time, and they had room to live in it, room that let human spirit grow—the wide green land, the untroubled shore, a little alabaster here and there, and places no one thought to pave yet that are almost all slipping away now.

Whatever let it happen, Eliot Porter's world had something in common with Stuart Little's about which E. B. White wrote a paragraph that ought to be displayed in every town hall in the land. Because Mr. White knows Maine, we hoped he would introduce Eliot Porter's island world, but he couldn't. Nevertheless, his paragraph does.

"In the loveliest town of all, where the houses were white and high and the elm trees were green and higher than the houses, where the front yards were wide and pleasant and the back yards were bushy and worth finding out about, where the streets sloped down to the stream and the stream flowed quietly under the bridge, where the lawns ended in orchards and the orchards ended in the fields and the fields ended in pastures and the pastures climbed the hill and disappeared over the top toward the wonderful wide sky, in this the loveliest of all towns Stuart stopped to get a drink of sarsaparilla."

Stuart could still find sarsaparilla if he asked for it, but he would need something stronger were he now to look at what they've done to the edge of his town.

Whoever they are, those who did this to Stuart Little's habitat, we don't want them to do it any more, and we are sure they don't need to. Enough of the lovely towns have already lost their loveliness. It will add too little to the material development of this land, and take too much from its spirit, to diminish any more loveliness. Better to go back to the places man has lessened, to add evidence not of man's grossness or his neglect or his callousness, but rather of his genius. Let man heal the hurt places, and revere whatever is still miraculously pristine.

That is our biased aim, one we hope will be increasingly understood and widely shared. If it succeeds, there may be more time for sarsaparilla and less need for LSD. No one should underestimate the power of the reawakening that comes when time runs along at its own pace and not under forced draft, and there is a place to spend it in we want to know, or approach knowing, through what all our senses will tell us if instead of merely counting we learn to listen, or look, taste, touch, and see, or to comprehend.

Do something silly for a moment. Toss a precious object into the air and catch it. Now consider the extraordinary device (you, yourself) that just accomplished this everyday miracle. You sensed the energy of the toss, knew the value and the importance of success. You triangulated the position of the object throughout its flight with your binocular vision, you edited out distractions by other senses that might divert your attention, you brought an extraordinary signal mechanism into precise operation that triggered one set of muscles after another into a sequence of ground-to-air-missile direction-control processes resulting in easy success as you caught the object without thinking.

What you did will not make headlines anywhere. It is the simplest example I can think of of what you do millions of times a day. But ask your friends who know micro-electronics best what it would cost, and how much space it would take, to achieve artificially what you just achieved naturally. He will admit that the problem of reconstituting these simple excellences of yours would require a major federal grant. But that's just for the easy part.

Remember that all the miraculous abilities you demonstrated can be naturally and automatically packaged, and preserved without the slightest impairment, for periods of twenty to fifty years or so, in an ultramicroscopic part of you, received by you at no cost and forwarded into the future at the same price, in a tiny segment of a gene in a chromosome in a solution so concentrated that a single teaspoon could contain all the instructions needed to build and operate the three billion people now on the planet.

All this comes free from nature, the nature too many of our best superficial minds think we can do without. We can't. We have already done too much of it in. There may yet be, in the untrammeled tenth of America, enough nature, unsecond-guessed by technological arrogance, to build a good future on. We must hope so, and treasure what we have. Not to make mass sandboxes out of, or Lake Powells, or highway and helicopter havens, but places where like Eliot Porter we perceive instead of just looking, where we listen a little and talk less, where we consider our beginnings and our beyondings, where we learn to absorb, and to respect and love and remember.

The wild places are where we began. When they end, so do we. We had better not speed their passing. Man's talent can keep them if he lets it.

Something happened and can still happen on a summer island to substantiate all this hypothesis. Drive near (you can't, happily, drive *to* places like this), park, and ask for a sarsaparilla, then think about the island and about the other places there ought to be that are like it enough to count, this year, next year, and forever after.

The Historical Roots
of Our Ecologic Crisis

Lynn White, Jr.

from Science

A conversation with Aldous Huxley not infrequently put one at the receiving end of an unforgettable monologue. About a year before his lamented death he was discoursing on a favorite topic: Man's unnatural treatment of nature and its sad results. To illustrate his point he told how, during the previous summer, he had returned to a little valley in England where he had spent many happy months as a child. Once it had been composed of delightful grassy glades; now it was becoming overgrown with unsightly brush because the rabbits that formerly kept such growth under control had largely succumbed to a disease, myxomatosis, that was deliberately introduced by the local farmers to reduce the rabbits' destruction of crops. Being something of a Philistine, I could be silent no longer, even in the interests of great rhetoric. I interrupted to point out that the rabbit itself had been brought as a domestic animal to England in 1176, presumably to improve the protein diet of the peasantry.

All forms of life modify their contexts. The most spectacular and benign instance is doubtless the coral polyp. By serving its own ends, it has created a vast undersea world favorable to thousands of other kinds of animals and plants. Ever since man became a numerous species he has affected his environment notably. The

12

hypothesis that his fire-drive method of hunting created the world's great grasslands and helped to exterminate the monster mammals of the Pleistocene from much of the globe is plausible, if not proved. For six millennia at least, the banks of the lower Nile have been a human artifact rather than the swampy African jungle which nature, apart from man, would have made it. The Aswan Dam, flooding 5000 square miles, is only the latest stage in a long process. In many regions terracing or irrigation, overgrazing, the cutting of forests by Romans to build ships to fight Carthaginians or by Crusaders to solve the logistics problems of their expeditions, have profoundly changed some ecologies. Observation that the French landscape falls into two basic types, the open fields of the north and the *bocage* of the south and west, inspired Marc Bloch to undertake his classic study of medieval agricultural methods. Quite unintentionally, changes in human ways often affect nonhuman nature. It has been noted, for example, that the advent of the automobile eliminated huge flocks of sparrows that once fed on the horse manure littering every street.

The history of ecologic change is still so rudimentary that we know little about what really happened, or what the results were. The extinction of the European aurochs, as late as 1627 would seem to have been a simple case of overenthusiastic hunting. On more intricate matters it often is impossible to find solid information. For a thousand years or more the Frisians and Hollanders have been pushing back the North Sea, and the process is culminating in our own time in the reclamation of the Zuider Zee. What, if any, species of animals, birds, fish, shore life, or plants have died out in the process? In their epic combat with Neptune have the Netherlanders overlooked ecological values in such a way that the quality of human life in the Netherlands has suffered? I cannot discover that the questions have ever been asked, much less answered.

People, then, have often been a dynamic element in their own environment, but in the present state of historical scholarship we usually do not know exactly when, where, or with what effects man-induced changes came. As we enter the last third of the twentieth century, however, concern for the problem of ecologic backlash is mounting feverishly. Natural science, conceived as the effort to understand the nature of things, had flourished in several eras and among several peoples. Similarly there had been an age-old accumulation of technological skills, sometimes growing rapidly, sometimes slowly. But it was not until about four generations ago that Western Europe and North America arranged a marriage between science and technology, a union of the theoretical and the empirical approaches to our natural environment. The emergence in widespread practice of the Baconian creed that scientific knowledge means technological power over nature can scarcely be dated before about 1850, save in the chemical industries, where it is anticipated in the eighteenth century. Its acceptance as a normal pattern of action may mark the greatest event in human history since the invention of agricultu. and perhaps in nonhuman terrestrial history as well.

Almost at once the new situation forced the crystallization of the novel concept of ecology; indeed, the word *ecology* first appeared in the English language in 1873. Today, less than a century later, the impact of our race upon the environment has so increased in force that it has charged in essence. When the first cannons were fired, in the early fourteenth century, they affected ecology by sending workers scrambling to the forests and mountains for more potash, sulfur, iron ore, and charcoal, with some resulting erosion and deforestation. Hydrogen bombs are of a different order: a war fought with them might alter the genetics of all life on this planet. By 1285 London had a smog problem arising from the burning of soft coal, but our present combustion of fossil fuels threatens to change the chemistry of the globe's atmosphere as a whole, with consequences which we are only beginning to guess. With the population explosion, the carcinoma of planless urbanism, the new geological deposits of sewage and garbage, surely no creature other than man has ever managed to foul its nest in such short order.

There are many calls to action, but specific proposals, however worthy as individual items, seem too partial, palliative, negative: ban the bomb, tear down the billboards, give the Hindus contraceptives and tell them to eat their sacred cows. The simplest solution to any suspect change is, of course, to stop it, or, better yet, to revert to a romanticized past: make those ugly gasoline stations look like Anne Hathaway's cottage or (in the Far West) like ghost-town saloons. The "wilderness-area" mentality invariably advocates deep-freezing an ecology, whether San Gimignano or the High Sierra, as it was before the first Kleenex was dropped. But neither atavism nor prettification will cope with the ecologic cr... or our time.

What shall we do? No one yet knows. Unless we think about fundamentals, our specific measures may produce new backlashes more serious than those they are designed to remedy.

As a beginning we should try to clarify our thinking by looking, in some historical depth, at the presuppositions that underlie modern technology and science. Science was traditionally aristocratic, speculative, intellectual in intent; technology was lower-class, empirical, action-oriented. The quite sudden fusion of these two, towards the middle of the nineteenth century, is surely related to the slightly prior and contemporary democratic revolutions which, by reducing social barriers, tended to assert a functional unity of brain and hand. Our ecologic crisis is the product of an emerging, entirely novel, democratic culture. The issue is whether a democratized world can survive its own implications. Presumably we cannot unless we rethink our axioms.

THE WESTERN TRADITIONS
OF TECHNOLOGY AND SCIENCE

One thing is so certain that it seems stupid to verbalize it: both modern technology and modern science are distinctively *occidental*. Our technology has absorbed elements from all over the world, notably from China; yet everywhere today, whether in Japan or in Nigeria, successful technology is Western. Our science is the heir to all the sciences of the past, especially perhaps to the work of the great Islamic scientists of the Middle Ages, who so often outdid the ancient Greeks in skill and perspicacity: al-Rāzī in medicine, for example; or ibn-al-Haytham in optics; or Omar Khāyyám in mathematics. Indeed, not a few works of such geniuses seem to have vanished in the original Arabic and to survive only in medieval Latin translations that helped to lay the foundations for later Western developments. Today, around the globe, all significant science is Western in style and method, whatever the pigmentation or language of the scientists.

A second pair of facts is less well recognized because they result from quite recent historical scholarship. The leadership of the West, both in technology and in science, is far older than the so-called scientific revolution of the seventeenth century or the so-called industrial revolution of the eighteenth century. These terms are in fact outmoded and obscure the true nature of what they try to describe—significant stages in two long and separate developments. By A.D. 1000 at the latest—and perhaps, feebly, as much as 200 years earlier—the West began to apply water power to industrial processes other than milling grain. This was followed in the late twelfth century by the harnessing of wind power. From simple beginnings, but with remarkable consistency of style, the West rapidly expanded its skills in the development of power machinery, laborsaving devices, and automation. Those who doubt should contemplate that most monumental achievement in the history of automation: the weight-driven mechanical clock, which appeared in two forms in the early fourteenth century. Not in craftsmanship but in basic technological capacity, the Latin West of the later Middle Ages far outstripped its elaborate, sophisticated, and esthetically magnificent sister cultures, Byzantium and Islam. In 1444 a great Greek ecclesiastic,

Bessarion, who had gone to Italy, wrote a letter to a prince in Greece. He is amazed by the superiority of Western ships, arms, textiles, glass. But above all he is astonished by the spectacle of waterwheels sawing timbers and pumping the bellows of blast furnaces. Clearly, he had seen nothing of the sort in the Near East.

By the end of the fifteenth century the technological superiority of Europe was such that its small, mutually hostile nations could spill out over all the rest of the world, conquering, looting, and colonizing. The symbol of this technological superiority is the fact that Portugal, one of the weakest states of the Occident, was able to become, and to remain for a century, mistress of the East Indies. And we must remember that the technology of Vasco da Gama and Albuquerque was built by pure empiricism, drawing remarkably little support or inspiration from science.

In the present-day vernacular understanding, modern science is supposed to have begun in 1543, when both Copernicus and Vesalius published their great works. It is no derogation of their accomplishments, however, to point out that such structures as the *Fabrica* and the *De revolutionibus* do not appear overnight. The distinctive Western tradition of science, in fact, began in the late eleventh century with a massive movement of translation of Arabic and Greek scientific works into Latin. A few notable books—Theophrastus, for example—escaped the West's avid new appetite for science, but within less than 200 years effectively the entire corpus of Greek and Muslim science was available in Latin, and was being eagerly read and criticized in the new European universities. Out of criticism arose new observation, speculation, and increasing distrust of ancient authorities. By the late thirteenth century Europe had seized global scientific leadership from the faltering hands of Islam. It would be as absurd to deny the profound originality of Newton, Galileo, or Copernicus as to deny that of the fourteenth century scholastic scientists like Buridan or Oresme on whose work they built. Before the eleventh century, science scarcely existed in the Latin

West, even in Roman times. From the eleventh century onward, the scientific sector of occidental culture has increased in a steady crescendo.

Since both our technological and our scientific movements got their start, acquired their character, and achieved world dominance in the Middle Ages, it would seem that we cannot understand their nature or their present impact upon ecology without examining fundamental medieval assumptions and developments.

MEDIEVAL VIEW
OF MAN AND NATURE

Until recently, agriculture has been the chief occupation even in "advanced" societies; hence, any change in methods of tillage has much importance. Early plows, drawn by two oxen, did not normally turn the sod but merely scratched it. Thus, cross-plowing was needed and fields tended to be squarish. In the fairly light soils and semi-arid climates of the Near East and Mediterranean, this worked well. But such a plow was inappropriate to the wet climate and often sticky soils of northern Europe. By the latter part of the seventh century after Christ, however, following obscure beginnings, certain northern peasants were using an entirely new kind of plow, equipped with a vertical knife to cut the line of the furrow, a horizontal share to slice under the sod, and a moldboard to turn it over. The friction of this plow with the soil was so great that it normally required not two but eight oxen. It attacked the land with such violence that cross-plowing was not needed, and fields tended to be shaped in long strips.

In the days of the scratch-plow, fields were distributed generally in units capable of supporting a single family. Subsistence farming was the presupposition. But no peasant owned eight oxen: to use the new and more efficient plow, peasants pooled their oxen to form large plow-teams, originally receiving (it would appear) plowed strips in proportion to their contribution. Thus, distribution of land was based no longer on the needs of a family but, rather, on the capacity of a power machine to till the earth. Man's relation to the soil was profoundly changed. Formerly man had been part of nature; now he was the exploiter of nature. Nowhere else in the world did farmers develop any analogous agricultural implement. Is it coincidence that modern technology, with its ruthlessness toward nature, has so largely been produced by descendants of these peasants of northern Europe?

This same exploitive attitude appears slightly before A.D. 830 in Western illustrated calendars. In older calendars the months were shown as passive personifications. The new Frankish calendars, which set the style for the Middle Ages, are very different: they show men coercing the world around them—plowing, harvesting, chopping trees, butchering pigs. Man and nature are two things, and man is master.

These novelties seem to be in harmony with larger intellectual patterns. What people do about their ecology depends on what they think about themselves in relation to things around them. Human ecology is deeply conditioned by beliefs about our nature and destiny—that is, by religion. To Western eyes this is very evident in, say, India or Ceylon. It is equally true of ourselves and of our medieval ancestors.

The victory of Christianity over paganism was the greatest psychic revolution in the history of our culture. It has become fashionable today to say that, for better or worse, we live in "the post-Christian age." Certainly the forms of our thinking and language have largely ceased to be Christian, but to my eye the substance often remains amazingly akin to that of the past. Our daily habits of action, for example, are dominated by an implicit faith in perpetual progress which was unknown either to Greco-Roman antiquity or to the Orient. It is rooted in, and is indefensible apart from, Judeo-Christian teleology. The fact that Communists share it merely helps to show what can be demonstrated on many other grounds: that Marxism, like Islam, is a Judeo-Christian heresy. We continue today to live, as we have lived for about 1700 years, very largely in a context of Christian axioms.

What did Christianity tell people about their relations with the environment?

While many of the world's mythologies provide stories of creation, Greco-Roman mythology was singularly incoherent in this respect. Like Aristotle, the intellectuals of the ancient West denied that the visible world had had a beginning. Indeed, the idea of a beginning was impossible in the framework of their cyclical notion of time. In sharp contrast, Christianity inherited from Judaism not only a concept of time as nonrepetitive and linear but also a striking story of creation. By gradual stages a loving and all-powerful God had created light and darkness, the heavenly bodies, the earth and all its plants, animals, birds, and fishes. Finally, God had created Adam and, as an afterthought, Eve, to keep man from being lonely. Man named all the animals, thus establishing his dominance over them. God planned all of this explicitly for man's benefit and rule: no item in the physical creation had any purpose save to serve man's purposes. And, although man's body is made of clay, he is not simply part of nature: he is made in God's image.

Especially in its Western form, Christianity is the most anthropocentric religion the world has seen. As early as the second century both Tertullian and Saint Irenaeus of Lyons were insisting that when God shaped Adam he was foreshadowing the image of the Incarnate Christ, the Second Adam. Man shares, in great measure, God's transcendence of nature. Christianity, in absolute contrast to ancient paganism and Asia's religions (except, perhaps, Zoroastrianism), not only established a dualism of man and nature but also insisted that it is God's will that man exploit nature for his proper ends.

At the level of the common people this worked out in an interesting way. In antiquity every tree, every spring, every stream, every hill had its own *genius loci,* its guardian spirit. These spirits were accessible to men, but were very unlike men; centaurs, fauns, and mermaids show their ambivalence. Before one cut a tree, mined a mountain, or dammed a brook, it was important to placate the spirit in charge of that particular situation, and to keep it placated. By destroying pagan animism, Christianity made it possible to exploit nature in a mood of indifference to the feelings of natural objects.

It is often said that for animism the Church substituted the cult of saints. True; but the cult of saints is functionally quite different from animism. The saint is not *in* natural objects; he may have special shrines, but his citizenship is in heaven. Moreover, a saint is entirely a man; he can be approached in human terms. In addition to saints, Christianity of course also had angels and demons inherited from Judaism and perhaps, at one remove, from Zoroastrianism. But these were all as mobile as the saints themselves. The spirits *in* natural objects, which formerly had protected nature from man, evaporated. Man's effective monopoly on spirit in this world was confirmed, and the old inhibitions to the exploitation of nature crumbled.

When one speaks in such sweeping terms, a note of caution is in order. Christianity is a complex faith, and its consequences differ in differing contexts. What I have said may well apply to the medieval West, where in fact technology made spectacular advances. But the Greek East, a highly civilized realm of equal Christian devotion, seems to have produced no marked technological innovation after the late seventh century, when Greek fire was invented. The key to the contrast may perhaps be found in a difference in the tonality of piety and thought which students of comparative theology find between the Greek and the Latin churches. The Greeks believed that sin was intellectual blindness, and that salvation was found in illumination, orthodoxy—that is, clear thinking. The Latins, on the other hand, felt that sin was moral evil, and that salvation was to be found in right conduct. Eastern theology has been intellectualist. Western theology has been voluntarist. The Greek saint contemplates; the Western saint acts. The implications of Christianity for the conquest of nature would emerge more easily in the Western atmosphere.

The Christian dogma of creation, which is found in the first clause of all the Creeds, has another meaning for our comprehension of today's ecologic crisis. By revelation, God had given man the Bible, the Book of Scripture. But since God had made nature, nature also must reveal the divine mentality. The religious study of nature for the better understanding of God was known as natural theology. In the early Church, and always in the Greek East, nature was conceived primarily as a symbolic system through which God speaks to men: the ant is a sermon to sluggards; rising flames are the symbol of the soul's aspiration. This view of nature was essentially artistic rather than scientific. While Byzantium preserved and copied great numbers of ancient Greek scientific texts, science as we conceive it could scarcely flourish in such an ambience.

However, in the Latin West by the early thirteenth century natural theology was following a very different bent. It was ceasing to be the decoding of the physical symbols of God's communication with man and was becoming the effort to understand God's mind by discovering how his creation operates. The rainbow was no longer simply a symbol of hope first sent to Noah after the Deluge: Robert Grosseteste, Friar Roger Bacon, and Theodoric of Freiberg produced startlingly sophisticated work on the optics of the rainbow, but they did it as a venture in religious understanding. From the thirteenth century onward, up to and including Leibnitz and Newton, every major scientist, in effect, explained his motivations in religious terms. Indeed, if Galileo had not been so expert an amateur theologian he would have got into far less trouble: the professionals resented his intrusion. And Newton seems to have regarded himself more as a theologian than as a scientist. It was not until the late eighteenth century that the hypothesis of God became unnecessary to many scientists.

It is often hard for the historian to judge, when men explain why they are doing what they want to do, whether they are offering real reasons or merely culturally acceptable reasons. The consistency with which scientists during the long formative centuries of Western science said that the task and the reward of the scientist was "to think God's thoughts after him" leads one to believe that this was their real motivation. If so, then modern Western science was cast in a matrix of Christian theology. The dynamism of religious devotion, shaped by the Judeo-Christian dogma of creation, gave it impetus.

AN ALTERNATIVE CHRISTIAN VIEW

We would seem to be headed toward conclusions unpalatable to many Christians. Since both *science* and *technology* are blessed words in our contemporary vocabulary, some may be happy at the notions, first, that, viewed historically, modern science is an extrapolation of natural theology and, second, that modern technology is at least partly to be explained as an occidental, voluntarist realization of the Christian dogma of man's transcendence of, and rightful mastery over, nature. But, as we now recognize, somewhat over a century ago science and technology—hitherto quite separate activities— joined to give mankind powers which, to judge by many of the ecologic effects, are out of control. If so, Christianity bears a huge burden of guilt.

I personally doubt that disastrous ecologic backlash can be avoided simply by applying to our problems more science and more technology. Our science and technology have grown out of Christian attitudes toward man's relation to nature which are almost universally held not only by Christians and neo-Christians but also by those who fondly regard themselves as post-Christians. Despite Copernicus, all the cosmos rotates around our little globe. Despite Darwin, we are *not,* in our hearts, part of the natural process. We are superior to nature, contemptuous of it, willing to use it for our slightest whim. The newly elected governor of California, like myself a churchman, but less troubled than I, spoke for the Christian tradition when he said (as is alleged), "when you've seen one redwood tree, you've seen them all." To a

Christian a tree can be no more than a physical fact. The whole concept of the sacred grove is alien to Christianity and to the ethos of the West. For nearly two millennia Christian missionaries have been chopping down sacred groves, which are idolatrous because they assume spirit in nature.

What we do about ecology depends on our ideas of the man-nature relationship. More science and more technology are not going to get us out of the present ecologic crisis until we find a new religion, or rethink our old one. The beatniks, who are the basic revolutionaries of our time, show a sound instinct in their affinity for Zen Buddhism, which conceives of the man-nature relationship as very nearly the mirror image of the Christian view. Zen, however, is as deeply conditioned by Asian history as Christianity is by the experience of the West, and I am dubious of its viability among us.

Possibly we should ponder the greatest radical in Christian history since Christ: Saint Francis of Assisi. The prime miracle of Saint Francis is the fact that he did not end at the stake, as many of his left-wing followers did. He was so clearly heretical that a general of the Franciscan Order, Saint Bonaventura, a great and perceptive Christian, tried to suppress the early accounts of Franciscanism. The key to an understanding of Francis is his belief in the virtue of humility—not merely for the individual but for man as a species. Francis tried to depose man from his monarchy over creation and set up a democracy of all God's creatures. With him the ant is no longer simply a homily for the lazy, flames a sign of the thrust of the soul toward union with God; now they are Brother Ant and Sister Fire, praising the Creator in their own ways as Brother Man does in his.

Later commentators have said that Francis preached to the birds as a rebuke to men who would not listen. The records do not read so: he urged the little birds to praise God, and in spiritual ecstasy they flapped their wings and chirped rejoicing. Legends of saints, especially the Irish saints, had long told of their dealings with animals but always, I believe, to show their human dominance over creatures. With Francis it is different. The land around Gubbio in the Apennines was being ravaged by a fierce wolf. Saint Francis, says the legend, talked to the wolf and persuaded him of the error of his ways. The wolf repented, died in the odor of sanctity, and was buried in consecrated ground.

What Sir Steven Ruciman calls "the Franciscan doctrine of the animal soul" was quickly stamped out. Quite possibly it was in part inspired, consciously or unconsciously, by the belief in reincarnation held by the Cathar heretics who at that time teemed in Italy and southern France, and who presumably had got it originally from India. It is significant that at just the same moment, about 1200, traces of metempsychosis are found also in western Judaism, in the Provençal *Cabbala*. But Francis held neither to transmigration of souls nor to pantheism. His view of nature and of man rested on a unique sort of pan-psychism of all things animate and inanimate, designed for the glorification of their transcendent Creator, who, in the ultimate gesture of cosmic humility, assumed flesh, lay helpless in a manger, and hung dying on a scaffold.

I am not suggesting that many contemporary Americans who are concerned about our ecologic crisis will be either able or willing to counsel with wolves or exhort birds. However, the present increasing disruption of the global environment is the product of a dynamic technology and science which were originating in the Western medieval world against which Saint Francis was rebelling in so original a way. Their growth cannot be understood historically apart from distinctive attitudes toward nature which are deeply grounded in Christian dogma. The fact that most people do not think of these attitudes as Christian is irrelevant. No new set of basic values has been accepted in our society to displace those of Christianity. Hence we shall continue to have a worsening ecologic crisis until we reject the Christian axiom that nature has no reason for existence save to serve man.

The greatest spiritual revolutionary in Western history, Saint Francis, proposed what he thought was an alternative Christian view of nature and man's relation to it: he tried to substitute the idea of the equality of all creatures, including man, for the idea of man's limitless rule of creation. He failed. Both our present science and our present technology are so tinctured with orthodox Christian arrogance toward nature that no solution for our ecologic crisis can be expected from them alone. Since the roots of our trouble are so largely religious, the remedy must also be essentially religious, whether we call it that or not. We must rethink and refeel our nature and destiny. The profoundly religious, but heretical, sense of the primitive Franciscans for the spiritual autonomy of all parts of nature may point a direction. I propose Francis as a patron saint for ecologists.

The Limits of Adaptability

René Dubos

Let me state why I believe that the health of the environment in which man functions is crucial for his well-being in the here and now and for the quality of life in the future.

The phrase "health of the environment" is not a literary convention. It has a real biological meaning, because the surface of the earth is truly a living organism. Without the countless and immensely varied forms of life that the earth harbors, our planet would be just another fragment of the universe with a surfac. ...rab as that of the moon and an atmosphere inho, .ิable to man. We human beings exist and enjoy life only by virtue of the conditions created and maintained on the surface of the earth by the microbes, plants, and animals that have converted its inanimate matter into a highly integrated living structure. Any profound disturbance in the ecological equilibrium is a threat to the maintenance of human life as we know it now. Admittedly, there are scientists who claim that it will soon be possible to alter man's genetic code so as to make it better suited to whatever conditions may arise in the future. But I do not take them seriously. Indeed I believe that any attempt to alter the fundamental being of man is a biological absurdity as well as an ethical monstrosity.

Man has a remarkable ability to develop some form of tolerance to conditions extremely different from those under which he evolved. This has led to the belief that, through social and technological innovations, he can

27

endlessly modify his ways of life without risk. But the facts do not justify this euphoric attitude. Modern man can adapt biologically to the technological environment only in so far as mechanisms of adaptation are potentially present in his genetic code. For this reason, we can almost take it for granted that he cannot achieve successful biological adaptation to insults with which he has had no experience in his evolutionary past, such as the shrill noises of modern equipment, the exhausts of automobiles and factories, the countless new synthetic products that get into air, water, and food. The limits that must be imposed on social and technological innovations are determined not by scientific knowledge or practical know-how, but by the biological and mental nature of man which is essentially unchangeable.

Some recent experiences appear at first sight to provide evidence that the immense adaptability of man is much greater than I suggest. For example, people of all races have survived the horrors of modern warfare and concentration camps. The population continues to grow even amidst the appalling misery prevailing in some underprivileged urban areas. The other side of the coin, however, is that continuous exposure to biological stresses always results in biological and mental alterations that mean hardships for the future. For example, people born and raised in the industrial areas of northern Europe have survived and multiplied despite constant exposure to smogs made worse by the inclemency of the Atlantic climate. But the long-range consequence of this so-called adaptation is a very large incidence of chronic pulmonary diseases. The same trend can be recognized in this country.

Social regimentation and standardization is compatible with the survival and multiplication of biological man, but not with the quality of human life. Step-by-step, people become tolerant of worse and worse environmental conditions without realizing that the expressions of this tolerance will emerge later in the form of debilitating ailments and what is even worse, in a form of life that will retain little of true humanness.

Experiments in animals and observations in man leave no doubt that environmental influences exert their most profound and lasting effects when they impinge on the organism during the early phases of its biological and mental development. In consequence, it can be anticipated that the deleterious effects of the present crisis will not reach their full expression until around the end of the present century, when today's children have become young adults. A very large percentage of these children will have been exposed from birth and throughout their formative years to conditions that will almost certainly elicit maladaptive responses in the long run—not only organic diseases but also, and perhaps most importantly, distortions of mental and emotional attributes.

We are naturally concerned with the unpleasant effects that the environmental crisis has for us in the here and now, but these are trivial when compared with the distant effects that it will have on the human beings who are being exposed to it throughout their development. Although I have emphasized—because of my professional specialization—the disease aspects of environmental insults, I do not believe that these are the most important. The mind is affected by environmental factors just as much as the body. Its expressions can be atrophied or distorted by the surroundings in which it develops, and by the hostile stimuli to which it has to respond.

The increase in the world population is one of the determinants of the ecological crisis and indeed may be at its root. But few persons realize that the dangers posed by overpopulation are more grave and more immediate in the U.S. than in less industrialized countries. This is due in part to the fact that each U.S. citizen uses more of the world's natural resources than any other human being and destroys them more rapidly, thereby contributing massively to the pollution of his own surroundings and of the earth as a whole—let alone the pollution of the moon and of space. Another reason is that the destructive impact of each U.S. citizen on the physical, biological, and human environment is enormously magnified by the variety of gadgets and by the amount of energy at his disposal.

American cities give the impression of being more crowded than Asian and European cities not because their population density is greater—it is in fact much lower—but because they expose their inhabitants to many more unwelcome stimuli. Much of the experience of crowding comes not from contacts with real human beings but from the telephones, radios, and television sets that bring us the mechanical expressions of mankind instead of the warmth of its biological nature.

The Tragedy of the Commons

Garrett Hardin

from Science

At the end of a thoughtful article on the future of nuclear war, Wiesner and York[1] concluded that: "Both sides in the arms race are . . . confronted by the dilemma of steadily increasing military power and steadily decreasing national security. *It is our considered professional judgment that this dilemma has no technical solution.* If the great powers continue to look for solutions in the area of science and technology only, the result will be to worsen the situation."

I would like to focus your attention not on the subject of the article (national security in a nuclear world) but on the kind of conclusion they reached, namely that there is no technical solution to the problem. An implicit and almost universal assumption of discussions published in professional and semipopular scientific journals is that the problem under discussion has a technical solution. A technical solution may be defined as one that requires a change only in the techniques of the natural sciences, demanding little or nothing in the way of change in human values or ideas of morality.

In our day (though not in earlier times) technical solutions are always welcome. Because of previous failures in prophecy, it takes courage to assert that a desired technical solution is not possible. Wiesner and York exhibited this courage; publishing in a science journal, they insisted that the solution to the problem was not to be found in the natural sciences. They cautiously qualified their statement with the phrase, "It is our considered professional judgment. . . ." Whether they were right or not is not the concern of the present article. Rather, the concern here is with the important concept of a class of human problems which can be called "no technical solution problems," and, more specifically, with the identification and discussion of one of these.

It is easy to show that the class is not a null class. Recall the game of tick-tack-toe. Consider the problem, "How can I win the game of tick-tack-toe?" It is well known that I cannot, if I assume (in keeping with the conventions of game theory) that my opponent understands the game perfectly. Put another way, there is no "technical solution" to the problem. I can win only by giving a radical meaning to the word "win." I can hit my opponent over the head; or I can drug him; or I can falsify the records. Every way in which I "win" involves, in some sense, an abandonment of the game, as we intuitively understand it. (I can also, of course, openly abandon the game—refuse to play it. This is what most adults do.)

The class of "No technical solution problems" has members. My thesis is that the "population problem," as conventionally conceived, is a member of this class. How it is conventionally conceived needs some comment. It is fair to say that most people who anguish over the population problem are trying to find a way to avoid the evils of overpopulation without relinquishing any of the privileges they now enjoy. They think that farming the seas or developing new strains of wheat will solve the problem—technologically. I try to show here that the solution they seek cannot be found. The population problem cannot be solved in a technical way, any more than can the problem of winning the game of tick-tack-toe.

What Shall We Maximize?

Population, as Malthus said, naturally tends to grow "geometrically," or, as we would now say, exponentially. In a finite world this means that the per capita share of the world's goods must steadily decrease. Is ours a finite world?

A fair defense can be put forward for the view that the world is infinite; or that we do not know that it is not. But, in terms of the practical problems that we must face in the next few generations with the foreseeable technology, it is clear that we will greatly increase human misery if we do not, during the immediate future, assume that the world available to the terrestrial human population is finite. "Space" is no escape.[2]

A finite world can support only a finite population; therefore, population growth must eventually equal zero. (The case of perpetual wide fluctuations above and below zero is a trivial variant that need not be discussed.) When this condition is met, what will be the situation of mankind? Specifically, can Bentham's goal of "the greatest good for the greatest number" be realized?

No—for two reasons, each sufficient by itself. The first is a theoretical one. It is not mathematically possible to maximize for two (or more) variables at the same time. This was clearly stated by von Neumann and Morgenstern[3], but the principle is implicit in the theory of partial differential equations, dating back at least to D'Alembert (1717–1783).

The second reason springs directly from biological facts. To live, any organism must have a source of energy (for example, food). This energy is utilized for two purposes: mere maintenance and work. For man, maintenance of life requires about 1600 kilo-calories a day ("maintenance calories"). Anything that he does over and above merely staying alive will be defined as work, and is supported by "work calories" which he takes in. Work calories are used not only for what we call work in common speech; they are also required for all forms of enjoyment, from swimming and automobile racing to playing music and writing poetry. If our goal is to maximize population it is obvious what we must do: We must make the work calories per person approach as close to zero as possible. No gourmet meals, no vacations, no sports, no music, no literature, no art.

. . . I think that everyone will grant, without argument or proof, that maximizing population does not maximize goods. Bentham's goal is impossible.

In reaching this conclusion I have made the usual assumption that it is the acquisition of energy that is the problem. The appearance of atomic energy has led some to question this assumption. However, given an infinite source of energy, population growth still produces an inescapable problem. The problem of the acquisition of energy is replaced by the problem of its dissipation, as J. H. Fremlin has so wittily shown.[4] The arithmetic signs in the analysis are, as it were, reversed; but Bentham's goal is still unobtainable.

The optimum population is, then, less than the maximum. The difficulty of defining the optimum is enormous; so far as I know, no one has seriously tackled this problem. Reaching an acceptable and stable solution will surely require more than one generation of hard analytical work—and much persuasion.

We want the maximum good per person; but what is good? To one person it is wilderness, to another it is ski lodges for thousands. To one it is estuaries to nourish ducks for hunters to shoot; to another it is factory land. Comparing one good with another is, we usually say, impossible because goods are incommensurable. Incommensurables cannot be compared.

Theoretically this may be true; but in real life incommensurables *are* commensurable. Only a criterion of judgment and a system of weighting are needed. In nature the criterion is survival. Is it better for a species to be small and hideable, or large and powerful? Natural selection commensurates the incommensurables. The compromise achieved depends on a natural weighting of the values of the variables.

Man must imitate this process. There is no doubt that in fact he already does, but unconsciously. It is when the hidden decisions are made explicit that the arguments begin. The problem for the years ahead is to work out an acceptable theory of weighting. Synergistic effects, nonlinear variation, and difficulties in discounting the future make the intellectual problem difficult, but not (in principle) insoluble.

Has any cultural group solved this practical problem at the present time, even on an intuitive level? One simple fact proves that none has: there is no prosperous population in the world today that has, or has had for some time, a growth rate of zero. Any people that has intuitively identified its optimum point will soon reach it, after which its growth rate becomes and remains zero.

Of course, a positive growth rate might be taken as evidence that a population is below its optimum. However, by any reasonable standards, the most rapidly growing populations on earth today are (in general) the most miserable. This association (which need not be invariable) casts doubt on the optimistic assumption that the positive growth rate of a population is evidence that it has yet to reach its optimum.

We can make little progress in working toward optimum population size until we explicitly exorcize the spirit of Adam Smith in the field of practical demography. In economic affairs, *The Wealth of Nations* (1776) popularized the "invisible hand," the idea that an individual who "intends only his own gain," is, as it were, "led by an invisible hand to promote . . . the public interest."[5] Adam Smith did not assert that this was invariably true, and perhaps neither did any of his followers. But he contributed to a dominant tendency of thought that has ever since interfered with positive action based on rational analysis, namely, the tendency to assume that decisions reached individually will, in fact, be the best decisions for an entire society. If this assumption is correct it justifies the continuance of our present policy of laissez-faire in reproduction. If it is correct we can assume that men will control their individual fecundity so as to produce the optimum population. If the assumption is not correct, we need to reexamine our individual freedoms to see which ones are defensible.

TRAGEDY OF FREEDOM IN A COMMONS

The rebuttal to the invisible hand in population control is to be found in a scenario first sketched in a little-known pamphlet[6] in 1833 by a mathematical amateur named William Forster Lloyd (1794–1852). We may well call it "the tragedy of the commons," using the word "tragedy" as the philosopher Whitehead used it[7]: "The essence of dramatic tragedy is not unhappiness. It resides in the solemnity of the remorseless working of things." He then goes on to say, "This inevitableness of destiny can only be illustrated in terms of human life by incidents which in fact involve unhappiness. For it is only by them that the futility of escape can be made evident in the drama."

The tragedy of the commons develops in this way. Picture a pasture open to all. It is to be expected that each herdsman will try to keep as many cattle as possible on the commons. Such an arrangement may work reasonably satisfactorily for centuries because tribal wars, poaching, and disease keep the numbers of both man and beast well below the carrying capacity of the land. Finally, however, comes the day of reckoning, that is, the day when the long-desired goal of social stability becomes a reality. At this point, the inherent logic of the commons remorselessly generates tragedy.

As a rational being, each herdsman seeks to maximize his gain. Explicitly or implicitly, more or less consciously, he asks, "What is the utility *to me* of adding one more animal to my herd?" This utility has one negative and one positive component.

1. The positive component is a function of the increment of one animal. Since the herdsman receives all the proceeds from the sale of the additional animal, the positive utility is nearly +1.

2. The negative component is a function of the additional overgrazing created by one more animal. Since, however, the effects of overgrazing are shared by all the herdsmen, the negative utility for any particular decision-making herdsman is only a fraction of −1.

Adding together the component partial utilities, the rational herdsman concludes that the only sensible course for him to pursue is to add another animal to his herd. And another; and another. . . . But this is the conclusion reached by each and every rational herdsman sharing a commons. Therein is the tragedy. Each man is locked into a system that compels him to increase his herd without limit—in a world that is limited. Ruin is the destination toward which all men rush, each pursuing his own best interest in a society that believes in the freedom of the commons. Freedom in a commons brings ruin to all.

Some would say that this is a platitude. Would that it were! In a sense, it was learned thousands of years ago, but natural selection favors the forces of psychological denial.[8] The individual benefits as an individual from his ability to deny the truth even though society as a whole, of which he is a part, suffers. Education can counteract the natural tendency to do the wrong thing, but the inexorable succession of generations requires that the basis for this knowledge be constantly refreshed.

A simple incident that occurred a few years ago in Leominster, Massachusetts, shows how perishable the knowledge is. During the Christmas shopping season the parking meters downtown were covered with plastic bags that bore tags reading: "Do not open until after Christmas. Free parking courtesy of the mayor and city council." In other words, facing the prospect of an increased demand for already scarce space, the city fathers reinstituted the system of the commons. (Cynically, we suspect that they gained more votes than they lost by this retrogressive act.)

In an approximate way, the logic of the commons has been understood for a long time, perhaps since the discovery of agriculture or the invention of private property in real estate. But it is understood mostly only in special cases which are not sufficiently generalized. Even at this late date, cattlemen leasing national land on the western ranges demonstrate no more than an ambivalent understanding, in constantly pressuring federal authorities to increase the head count to the point where over-grazing produces erosion and weed-dominance. Like-wise, the oceans of the world continue to suffer from the survival of the philosophy of the commons. Maritime nations still respond automatically to the shibboleth of the "freedom of the seas." Professing to believe in the "inexhaustible resources of the oceans," they bring species after species of fish and whales closer to extinction.[9]

The national parks present another instance of the working out of the tragedy of the commons. At present, they are open to all, without limit. The parks themselves are limited in extent—there is only one Yosemite Valley —whereas population seems to grow without limit. The values that visitors seek in the parks are steadily eroded. Plainly, we must soon cease to treat the parks as com-mons or they will be of no value to anyone.

What shall we do? We have several options. We might sell them off as private property. We might keep them as public property, but allocate the right to enter them. The allocation might be on the basis of wealth, by the use of an auction system. It might be on the basis of merit, as defined by some agreed-upon standards. It might be by lottery. Or it might be on a first-come, first-served basis, administered to long queues. These, I think, are all the reasonable possibilities. They are all objec-tionable. But we must choose—or acquiesce in the destruction of the commons that we call our national parks.

POLLUTION

In a reverse way, the tragedy of the commons re-appears in problems of pollution. Here it is not a ques-tion of taking something out of the commons, but of putting something in—sewage, or chemical, radioactive, and heat wastes into water; noxious and dangerous fumes into the air; and distracting and unpleasant advertising signs into the line of sight. The calculations of utility are much the same as before. The rational man finds that his share of the cost of the wastes he discharges into the commons is less than the cost of purifying his wastes before releasing them. Since this is true for everyone, we are locked into a system of "fouling our own nest," so long as we behave only as independent, rational, free-enterprisers.

The tragedy of the commons as a food basket is averted by private property, or something formally like it. But the air and waters surrounding us cannot readily be fenced, and so the tragedy of the commons as a cesspool must be prevented by different means, by coercive laws or taxing devices that make it cheaper for the polluter to treat his pollutants than to discharge them untreated. We have not progressed as far with the solution of this problem as we have with the first. Indeed, our particular concept of private property, which deters us from exhausting the positive resources of the earth, favors pollution. The owner of a factory on the bank of a stream—whose property extends to the middle of the stream—often has difficulty seeing why it is not his natural right to muddy the waters flowing past his door. The law, always behind the times, requires elaborate stitching and fitting to adapt it to this newly perceived aspect of the commons.

The pollution problem is a consequence of population. It did not much matter how a lonely American frontiersman disposed of his waste. "Flowing water purifies itself every ten miles," my grandfather used to say, and the myth was near enough to the truth when he was a boy, for there were not too many people. But as population became denser, the natural chemical and biological recycling processes became overloaded, calling for a redefinition of property rights.

How To Legislate Temperance?

Analysis of the pollution problem as a function of population density uncovers a not generally recognized principle of morality, namely: *the morality of an act is a function of the state of the system at the time it is performed*.[10] Using the commons as a cesspool does not harm the general public under frontier conditions, because there is no public; the same behavior in a metropolis is unbearable. A hundred and fifty years ago a plainsman could kill an American bison, cut out only the tongue for his dinner, and discard the rest of the animal. He was not in any important sense being wasteful. Today, with only a few thousand bison left, we would be appalled at such behavior.

In passing, it is worth noting that the morality of an act cannot be determined from a photograph. One does not know whether a man killing an elephant or setting fire to the grassland is harming others until one knows the total system in which his act appears. "One picture is worth a thousand words," said an ancient Chinese; but it may take 10,000 words to validate it. It is as tempting to ecologists as it is to reformers in general to try to persuade others by way of the photographic shortcut. But the essence of an argument cannot be photographed: it must be presented rationally—in words.

That morality is system-sensitive escaped the attention of most codifiers of ethics in the past. "Thou shalt not . . ." is the form of traditional ethical directives which make no allowance for particular circumstances. The laws of our society follow the pattern of ancient ethics, and therefore are poorly suited to governing a complex, crowded, changeable world. Our epicyclic solution is to augment statutory law with administrative law. Since it is practically impossible to spell out all the conditions under which it is safe to burn trash in the back yard or to run an automobile without smog-control, by law we delegate the details to bureaus. The result is administrative law, which is rightly feared for an ancient reason—*Quis custodiet ipsos custodes?*—"Who shall watch the watchers themselves?" John Adams said that we must have "a government of laws and not men." Bureau administrators, trying to evaluate the morality of acts in the total system, are singularly liable to corruption, producing a government by men, not laws.

Prohibition is easy to legislate (though not necessarily to enforce); but how do we legislate temperance? Experience indicates that it can be accomplished best through the mediation of administrative law. We limit possibilities unnecessarily if we suppose that the sentiment of *Quis custodiet* denies us the use of administrative law. We should rather retain the phrase as a perpetual reminder of fearful dangers we cannot avoid. The great challenge facing us now is to invent the corrective feedbacks that are needed to keep custodians honest. We must find ways to legitimate the needed authority of both the custodians and the corrective feedbacks.

FREEDOM TO BREED IS INTOLERABLE

The tragedy of the commons is involved in population problems in another way. In a world governed solely by the principle of "dog eat dog"—if indeed there ever was such a world—how many children a family had would not be a matter of public concern. Parents who bred too exuberantly would leave fewer descendants, not more, because they would be unable to care adequately for their children. David Lack and others have found that such a negative feedback demonstrably controls the fecundity of birds.[11] But men are not birds, and have not acted like them for millenniums, at least.

If each human family were dependent only on its own resources; *if* the children of improvident parents starved to death; *if,* thus, overbreeding brought its own "punishment" to the germ line—*then* there would be no public interest in controlling the breeding of families. But our society is deeply committed to the welfare state,[12] and hence is confronted with another aspect of the tragedy of the commons.

In a welfare state, how shall we deal with the family, the religion, the race, or the class (or indeed any distinguishable and cohesive group) that adopts overbreeding as a policy to secure its own aggrandizement?[13] To couple the concept of freedom to breed with the belief that everyone born has an equal right to the commons is to lock the world into a tragic course of action.

Unfortunately this is just the course of action that is being pursued by the United Nations. In late 1967, some thirty nations agreed to the following:[14]

> The Universal Declaration of Human Rights describes the family as the natural and fundamental unit of society. It follows that any choice and decision with regard to the size of the family must irrevocably rest with the family itself, and cannot be made by anyone else.

It is painful to have to deny categorically the validity of this right; denying it, one feels as uncomfortable as a resident of Salem, Massachusetts, who denied the reality of witches in the seventeenth century. At the present time, in liberal quarters, something like a taboo acts to inhibit criticism of the United Nations. There is a feeling that the United Nations is "our last and best hope," that we shouldn't find fault with it; we shouldn't play into the hands of the archconservatives. However, let us not forget what Robert Louis Stevenson said: "The truth that is suppressed by friends is the readiest weapon of the enemy." If we love the truth we must openly deny the validity of the Universal Declaration of Human Rights, even though it is promoted by the United Nations. We should also join with Kingsley Davis[15] in attempting to get Planned Parenthood-World Population to see the error of its ways in embracing the same tragic ideal.

CONSCIENCE IS SELF-ELIMINATING

It is a mistake to think that we can control the breeding of mankind in the long run by an appeal to conscience. Charles Galton Darwin made this point when he spoke on the centennial of the publication of his grandfather's great book. The argument is straightforward and Darwinian.

People vary. Confronted with appeals to limit breeding, some people will undoubtedly respond to the plea more than others. Those who have more children will produce a larger fraction of the next generation than those with more susceptible consciences. The difference will be accentuated, generation by generation.

In C. G. Darwin's words: "It may well be that it would take hundreds of generations for the progenitive instinct to develop in this way, but if it should do so, nature would have taken her revenge, and the variety *Homo contracipiens* would become extinct and would be replaced by the variety *Homo progenitivus*."[16]

The argument assumes that conscience or the desire for children (no matter which) is hereditary—but hereditary only in the most general formal sense. The result will be the same whether the attitude is transmitted through germ cells, or exosomatically, to use A. J. Lotka's term. (If one denies the latter possibility as well as the former, then what's the point of education?) The argument has here been stated in the context of the population problem, but it applies equally well to any instance in which society appeals to an individual exploiting a commons to restrain himself for the general good—by means of his conscience. To make such an appeal is to set up a selective system that works toward the elimination of conscience from the race.

PATHOGENIC EFFECTS OF CONSCIENCE

The long-term disadvantage of an appeal to conscience should be enough to condemn it; but has serious short-term disadvantages as well. If we ask a man who is exploiting a commons to desist "in the name of conscience," what are we saying to him? What does he hear?—not only at the moment but also in the wee small hours of the night when, half asleep, he remembers not merely the words we used but also the nonverbal communication cues we gave him unawares? Sooner or later, consciously or subconsciously, he senses that he has received two communications, and that they are contradictory: (i) (intended communication) "If you don't do as we ask, we will openly condemn you for not acting like a responsible citizen"; (ii) (the unintended communication) "If you *do* behave as we ask, we will secretly condemn you for a simpleton who can be shamed into standing aside while the rest of us exploit the commons."

Every man then is caught in what Bateson has called a "double bind." Bateson and his coworkers have made a plausible case for viewing the double bind as an important causative factor in the genesis of schizophrenia.[17] The double bind may not always be so damaging, but it always endangers the mental health of anyone to whom it is applied. "A bad conscience," said Nietzsche, "is a kind of illness."

To conjure up a conscience in others is tempting to anyone who wishes to extend his control beyond the legal limits. Leaders at the highest level succumb to this temptation. Has any president during the past generation failed to call on labor unions to moderate voluntarily their demands for higher wages, or to steel companies to honor voluntary guidelines on prices? I can recall none. The rhetoric used on such occasions is designed to produce feelings of guilt in noncooperators.

For centuries it was assumed without proof that guilt was a valuable, perhaps even an indispensable, ingredient of the civilized life. Now, in this post-Freudian world, we doubt it.

Paul Goodman speaks from the modern point of view when he says: "No good has ever come from feeling guilty, neither intelligence, policy, nor compassion. The guilty do not pay attention to the object but only to themselves, and not even to their own interests, which might make sense, but to their anxieties." [18]

One does not have to be a professional psychiatrist to see the consequences of anxiety. We in the Western world are just emerging from a dreadful two-centuries-long Dark Ages of Eros that was sustained partly by prohibition laws, but perhaps more effectively by the anxiety-generating mechanisms of education. Alex Comfort has told the story well in *The Anxiety Makers;*[19] it is not a pretty one.

Since proof is difficult, we may even concede that the results of anxiety may sometimes, from certain points of view, be desirable. The larger question we should ask is whether, as a matter of policy, we should ever encourage the use of a technique the tendency (if not the intention) of which is psychologically pathogenic. We hear much talk these days of responsible parenthood; the coupled words are incorporated into the titles of some organizations devoted to birth control. Some people have proposed massive propaganda campaigns to instill responsibility into the nation's (or the world's) breeders, But what is the meaning of the word responsibility in this context? Is it not merely a synonym for the word conscience? When we use the word responsibility in the absence of substantial sanctions are we not trying to browbeat a free man in a commons into acting against his own interest? Responsibility is a verbal counterfeit for a substantial *quid pro quo*. It is an attempt to get something for nothing.

If the word responsibility is to be used at all, I suggest that it be in the sense Charles Frankel uses it.[20] "Responsibility," says this philosopher, "is the product of definite social arrangements." Notice that Frankel calls for social arrangements—not propaganda.

MUTUAL COERCION
MUTUALLY AGREED UPON

The social arrangements that produce responsibility are arrangements that create coercion, of some sort. Consider bank-robbing. The man who takes money from a bank acts as if the bank were a commons. How do we prevent such action? Certainly not by trying to control his behavior solely by a verbal appeal to his sense of responsibility. Rather than rely on propaganda we follow Frankel's lead and insist that a bank is not a commons; we seek the definite social arrangements that will keep it from becoming a commons. That we thereby infringe on the freedom of would-be robbers we neither deny nor regret.

The morality of bank-robbing is particularly easy to understand because we accept complete prohibition of this activity. We are willing to say "Thou shalt not rob banks," without providing for exceptions. But temperance also can be created by coercion. Taxing is a good coercive device. To keep downtown shoppers temperate in their use of parking space we introduce parking meters for short periods, and traffic fines for longer ones. We need not actually forbid a citizen to park as long as he wants to; we need merely make it increasingly expensive for him to do so. Not prohibition, but carefully biased options are what we offer him. A Madison Avenue man might call this persuasion; I prefer the greater candor of the word coercion.

Coercion is a dirty word to most liberals now, but it need not forever be so. As with the four-letter words, its dirtiness can be cleansed away by exposure to the light, by saying it over and over without apology or embarrassment. To many, the word coercion implies arbitrary decisions of distant and irresponsible bureaucrats; but this is not a necessary part of its meaning. The only kind of coercion I recommend is mutual coercion, mutually agreed upon by the majority of the people affected.

To say that we mutually agree to coercion is not to say that we are required to enjoy it, or even to pretend we enjoy it. Who enjoys taxes? We all grumble about them. But we accept compulsory taxes because we recognize that voluntary taxes would favor the conscienceless. We institute and (grumblingly) support taxes and other coercive devices to escape the horror of the commons.

An alternative to the commons need not be perfectly just to be preferable. With real estate and other material goods, the alternative we have chosen is the institution of private property coupled with legal inheritance. Is this system perfectly just? As a genetically trained biologist I deny that it is. It seems to me that, if there are to be differences in individual inheritance, legal possession should be perfectly correlated with biological inheritance—that those who are biologically more fit to be the custodians of property and power should legally inherit more. But genetic recombination continually makes a mockery of the doctrine of "like father, like son" implicit in our laws of legal inheritance. An idiot can inherit millions, and a trust fund can keep his estate intact. We must admit that our legal system of private property plus inheritance is unjust—but we put up with it because we are not convinced, at the moment, that anyone has invented a better system. The alternative of the commons is too horrifying to contemplate. Injustice is preferable to total ruin.

It is one of the peculiarities of the warfare between reform and the status quo that it is thoughtlessly governed by a double standard. Whenever a reform measure is proposed it is often defeated when its opponents triumphantly discover a flaw in it. As Kingsley Davis has pointed out,[21] worshippers of the status quo sometimes imply that no reform is possible without unanimous agreement, an implication contrary to historical fact. As nearly as I can make out, automatic rejection of proposed reforms is based on one of two unconscious assumptions: (i) that the status quo is perfect; or (ii) that the choice we face is between reform and no action; if the proposed reform is imperfect, we presumably should take no action at all, while we wait for a perfect proposal.

But we can never do nothing. That which we have done for thousands of years is also action. It also produces evils. Once we are aware that the status quo is action, we can then compare its discoverable advantages and disadvantages with the predicted advantages and disadvantages of the proposed reform, discounting as best we can for our lack of experience. On the basis of such a comparison, we can make a rational decision which will not involve the unworkable assumption that only perfect systems are tolerable.

Recognition of Necessity

Perhaps the simplest summary of this analysis of man's population problems is this: the commons, if justifiable at all, is justifiable only under conditions of low-population density. As the human population has increased, the commons has had to be abandoned in one aspect after another.

First we abandoned the commons in food gathering, enclosing farm land and restricting pastures and hunting and fishing areas. These restrictions are still not complete throughout the world.

Somewhat later we saw that the commons as a place for waste disposal would also have to be abandoned. Restrictions on the disposal of domestic sewage are widely accepted in the Western world; we are still struggling to close the commons to pollution by automobiles, factories, insecticide sprayers, fertilizing operations, and atomic energy installations.

In a still more embryonic state is our recognition of the evils of the commons in matters of pleasure. There is almost no restriction on the propagation of sound waves in the public medium. The shopping public is assaulted with mindless music, without its consent. Our government is paying out billions of dollars to create supersonic transport which will disturb 50,000 people for every one person who is whisked from coast to coast three hours faster. Advertisers muddy the airwaves of radio and television and pollute the view of travelers. We are a long way from outlawing the commons in matters of pleasure. Is this because our Puritan inheritance makes us view pleasure as something of a sin, and pain (that is, the pollution of advertising) as the sign of virtue?

Every new enclosure of the commons involves the infringement of somebody's personal liberty. Infringements made in the distant past are accepted because no contemporary complains of a loss. It is the newly proposed infringements that we vigorously oppose; cries of "rights" and "freedom" fill the air. But what does "freedom" mean? When men mutually agreed to pass laws against robbing, mankind became more free, not less so. Individuals locked into the logic of the commons are free only to bring on universal ruin; once they see the necessity of mutual coercion, they become free to pursue other goals. I believe it was Hegel who said, "Freedom is the recognition of necessity."

The most important aspect of necessity that we must now recognize, is the necessity of abandoning the commons in breeding. No technical solution can rescue us from the misery of overpopulation. Freedom to breed will bring ruin to all. At the moment, to avoid hard decisions many of us are tempted to propagandize for conscience and responsible parenthood. The temptation must be resisted, because an appeal to independently acting consciences selects for the disappearance of all conscience in the long run, and an increase in anxiety in the short.

The only way we can preserve and nurture other and more precious freedoms is by relinquishing the freedom to breed, and that very soon. "Freedom is the recognition of necessity"—and it is the role of education to reveal to all the necessity of abandoning the freedom to breed. Only so, can we put an end to this aspect of the tragedy of the commons.

Notes

1. J. B. Wiesner and H. F. York, *Sci. Amer.* **211** (No. 4), 27 (1964).

2. G. Hardin, *J. Hered.* **50**, 68 (1959); S. von Hoerner, *Science,* **137**, 18 (1962).

3. J. von Neumann and O. Morgenstern, *Theory of Games and Economic Behavior* (Princeton Univ. Press, Princeton, N.J., 1947), p. 11.

4. J. H. Fremlin, *New Sci.*, No. 415 (1964), p. 285.

5. A. Smith, *The Wealth of Nations* (Modern Library, New York, 1937), p. 423.

6. W. F. Lloyd, *Two Lectures on the Checks to Population* (Oxford Univ. Press, Oxford, England, 1833), reprinted (in part) in *Population, Evolution, and Birth Control,* G. Hardin, ed. (Freeman, San Francisco, 1964), p. 37.

7. A. N. Whitehead, *Science and the Modern World* (Mentor, New York, 1948), p. 17.

8. G. Hardin, Ed. *Population, Evolution, and Birth Control* (Freeman, San Francisco, 1964), p. 56.

9. S. McVay, *Sci. Amer.* **216** (No. 8), 13 (1966).

10. J. Fletcher, *Situation Ethics* (Westminster, Philadelphia, 1966).

11. D. Lack, *The Natural Regulation of Animal Numbers* (Clarendon Press, Oxford, 1954).

12. H. Girvetz, *From Wealth to Welfare* (Stanford Univ. Press, Stanford, Calif., 1950).

13. G. Hardin, *Perspec. Biol. Med.* **6**, 366 (1963).

14. U. Thant, *Int. Planned Parenthood News*, No. 168 (February, 1968), p. 3.

15. K. Davis, *Science* **158**, 730 (1967).

16. S. Tax, ed., *Evolution after Darwin* (Univ. of Chicago Press, Chicago, 1960), vol. 2, p. 469.

17. G. Bateson, D. D. Jackson, J. Haley, J. Weakland, *Behav. Sci.* **1**, 251 (1956).

18. P. Goodman, *New York Rev. Books* **10** (8), 22 (23 May 1968).

19. A. Comfort, *The Anxiety Makers* (Nelson, London, 1967).

20. C. Frankel, *The Case for Modern Man* (Harper, New York, 1955), p. 203.

21. J. D. Roslansky, *Genetics and the Future of Man* (Appleton-Century-Crofts, New York, 1966), p. 177.

The Tainted Sea

Wesley Marx

from The Frail Ocean

The sea is not always blue. Sometimes it is stained with a dull red that shrimp fishermen compare with tobacco juice and tourists with tomato soup. In the evening a much more dazzling color may emerge. A wave that feels the bottom, crests, and topples will release a phosphorescent surf of pale green or red hue. This glowing, advancing surf can be stunning, like lambent lightning across the sky or a rainbow on the horizon. Once, while viewing this radiance from a Malibu beach, I happened to glance back over my shoulder and noticed that my footprints also glowed for an instant in the wet sand.

To the residents of the Florida Gulf Coast a dull red sea is far more than just a curiosity, for it signifies the advent of a distressing chain of events commonly referred to as the "red tide." Amazed fishermen watch schools of mullet suddenly splashing about in a frenzy. Some leap out of the water, as if trying to escape their very home. This frantic activity gradually subsides, as fish after fish begins to float belly up. Soon a windrow of dead fish winds through the reddish sea. The entire school has perished.

Like a massive janitor's broom, the tides and the winds sweep fish windrow after fish windrow onto the glistening white Gulf beaches. Municipal bulldozers and roadscrapers hastily push the stinking, sun-basted wind-

51

rows into lime-filled pits. An odorless and colorless gas, swirling above this makeshift burial ground, causes beach visitors and vendors to tear, gasp, gag, and even vomit. Motel operators and hotel managers are besieged by guests suddenly turned hostile. The beauty of the night-tide surf hardly serves to compensate for the other properties of the red tide.

Although of little solace to a motel operator counting canceled vacation reservations, the phenomenon of discolored water—the scientifically accepted phrase for red tide—appears throughout the world. It occurs in a variety of shades and has been doing so for some time. The *Iliad* spoke of the Mediterranean's changing color, and the seventh chapter of Exodus observed the same chameleon quality on the lower Nile:

> And all of the waters that were in the river were turned to blood and the fish that was in the river died; and the river stank, and the Egyptians could not drink of the water of the river.

What this did to the Nile tourist trade is not mentioned.

The sea can and does turn white off Ceylon, yellow off Brazil, green off Spain, black off western Africa, and dull red off California. Puget Sound, in the state of Washington, and Delaware and Narrangansett bays on the eastern seaboard are also afflicted by "bloody waters." The sea turns red off Peru, but Peruvians call the lethal tide *el pintor,* in honor of the sulfurous fumes of accompanying decay that blacken ship's brass.

Although discolored water is worldwide, its impact on sea life varies enormously. In some areas it remains unaffected, and sea breezes stir as fresh as ever. In others discolored water mocks the ocean's beauty and fertility and indulges in an orgy of destruction. "The sea just gives up and dies," observed one perplexed oceanographer. That this is the occasional lot of Florida Gulf Coast waters is of great concern to state officials. In the pecking order of state problems one official has ranked the red tide as "second only to the weather." Such lofty concern has fostered a major attempt to eradicate the ocean's most incongruous phenomenon.

The Florida Gulf Coast has always considered itself blessed by its proximity to the Gulf of Mexico. "There seems to be no end to the oysters, the fish, the sea birds, the shells, the turtles along these waters," exulted Sidney Lanier, commissioned a century ago by the Atlantic Seaboard Railroad to write about the Florida Gulf Coast. Lanier was even more impressed by the coastline itself, grooved with spacious bays, rimmed by endless white beaches, and shadowed by leafy palms and sprawling mangrove trees. "This suave region," declared the poet-promoter, "is a sort of Arabian nights, vaguely diffused and beaten out into a long, glittering, sleepy expanse and the water presently cease to be waters and seem only great level enchantments-that-shine."

Cities devoted to cultivating such assets have long since sprung up: St. Petersburg, Pensacola, Tampa, Sarasota. Fishing fleets take mullet, red snapper, menhaden, and shrimp. Descendants of Greek divers venture out in boats called *Venus, Apollo,* and *Bozzaris* to dive to the rich sponge beds off Tarpon Springs. New York bankers and retired Chicago shopkeepers risk blisters and coronaries to pole marlin, sailfish, and the "silver king" of leaping sportfish, the tarpon. No coastline in the United States is favored with such a variety of marine species—more than three hundred of them.

Already a prominent fish hole and retirement haven (shuffleboard clubs in St. Petersburg boast memberships of three thousand plus), the Florida Gulf Coast now seeks to market its marine surroundings as a setting for industries that shape advanced technology. Toledo, Grand Rapids, Chicago, and St. Paul may have plenty of coal, iron, and synthetic rubber, but the Gulf Coast possesses the resource of the future—a marketable environment that can snare choosy scientists and engineers. There is nothing like a sunny beach and blue waves to spruce up a recruitment brochure.

The ominous red blemish on these southern waters first appeared in 1946. Up until that time the Florida

Gulf Coast had considered itself relatively immune to red tides, the last one having appeared in 1932, the one before that in 1916. But in November the water began turning red, and the severity of the ensuing red tide shattered any complacency. Dead fish accumulated on the Fort Myers shoreline at the rate of a hundred pounds per linear foot. A windrow ten yards wide stretched for some five miles on one beach. Road scrapers worked furiously to avert a public health menace. On serene Captiva Island one homeowner had to bury sixty thousand fish before regaining the use of his sandy front yard. Amid the piles of mullet and snapper lay the bloated forms of once-magnificent tarpon and frisky porpoises. Only true crabs and sponges managed to escape the vast marine purge. Biologist Gordon Gunter's conservative estimate was fifty million dead fish.

The red tide outbreak was not only severe but of long duration, lingering on until August of 1947, a period of ten months. The outbreak quickly assumed an exasperating enonomic form. Sport-boat skippers would take out a dwindling number of clients to catch snapper or tarpon. Whenever their boats passed through a reddish patch, the live bait in the stern tanks would suddenly splash spasmodically and then perish en masse. The water pump designed to keep the tank water fresh had cycled in a dose of the deadly red water. Skippers were forced to tell their clients that they could no longer offer them the means to catch whatever fish had managed to evade the red tide. Commercial fishing as well as sport fishing was sharply curtailed.

On shore the stinking beaches and choking air took their own toll. Demand for tourist accommodations in St. Petersburg almost stopped in one six-week period. Hotel and motel managers in Fort Myers reported a half-million-dollar loss in canceled reservations. Real estate prices in Sarasota plummeted. The fact that bathers could swim in the red waters and that vacationing fishermen could eat fish caught in them was of little consolation. If the stinking windrows and the invisible gas did not discourage Gulf visitors, the thick slimy nature of the discolored water usually did. "When taken up in the hand," noted Robert Ingle of the Florida State Board of Conservation, "the water runs from the fingers in strings like thin syrup." For travel agents the region was becoming a place to send expendable clients. The Florida Gulf Coast's prize asset, its waters, was contriving to place the region under economic quarantine.

Distress over the red tide was intensified by the fact that no one could fathom its cause. Rumor soon had it that the red tide was a Russian form of chemical warfare. This set others to speculating that the U.S. Navy had made a miscalculation during similar experiments. Almost routinely, atomic fallout was added to the rumor mill. A charge that particularly appealed to consumers was that fishermen were dumping their catches to keep prices high. But the rumor with the most staying power maintained that dumped nerve gas was the cause. The genesis of this theory lay in the fact that the Army had dumped quantities of nerve gas into the Gulf.

Added to the clamor of rumors were demands that the State Division of Salt Water Fisheries and the U.S. Fish and Wildlife Service poison, spray, disinfect or otherwise treat the red tide. Initially, these agencies were ill-equipped to cope with it. Although the United States began as a maritime nation, its interests—scientific as well as economic—have gravitated to land resources. Consequently the Department of Agriculture can sponsor broad scientific investigations, but the U.S. Fish and Wildlife Service and its state counterparts have too often been restricted to stocking fresh-water lakes with trout. This may have placated sport-fishing clubs, but it has hardly fostered a useful appreciation or understanding of the ocean.

Marine biologists from state and federal agencies were soon able to absolve Russia and the United States Navy. ("The Red Tide has nothing to do with Communism," observed *Science Newsletter* drily.) They were also able to squelch the nerve-gas rumor. The Army had indeed dumped nerve gas into the Gulf, but some three hundred miles away, off Mobile, and well after the initial red-tide outbreak.

A university biologist even succeeded in identifying the principal agent of death. Dr. C. C. Davis found one marine organism teeming in the red waters. Gymnodinium breve (nicknamed "Jim Brevis") measures one thousandth of an inch in width. This organism was tinting the Gulf red and killing fish by the millions.

G. breve belongs to the dinoflagellates (whirling organisms with whiplike appendages), an uncommonly talented class of plankton. Like plants, dinoflagellates use sunlight to transform sea nutrients into energy (photosynthesis). A red eyespot guides them to their proper light levels. Like animals, dinoflagellates are mobile, driven by currents, winds and their slim whiplike appendages. Under a microscope they are as exquisite as tiny jewel boxes. These unique organisms, half-animal, half-plant, drift cloudlike inside the sea, fine as fog, providing good grazing for fish and baleen whales.

These clouds can, however, burst into frantic fertility. G. breve will suddenly jump from one thousand to the quart to an incredible sixty million. A "bloom" becomes so dense that the eyespots of its members color the sea.

Some blooms, particularly those off California, emit a green or red phosphorescence. Sailors once regarded this nighttime radiance as the reflected flames of hell. One can even read a newspaper in the brilliance of a bloom in a Puerto Rican bay. The reason for such brilliance is not well understood; with their high phosphorous content, dinoflagellates may be literally striking themselves like matches. G. breve is not considered luminous; this quality in a Florida red tide comes from another dinoflagellate.

Most blooms provide a magnificent banquet for fish and whales. Others breed death, and the blooms of G. breve fall into this death-dealing category. G. breve blooms excrete a waste that immobilizes the nervous systems of fish, including their gills. This nerve toxin accounts for the spasmodic dance of the mullet just before death. The massive decomposition that results from the fish pogroms has another lethal aspect. At the same time that the products of decomposition provide more fuel for the blooms, the process of decomposition itself exhausts the oxygen content of the water and serves to suffocate the fish that have not yet breathed the toxin.

After the ominous rumors of atomic fallout and dumped nerve gas the residents of the Florida Gulf Coast had difficulty in believing that an invisible organism could be fostering the red tide and jeopardizing their sunshine and retirement economy. For the scientists the identification of the cause of the red tide led only to a more difficult question: what caused the *G. breve* to bloom? Blooms of dinoflagellates are as natural as the budding of flowers or the occurrence of earthquakes. The combinations of causative possibilities were almost infinite: winds, weather, supply of nutrients, light conditions, salinity, and so on. A precise knowledge of sea processes was a prerequisite to deciphering the *G. breve* blooms, and knowledge gained from trout-propagation programs and oyster-bed cultivation was hardly equal to this task. Obviously a major research program was in order. Scientists, unfortunately, were unable to cultivate *G. breve* in the laboratory, a situation that effectively cramped research once a red tide—with its abundant supply of *G. breve* specimens—had ebbed.

The residents of the Florida Gulf Coast thought there was a better way of dealing with this phenomenon—writing it off as a freakish occurrence. After all, only three had occurred in an equal number of decades. Four years then passed without another outbreak. A government laboratory studying *G. breve* blooms was closed for purposes of economy. Shortly afterward, the sea off Fort Myers again turned red. Only a seaward wind prevented fish corpses from inundating the beaches. A year later, another red tide bloomed. This time the winds were blowing the other way. The roadscrapers were back in business on the beaches. The following year, 1954, a new red tide ranged from Sarasota to Fort Myers—a span of fifty miles—and extended as far as fifteen miles out to sea. An extensive fish kill and clean-up ensued.

In the manner of a chamber of commerce dealing with a local hurricane, the tendency was to play down the reappearance of the red tide in order to stave off national publicity. But soon a group of Florida organizations petitioned President Eisenhower for federal money to control the latest bloom, which threatened "to make three hundred miles of highly developed Florida coastline uninhabitable." "Panic in Paradise" was the way one journalist sized up the local reaction.

Eight years after the 1946 outbreak the Fish and Wildlife Service was finally able to mount a modest research program. Cultures of *G. breve* were cultivated in laboratories as carefully as "orchids in a hothouse" to permit year-round study. All the moods of the sea—temperature, salinity, winds, and currents—were systematically observed and recorded in an attempt to isolate circumstances associated with *G. breve* blooms. A daily sea was virtually recreated on graph paper.

Gradually, a pattern began to emerge. Two of the severest red-tide outbreaks occurred in 1947 and 1953, years in which Florida's annual rainfall topped sixty inches, well above normal. Under the impact of the rain clouds the Peace River discharged into the Gulf at the rate of two thousand cubic feet per second, twice its rate during dry years. The correspondence between red-tide outbreaks and high rainfall led to an interesting speculation. Was the resulting high runoff from lands and rivers injecting massive doses of nutrients into the sea and "fertilizing" *G. breve* blooms? Suspicion began centering on phosphate, one particular nutrient in river discharges supplied copiously by inland phosphate mines. Such suspicion was allayed, however, by two subsequent disclosures. Red tides bloomed in waters low in phosphate content, and researchers discovered that seafloor deposits already supplied ample amounts of phosphate.

On the other hand, trace elements of iron, another ingredient of river discharges, was in much less generous sea supply. Researchers in the laboratory noted that iron stimulated the growth of G. breve. Another ingredient of high runoff, tannic acid, tended to make trace iron more soluble in seawater and thus more available to G. breve.

Researchers found that a prominent by-product of bacterial action in bays and harbors—vitamin B_{12}—also contributed to the growth of G. breve. The quiet, settling waters of bays and harbors could foster G. breve concentrations and thus make the B_{12} available for bloom enrichment.

While potential causes began to proliferate like G. breve blooms public pressure to control these deadly blossoms increased. The Fish and Wildlife Service and the State Board of Conservation found themselves trying to stamp out a scourge they were unable to explain. Setting natural predators on pests in one patented method of control. Unfortunately, the chief predator on the microscopic G. breve is another microscopic dino-flagellate, the luminous Noctiluca, which cannot be cultivated in predatory quantities. Chemical control agents can counteract known toxins, but even the Army's chemical warfare branch has failed to isolate and chemically identify G. breve toxin.

Prospective control measures then escalated to the extermination of the G. breve blooms themselves. Copper sulfate crystals can control algal blooms in lakes, observed researchers; why not G. breve blooms? Ernest Mitts of the Florida State Board of Conservation eagerly explained a heartening experiment to reporters. Within seconds after a copper penny was dropped into a quart of sea water containing sixty million G. breve all the G. breve perished. In 1957 a red tide obligingly appeared for field tests. Some fifty thousand dollars was released from a state red-tide emergency fund to underwrite an airborne assault by the Fish and Wildlife Service. Airplanes carrying tons of copper sulfate flew out over the ocean. Crop-dusting pilots, accustomed to guiding on orange-tree groves, were led to random red sea patches by smoke bombs dropped by spotter planes. A brilliant blue cloud of copper sulfate crystals descended on the patches. The control program, billed as the largest in marine history, at first fulfilled official hopes. The reddish patches vanished. "I think we have seen, in the last week and a half, the beginning of the end of the red tide as a menace to Florida," John Evans of the Fish and Wildlife Service told a reporter for *The Fisherman*. Unfortunately, within a week, the reddish patches reappeared. The copper sulfate had precipitated to the sea floor, a region shunned by *G. breve*. Spraying costs spiraled to one thousand and fifty dollars per square mile, a rather expensive proposition in dealing with a phenomenon of one hundred-square-mile dimensions. "In conclusion, we cannot recommend the dusting of copper sulfate as a control for a red tide outbreak of serious proportions," stated a Fish and Wildlife report coauthored by Mr. Evans.

The Fish and Wildlife Service then began a study of other measures of control. At last count the compounds tested numbered nearly five thousand. It seems that a certain compound in the Gulf waters inhibits toxic ambitions, but it has yet to be identified. Carbonic acid, the one control candidate that fulfills toxic requirements of one hundred per cent lethality in twenty-four hours, also happens to be toxic to agency budgets and to shrimp, the Gulf's most valuable marine crop.

A new approach in control programs has emerged from the association of red-tide outbreaks with high river discharges. Florida officials now feel that by a system of river dams high flow periods could be discharged over a number of months. Such river regulation would reduce the flow of *G. breve* nutrients such as tannic acid and B_{12}. *G. breve* would thus be placed on a diet—a diet enforced by dams. (A corollary project may involve the placement of giant air-bubbling hoses in the bays to induce motion and reduce *G. breve* and B_{12} concentrations.)

Besides requiring a major state expenditure, a dietary dam system would entail certain risks. The dams would have to be carefully located and regulated not to flood out or dry up the estuaries, the nurseries of the sea. (As Chapter 3 will reveal, however, dams do not combine well with beaches either. Indeed, the Gulf beaches, as well as *G. breve,* might wind up on a starvation diet.) Perhaps most ominously, the dams may turn into a case of putting out the fire by burning the building down. Dr. George Rounsefell of the University of Alabama, a veteran of red-tide investigations, notes that it can be quite difficult "to distinguish the poison ivy from the alfalfa." The importance of *G. breve,* trace iron, tannic acid, and B_{12} in the marine food chain is not precisely understood. Severe restrictions on their abundance might restrict the general fertility of the Gulf waters.

The acceptance of such large costs and risks becomes questionable in light of the actual damage caused by red tides. The large-scale fish kills have not resulted in any long-term reduction on commercial fish catches. Far from being rendered uninhabitable, the Florida Gulf Coast continues to grow bullishly. National articles with titles like "Blood in the Gulf" have failed to discourage migrants.

Why, if the red tide appears as nothing more than a mystifying nuisance, is Florida preparing to escalate from municipal roadscrapers to public dams? The answer lies partly in the aftermath of an oyster-gathering party on a bar in Little Sarasota Bay in December 1962. After collecting about one and one half bushels of oysters, a family of three began consuming the harvest—both raw and roasted—at the rate of ten to fifteen per meal. Soon they experienced a tingling sensation in the face that spread to the fingers and toes. Hot coffee tasted cold, and a cold drink of water seemed to "burn" the throat. Diarrhea set in. The father had difficulty keeping his car on the right side of the road, and his nineteen-year-old son complained of feeling drunk.

These symptoms all subsided within a day or so, but the Charlotte County Health Department was disturbed enough to send refrigerated oyster samples to the Public Health Service's research branch in Cincinnati. The Taft Sanitary Engineering Center injected extracts from the oysters into mice. The mice died, but not instantly as they would have of paralytic shellfish poison. Death was preceded by four hours of labored breathing, a symptom that suggested a poison called ciguatera. Ciguatera's unpredictable occurrence in barracuda, snapper, and reef fishes in tropical areas has already produced elaborate taboos that frustrate attempts to expand South Sea fisheries.

Researchers were unable to determine where the oysters picked up such toxicity. When it was noted, however, that its emergence coincided with a red-tide outbreak, *G. breve* extracts were injected into mice. The same deadly symptoms recurred. The oysters of Little Sarasota Bay were apparently not only picking up *G. breve* toxin but were concentrating it into levels harmful to man.

As a result of this perilous magnification, the harvesting of mussels, clams, and other shellfish is prohibited between the months of May and September on the California coast. These shellfish too effectively concentrate toxins secreted by dinoflagellates peculiar to the Pacific Coast. Before the prohibition some three hundred forty-six cases of shellfish poisoning were reported, twenty-four ending in death. "The afflicted person acts as though he were drunk," says zoologist Eugene Bouvee of the University of California at Los Angeles. "No antidote for this poisoning is known." The occurrence of ciguateralike poison in shellfish exposed to *G. breve* has shaken the original assumption that their blooms could not be toxic to man. Man can apparently swim safely in waters tainted by the bloom, yet become sick after eating a juicy clam plucked from identical waters.

The periodic closure of shellfish harvesting areas has become a new and unfortunate feature of red-tide outbreaks in Florida. Concern over these outbreaks is further heightened by an ominous recitation. Red-tide outbreaks of varying severity have occurred in 1952, 1953, 1954, 1957, 1958, 1959, 1960, 1961, 1962, 1963, and 1964. What was once only rarely seen has now become a feature of the Florida Gulf Coast as common as mangrove trees and tarpon. This situation inspires haunting speculation. Will the cycle of red tides recede to pre-1946 levels or will it intensify—intensify in severity and duration as well as in frequency—and thus imperil the Gulf Coast's "great level enchantments-that-shine"? Do man's increasing waste discharges into ocean-bound rivers account for such an upward cycle or is it propelled by forces that heed only the impersonal laws of nature? Unable to answer these questions, Florida finds itself seriously considering such expensive and risky projects as regulating the diet of a microscopic creature by means of dams. The Gulf of Mexico may be able to take red tides in stride, but Florida feels it cannot afford such nonchalance.

Meanwhile, red tides in southern California are on the increase. The offending dinoflagellate in this area is *Gonyaulax polyhedra*. Perplexed investigators with the California State Fish and Game Department cannot very well implicate river discharges in *G. polyhedra* blooms. As the California beaches demonstrate so well, river runoff has been virtually dammed up. The quiet settling waters of harbors and proliferating marinas are suspects; under consideration is the use of bubbling air hoses to agitate the calm waters. Recent red-tide outbreaks have left ten million fish floating belly up in harbor waters. The Sea World Oceanarium in San Diego was forced on one occasion to cancel half its shows. The star performer, a female pilot whale housed in an ocean-connected lagoon, died in the wake of a red-tide outbreak. Oceanarium officials blamed the death on *G. polyhedra*. As in Florida, such monumental kills generate public pressure on conservation officials. "But stopping a red tide," says John Carlisle of the Fish and Game Department, "is like trying to stop an earthquake."

Red-tide outbreaks off Peru pose a grave problem. Over the last decade Peru has surpassed the United States, Russia, Communist China, and Japan in annual fish landings, with 9.1 metric tons. That Peru paces world fishing activity is all the more remarkable, for a single fish, the small anchoveta, ground to fishmeal, is responsible. The susceptibility of anchoveta to periodic red-tide (*el-pintor*) outbreaks jeopardizes the stability of the world's leading fishmeal industry. Another major industry is similarly affected. Cormorants feed on the anchoveta and then deposit their excrement on "guano island." These prodigious droppings support a flourishing fertilizer industry. When the sea turns red, Peruvians worry, not about show whales and the tourist trade, but about their country's entire economy. At the same time the world fishmeal and fertilizer markets go into a price tizzy.

Such encounters with the phenomenon of discolored water are instructive to a world with pretensions of conquering the ocean. Twenty-two years after the alarming Florida red tide of 1946–1947 the understanding, prediction, and control of *G. breve* blooms still lie in the future. More appropriate allocation of funds is finally modifying this lingering ignorance. (Although the Fish and Wildlife Service began devoting more substantial resources to investigations by 1954, the Florida State Legislature dallied until 1963 before supporting a large-scale state research project.) The resulting imbalance between public interest in the ocean and public funding of ocean research fosters a disconcerting situation. Although we seem to know a good deal about the ocean as a resource, we know little about the ocean as an environment. As long as this imbalance persists, phenomena like discolored water will rebuke our claims to ocean conquest.

As this imbalance is righted in the Florida red-tide situation, a most ironic situation begins to emerge. Scientists are fascinated by the way in which a marine organism such as *G. breve* can immobilize creatures ten times its size by excreting a toxin. A study of this constant chemical warfare promises to produce a rich source of pharmaceuticals. Dr. Ross Nigrelli of the New York Aquarium injected poison from a sea cucumber into cancers induced in mice. The cancer tumor stopped growing. Dr. Nigrelli told a *New Yorker* reporter that he has also been able to isolate chemicals in marine organisms "that have antiviral, antimicrobial, tumor-inhibiting, nerve-blocking, and heart-stimulating properties." In another area of investigation Dr. S. H. Hunter of Haskins Laboratory, New York, has been intrigued by marine blooms ever since as a boy he watched purple and green algal blooms in city drainage ditches. Although New York drainage ditches and the Gulf of Mexico suffer from blooms of over-fertility, Dr. Hunter points out that substantial parts of the ocean appear to suffer from under-fertility. If prediction and even control of the red tide materializes, Dr. Hunter wonders if man may not then be able to "set off nutritious tides, cultivating the sea as we do the land." In the marine realm opportunity and calamity are not far separated.

Energy

Garrett De Bell

All power pollutes.

Each of the major forms of power generation does its own kind of harm to the environment. Fossil fuels—coal and oil—produce smoke and sulfur dioxide at worst; even under ideal conditions they convert oxygen to carbon dioxide. Hydroelectric power requires dams that cover up land, spoil wild rivers, increase water loss by evaporation, and eventually produce valleys full of silt. Nuclear power plants produce thermal and radioactive pollution and introduce the probability of disaster.

We are often told that it is essential to increase the amount of energy we use in order to meet demand. This "demand," we are told, must be met in order to increase or maintain our "standard of living." What these statements mean is that if population continues to increase, and if per capita power continues to increase as in the past, then power generation facilities must be increased indefinitely.

Such statements ignore the environmental consequences of building more and more power generation facilities. They ignore the destruction of wild rivers by dams, the air pollution by power plants, the increasing danger of disease and disaster from nuclear power facilities.

These effects can no longer be ignored, but must be directly confronted. *The perpetually accelerating expansion of power output is not necessary.*

It is assumed by the utilities that the demand for

power is real because people continue to purchase it. However, we are all bombarded with massive amounts of advertising encouraging us to buy appliances, gadgets, new cars, and so on. There is no comparable public service advertising pointing up the harmful effects of over-purchase of "convenience" appliances that increase use of power. Public utilities aggressively advertise to encourage increasing use of power. For instance, Pacific Gas and Electric advertises: "Beautify America—use electric clothes dryers." The unbeautifying results of building more power plants is, of course, not mentioned.

For the lopsided advertising, public utilities use public monies, paid in by the consumer. This is allowed by the regulatory agencies on the theory that increasing use of power lowers the per unit cost, which is beneficial to the consumer. However, the consumer is also the person who breathes the polluted air and has his view spoiled by a power plant. Therefore, this sort of advertising should be prohibited.

But perhaps it is unrealistic to expect the power companies and the appliance and car builders to call a halt, to flatly say, "This is where we stop. The limits have been reached, even exceeded." The limits can, and must, be set by the consumer. It is the consumer, ultimately, who must decide for himself what appliances he needs and which he can forego. The producers of power and power-using appliances will feel the pinch but they will, ultimately, cease to produce that which will not *sell*.

We *can* control our population and thus decrease our per capita use of power. Population may be stabilized, and use of power reduced to what is necessary for a high quality of life. But population control will take time. We can begin now by ceasing to use power for trivial purposes.

Power use is presently divided about as follows in the United States: household and commercial, 33 percent; industrial, 42 percent; transportation, 24 percent. We must decide which uses, within each category, improve the quality of peoples' lives sufficiently to justify the inevitable pollution that results from power generation and use.

HOUSEHOLD AND COMMERCIAL

The term "standard of living" as used by utility spokesmen in the United States today generally means abundant luxuries, such as the following, for the affluent: electric blenders, toothbrushes and can openers, power saws, toys and mowers, dune buggies, luxury cars and golf carts, electric clothes dryers and garbage grinders, air conditioners, electric blankets and hair dryers.

Are these necessary for a high quality of life? We must realize that a decision made to purchase one of these "conveniences" is also a decision to accept the environmental deterioration that results from the production, use and disposal of the "convenience." Hand-operated blenders, toothbrushes, can openers and saws, clotheslines, blankets, bicycles, and feet produce much less pollution than the powered equivalents.

We can make the ecologically sensible decision to reject the concept of increasing perpetually the "standard of living" regardless of the human or ecological consequences. We can replace the outmoded industrial imperative—the "standard of living" concept—by the more human "quality of life" concept.

Many of us feel that the quality of our lives would be higher with far less use of energy in this country. We would be happy to do with fewer cars, substituting a transportation system that can make us mobile without dependence on the expensive, polluting, and dangerous automobile. We would be happy to see the last of glaring searchlights, neon signs, noisy power mowers and private airplanes, infernally noisy garbage trucks, dune buggies, and motorcycles. The quality of our lives is improved by each power plant not constructed near our homes or recreation areas, by each dam not constructed on a river used for canoeing. Quality of life is a positive ethic. Peace and quiet and fresh air are positive values; noisy smoking machines are negative ones.

Industry

Industry has been rapidly increasing its use of energy to increase production. An *Electrical World* pamphlet cheerfully describes this trend as follows:

> Industry's use of electric power has been increasing rapidly, too. The index of consumer use of electricity is kilowatts-per-hour. Industry's use is measured as the amount used per employee. Ten years ago, American industry used 24,810 kilowatt hours per year for each person employed. Today, the figure is estimated at 37,-912. As industry finds more ways to use power to improve production, the output and wages of the individual employee rise.

Since unemployment is a problem and power use causes pollution, perhaps automation which uses energy to replace workers isn't a very good idea. Of course we could have full employment, a shorter work week, and less power use if we just wouldn't bother producing things that don't really improve the quality of life—pay for, and that complicate our lives.

Transportation

If you wanted to design a transportation system to waste the earth's energy reserves and pollute the air as much as possible, you couldn't do much better than our present system dominated by the automobile. Only by following the advice of the popular science journals, placing in every garage a helicopter (using three times as much gasoline per passenger mile as a car) could you manage to do greater environmental damage.

Compared to a bus, the automobile uses from four to five times as much fuel per passenger mile. Compared to a train, it uses ten times as much. Walking and bicycling, of course, require no fuel at all.[1]

Switching from the system of automobilism to a system of rapid transit, with more bicycling and walking in cities, would reduce fossil fuel consumption for transportation by a factor of almost 10. As transportation now accounts for 24 percent of the fuel expended, a saving of even 50 percent in this category would be helpful in reducing the rapid consumption of fossil fuels. Added benefits would be fewer deaths and injuries by automobiles, which have much higher injury rates than any form of public transportation; the liberation of much of the cities' space presently dedicated to the automobile; and less smog.

The term "standard of living" usually seems to apply only to Americans, and usually just to the present generation. It is important to think of all people in the world, and of future generations. The question must be asked whether it is fair to the rest of the world for the United States to use up such a disproportionate share of the world's energy resources. Even looking solely to United States interests, is it the best policy to use up our allotment as fast as possible?

If the whole world had equal rights and everyone burned fuel as fast as the U.S., the reserves would be gone very soon. The U.S. per capita rate of use of fossil fuels is from ten to a hundred times as great as the majority of people (the Silent Majority?) who live in the underdeveloped countries.

Each person in India uses only 1/83 as much power as an American. India now has 500,000,000 people or 2½ times the population of the U.S. Yet since each person uses so much less power, India's total power use is only 1/33 of that of the U.S. Its fair share would be 2½ times as much power as the U.S. The same argument, with somewhat different figures, holds for China, Southeast Asia, Pakistan, the Middle East, South America and Africa.

Not only does the burning of fossil fuels produce local pollution, but it also increases the carbon dioxide-to-oxygen ratio in the atmosphere. This occurs because each molecule of oxygen consumed in burning fuels results in the production of a carbon dioxide molecule (CH_2O plus O_2 yields CO_2 plus H_2O). This has the doubly adverse effect of taking oxygen out of the atmosphere, and putting carbon dioxide in, in equal amounts. The latter effect is of most concern to us because the CO_2 percentage in the atmosphere is minute compared to the huge reservoir of oxygen. While the atmosphere contains 20 percent oxygen, it has only 0.02 percent CO_2. Thus, fuel combustion reducing the O_2 concentration by only 1 percent would simultaneously increase the CO_2 concentration *tenfold*.

Each year the burning of fossil fuels produces an amount of carbon dioxide equal to about 0.5 percent of the existing carbon dioxide reservoir in the atmosphere. Of this production, half stays in the atmosphere, resulting in a 0.25 percent increase in atmospheric CO_2 per year. Of the other half, some becomes bound up with calcium or magnesium to become limestone, some becomes dissolved in the sea, and some is stored as the bodies of plants that fall to the deep, oxygen-poor sediments of the ocean and do not decompose.

If no CO_2 were being disposed of by the physical and biological processes in the ocean, then the CO_2 concentration of the atmosphere would increase by twice the present rate, because all of the CO_2 produced each year would remain in the atmosphere.

Burning all the recoverable reserves of fossil fuels would produce three times as much carbon dioxide as is now present in the atmosphere. If the present rate of increase in fuel use continues, and the rate of CO_2 dispersal continues unchanged, there will be an increase of about 170 percent in the CO_2 level in the next 150 years (which is the minimum estimate of the amount of time our fossil fuels will last). If the fuels last longer, say up to the "optimistic" 400 years that some predict, we will have that much more CO_2 increase, with the attendant smog and oil spills.

Scientists are becoming worried about increasing CO_2 levels because of the greenhouse effect, with its possible repercussions on the world climate. Most of the sun's energy striking the earth's surface is in the form of visible and ultraviolet rays from the sun. Energy leaves the earth as heat radiation or infrared rays. Carbon dioxide absorbs infrared rays more strongly than visible or ultraviolet rays. Energy coming toward the earth's surface thus readily passes through atmospheric carbon dioxide, but some escaping heat energy is absorbed and trapped in the atmosphere by carbon dioxide, much as heat is trapped in a greenhouse. This effect of carbon dioxide on the earth's climate has, in fact, been called the "greenhouse effect." Scientists differ in their opinions as to the eventual result this will have on our climate. Some believe that the earth's average temperature will increase, resulting in the melting of polar ice caps with an accompanying increase of sea levels and inundation of coastal cities. Others feel that there will be a temporary warming and partial melting of polar ice, but then greater evaporation from the open Arctic seas will cause a vast increase in snowfall, with an ensuing ice age.

Many people believe that green plants can produce a surplus of oxygen to compensate for that converted to CO_2 in burning fuels. This is not true. A plant produces only enough oxygen for its own use during its life plus enough extra for the oxidation of the plant after death to its original buildings blocks (CO_2 plus H_2O). Whether this oxidation occurs by fire, by bacterial decay, or by respiration of an animal eating the plant, has no effect on the ultimate outcome. When the plant is totally consumed by any of these three means, all of the oxygen it produced over its life is also consumed. The only way a plant leaves an oxygen surplus is if it fails to decompose, a relatively rare occurrence.

The important point is that fossil fuel combustion results in a change in the ratio of carbon dioxide to oxygen in the atmosphere, whereas use of oxygen by animals does not. This point is not generally understood, so two examples are discussed below.

First, since 70 percent of the world's oxygen is produced in the ocean, it has been forecast that death of the plankton in the ocean would cause asphyxiation of the animals of the earth. This is not the case because oxygen and carbon dioxide cycle in what is called the carbon cycle. A plant, be it a redwood tree or an algal cell, produces just enough oxygen to be used in consuming its carcass after death. The ocean plankton now produce 70 percent of the oxygen, but animals in the ocean use it up in the process of eating the plants. Very little of it is left over. The small amount that is left over is produced by plankton that have dropped to the oxygen-poor deep sediments and are essentially forming new fossil fuel.

If the plankton in the ocean were all to die tomorrow, all of the animals in the ocean would starve. The effect of this on the world's oxygen supply would be very small. The effect on the world's food supply, however, would be catastrophic. A large number of nations rely significantly on the ocean for food, particularly for high-quality protein. Japan, for example, is very heavily dependent on fisheries to feed itself.

"Eco-catastrophe" by Paul Ehrlich, reprinted below, stresses the danger of poisoning plankton, and puts the emphasis where it belongs, on the effect on animal life.

Second, fears about reducing the world's oxygen supply have been expressed in reference to the cutting down of large forest areas, particularly in the tropics, where the soil will become hardened into bricklike laterite and no plant growth of any sort will be possible in the future. It will be a disaster if the Amazon rain forest is turned into laterite because the animals and people dependent on it could not exist. But this would have no effect on the world's oxygen balance. If the Amazon Basin were simply bricklike laterite, the area would produce no oxygen and consume no oxygen. At present the Amazon Basin is not producing surplus organic material. The same amount of organic material is present in the form of animal bodies, trees, stumps, and humus from year to year; therefore no net production of oxygen exists. The oxygen produced in the forest each year, which obviously is a large amount, is used up by the animals and microorganisms living in the forest in the consumption of the plant material produced over the preceding year.

In summary, I suggest that one goal of the environmental movement should be the reduction of total energy use in this country by 25 percent over the next decade.

By doing this, we will have made a start toward preventing possibly disastrous climatic changes due to CO_2 buildup and the greenhouse effect. We will so reduce the need for oil that we can leave Alaska as wilderness and its oil in the ground. We will be able to stop offshore drilling with its ever-present probability of oil slick disasters, and won't need new supertankers which can spill more oil than the *Torrey Canyon* dumped on the beaches of Britain and France. We will be able to do without the risks of disease and accident from nuclear power plants. We won't need to dam more rivers for power. And perhaps most important, we can liberate the people from the automobile, whose exhausts turn the air over our cities oily brown (which causes, 50,000 deaths a year) and which is turning our landscape into a sea of concrete.

Many of the steps needed to reduce energy consumption are clear. We can press for:

1. Bond issues for public transit
2. Gas tax money to go to public transportation, not more highways
3. Ending of oil depletion allowance, which encourages use of fuel
4. More bicycle and walking paths
5. Better train service for intermediate length runs
6. A reverse of the present price system for power use where rates are lower for big consumers. Put a premium on conserving resources. Give householders power for essential needs at cost with heavy rate increases for extra energy for luxuries.

BIBLIOGRAPHY

Dreisbach, R., *Handbook of the San Francisco Region*. Environmental Studies, Palo Alto, California.

"The Power Crisis," *Electrical World*, New York, New York.

Environmental Pollution Panel, President's Science Advisory Committee, *Restoring the Quality of Our Environment*. U.S. Government Printing Office, Washington,

D.C. (especially Section I, "Carbon Dioxide from Fossil Fuels—The Invisible Pollutant").

Annual Report 1968. Resources for the Future, Inc., Washington, D.C. (especially Special Report, "Patterns of U.S. Energy Use and How They Have Evolved").

Plass, G. N., "Carbon Dioxide and Climate" in *Scientific American*, July, 1959 (or offprint #823).

NOTES

1. Driesbach, R., *Handbook of the San Francisco Region*. Environmental Studies, Palo Alto, California, p. 322.

Pesticides Since *Silent Spring*

Steven H. Wodka

If one considers that almost every fruit, vegetable, or grain that he eats has been sprayed, dusted, or gassed by some type of poison at least once during its lifetime, one wonders when the system is going to break down. According to the Food and Drug Administration, at least 800 to 1,000 people die each year from pesticide poisoning and another 80,000 to 90,000 people are injured from these chemicals. There have been massive kills of fish, birds, and beneficial insects. But worse yet will be the slow but increased number of human deaths caused by the carcinogenic, mutagenic, and teratogenic effects of chemicals like DDT or 2,4,5–T after a lifetime of exposure.

This was the warning of Rachel Carson more than eight years ago in her monumental *Silent Spring*. But today's news media, especially after the Mrak Commission report on pesticides, speak of DDT in unborn infants as if it was a new discovery. In 1962, Rachel Carson wrote:

In experimental animals, the chlorinated hydrocarbon insecticides freely cross the barrier of the placenta, the traditional protective shield between the embryo and the harmful substances in the mother's body. While the quantities so received by human infants would normally be small, they are not unimportant because children are more susceptible to poisoning than adults. This situation also means that today the average individual almost certainly starts life with the first deposit of the growing load

76

of chemicals his body will be required to carry thenceforth.[1]

Even as early as 1950, FDA scientists declared that it is "extremely likely the potential hazard of DDT has been underestimated." [2] Thus the validity of *Silent Spring* is still great today and it should be read.

Since 1962, new studies have underscored the hazard of DDT. This "thin-shelled phenomenon" has become quite widespread in certain birds across the United States. DDT provokes the livers of mother birds into excess production of an enzyme which breaks down the steroid hormones essential to the manufacture of calcium. Lacking adequate calcium, the birds' eggs emerge thin-shelled and flaky, offering scant protection for the embryo. The National Audubon Society reported finding a bald-eagle egg on the shores of Lake Superior with no shell at all—just a fragile membrane. Other bird species are experiencing declining populations from the thin-shelled phenomenon—the osprey, the peregrine falcon, the brown pelican, and the Bermuda petrel.

The possibility of upsetting oceanic food chains was raised in 1968 concerning the action of minute concentrations of DDT on photosynthesis in algae.[3] In a species of freshwater algae, as well as in five species of marine algae, concentrations of only a few parts per billion of DDT were accompanied by depressions in the rate of photosynthesis and cell reproduction in the plants. These microscopic marine plants are the base of the oceanic food chain upon which all fisheries depend. Thus Dr. Charles Wurster of the New York State University at Stony Brook warned: "Such effects [on algae] are insidious and their cause may be obscure, yet they may be ecologically more important than the obvious, direct mortality of larger organisms."

A third area of significance concerns genetic effects on natural populations caused by DDT. Dr. Lawrence Cory, professor of biology at St. Mary's College in California, has found high correlations between DDT spraying in the western United States and geographic distribution of chromosomal changes in fruit flies that were in the path of those DDT residues. Cory claims that this evidence may "constitute a serious situation having implications for populations of all organisms."

The outlook for DDT's direct effect on man also looks quite bleak. Dr. William B. Deichmann of the University of Miami School of Medicine has found that persons who had liver cancer, leukemia, high blood pressure, and carcinoma at the time of death had two to three times more residues of DDT and related pesticides stored in their body tissues than did persons who died accidental deaths.[4] The National Cancer Institute in Bethesda, Maryland, has produced evidence incriminating DDT and related pesticides as the cause of tumors of the liver and lung in mice. When men are consistently exposed to such chemicals, adds the University of Colorado's Dr. David Metcalf, there is deterioration of memory and reaction time.[5] Dr. Richard Welch, senior pharmacologist at the Burroughs-Wellcome Research Lab in Tuckahoe, New York, ran studies on rats which show that DDT produces an increase in the size of the uterus. This causes a breakdown of sex hormones, reduces the effectiveness of some drugs, and may cause "a possible calcium deficiency" in bones. He also pointed out that because of the similarities between rats and humans, some of the same effects "probably do occur in man."[6]

Furthermore, the Russians warn us that their workers who are occupationally exposed to DDT and other organo-chlorine pesticides have shown disturbances of stomach and liver functions after ten years of contact. Even the workers exposed less than ten years had increased acid and pepsin secretion in their stomachs with slight disturbances of liver function. Those who were exposed more than ten years showed an inhibition of acid and pepsin secretion in the stomach; in the liver there was pronounced disturbance of protein and sugar metabolism.[7] At least there is a wide variety of symptoms that we can sadly look forward to from the 10 to 110 ppm of DDT that we store on the average in our fat.[8]

In November, 1969, the federal government announced an official ban of this programmed madness by the end of 1970. By that time DDT can only be used for "emergencies." Unfortunately, that will not spell the end of man and nature's exposure to DDT. According to Taylor Pryor, president of the Oceanic Foundation, "most of the DDT ever used is still active in the atmosphere or locked in soils ready to be removed by evaporation or by run-off into the sea. [Over 1 billion pounds of DDT are still in the biosphere.][9] With a 10-50 year half-life remaining, what effects will follow?"[10] The effects look rather clear—the extinction of several bird species and massive fish kills. But more morbid are the potential effects on the subjects in the largest experiment ever run—200 million human guinea pigs.

THE HERBICIDES

Herbicides, the weed-killing chemicals, are not immune from suspicion. In October, 1969, a report of tests commissioned by the National Cancer Institute showed that some of the herbicides used extensively in Vietnam for defoliation can cause birth malformations in experimental animals. The study found that 2,4,5–Trichlorophenoxyacetic acid (2,4,5–T) causes birth malformations in rats and mice and concludes that it is probably dangerous to man. The herbicide 2,4–D also causes birth malformations and is classified as potentially dangerous, but needing further study. Since 1962, United States military aircraft have been spraying herbicides containing 2,4,5–T and 2,4–D over forests and crop lands in South Vietnam. About 100 million pounds of herbicides have been sprayed over 4 million acres.[11]

In view of these findings, there is a distinct possibility that the use of herbicides in Vietnam is causing birth malformations among infants of exposed mothers. The amount of 2,4,5–T and 2,4–D sprayed is generally 20-30 pounds per acre. In rural districts, drinking and cooking water is often taken directly from rain-fed cisterns and ponds. Ingestion of several milligrams a day could occur from this source for several days following aerial spraying.

The lowest dose of 2,4,5–T administered orally to rats in the above study was 4.6 milligrams per kilogram of body weight for each of the 6 days during pregnancy. Thirty of the 66 fetuses found in these animals were grossly abnormal, nearly 4 times the proportion found in animals not given 2,4,5–T. Higher doses gave higher proportions of malformed fetuses, reaching 100 percent. Scaled up for a 44-kilogram human, the low dose corresponds to 200 milligrams per day for several weeks. Although the doses received by exposed persons in Vietnam may seldom be this high, it cannot be said that the margin of safety is adequate. The sensitivity of humans may be quite different from that of rats. Although the laboratory tests do not prove that 2,4,5–T (or 2,4–D) causes birth malformations in humans at the dose levels experienced in Vietnam, the tests do suggest this possibility.

Since late 1967, according to testimony in front of the House Foreign Affairs Committee on December 2, 1969 by Hans Swyter, a former aide to Secretary of Defense McNamara, there have been increasing reports and pictures in the Saigon press of a new kind of abnormality in newly born children.

At least four newspapers in South Vietnam printed stories—and pictures—in the summer of 1969 of deformed babies born in villages sprayed with 2,4,5–T and the newspapers were promptly closed down by the Thieu government for "interfering with the war effort."[12]

Since the hazard became known, the Defense Department has announced that it would no longer spray 2,4,5–T near populated areas with two exceptions: it would be used against enemy "training and regroupment centers"[13] and in areas where the population is not loyal to the Saigon government.[14] Rural areas will still receive the heavy dose. According to Mankiewicz and Braden, "Not since the Romans salted the land after destroying Carthage has a nation taken pains to visit the war upon future generations."

In this country, individual exposure to these chemicals is generally much lower than in Vietnam, but it too may represent a hazard. Thus the Department of Agriculture will ban 2,4,5–T from use on food crops effective January 1, 1970, unless by that time FDA has found a basis for establishing a safe legal tolerance in and on foods. No action was announced for 2,4–D which was labelled "potentially dangerous." This chemical is much more widely used than 2,4,5–T and is depended on in corn and wheat production. It is one of the 6 best selling pesticides in the United States. Banning it would deprive the U.S. pesticide industry of more than $25 million annually in sales. For such reasons, our health and the health of future generations has been forfeited.

AND FOR THE AMERICAN PEASANT . . .

For one group in this country the plight of the Vietnamese peasant does not seem remote. The farm worker, upon whom we depend so much to harvest our nation's food supply, lives and works in near slavery. This is especially true for the migrant worker. There is work only during the warm months of the year, and even then the boss does not have to pay him the legal minimum wage (average income for farm workers: $1232 a year). So the whole family goes to work, including the children, to earn as much as possible. Thus the farm-worker family has close exposure to dangerous pesticides—from contaminated drinking water, from living in close proximity to sprayed fields, from "accidentally" being sprayed while working in the fields, and from working among crops on which the residues of dangerous pesticides are still active.

In farming areas where there is a dangerous job to be done, like spraying a highly toxic chemical, it is common to hear the boss say, "*I* wouldn't do that. I'll get some Mexican to do it." So here is a fifth source of pesticide contamination for the farm worker—applying the chemical. Furthermore, the farm worker may not be able to read English or may be illiterate. In this case he cannot partake of that great panacea (according to the U. S. Department of Agriculture) for all ecological and hygienic problems from pesticides—the label. The label, which manufacturers spend thousands of dollars to have approved by the USDA and over which scientists feud, is usually too complicated for a farm worker to understand in the short time before the boss orders him to get moving. And I have yet to see such a label in Spanish.

Thus, according to Professor Matthew Meselsen of Harvard University, the effects of chemicals such as 2,4,5–T may already be evident in those deep rural areas of the U. S. where the farm worker lives. Right now someone could begin a statistical study of miscarriages and stillbirths among farm-worker women in comparison with a control group.

Though the farm worker is a victim of some of the worst exposure to pesticides, he is now organizing himself into one of the most effective power blocs for controls over the use of these dangerous chemicals. Through the efforts of the United Farm Workers Organizing Committee (UFWOC), the workers at the Perelli-Minetti Ranch near Delano, California, have achieved an historic breakthrough for farm workers. In 1969 Perelli-Minetti, which raises wine grapes, signed an agreement with their unionized farm workers in which the workers asked for and received a ban on the use of DDT, aldrin, dieldrin, and endrin. The agreement also provides for safety controls over the use of the organophosphate pesticides, including blood tests paid for by the company. The company will also provide the union with the detailed records of all its pesticide and herbicide programs so the union can effectively advise workers and consumers and also negotiate knowledgeably with the company.

Thus for a while, at least, effective environmental and consumer protection from pesticides depends on the success of the United Farm Workers in organizing farm workers and winning contracts. The workers, in contrast to federal and state officials, have their lives at stake and will rigidly enforce pesticide safety clauses. In the current table-grape strike, the workers are left with only one nonviolent means of keeping pressure on the growers—the grape boycott. But the farm workers have even used the boycott operation to warn consumers of pesticide dangers. During the summer of 1969, the Washington, D. C. office of the grape boycott sponsored a test by an independent testing lab to determine the amount of pesticide residues on grapes sold in local stores. The lab found residues of aldrin, a DDT-like pesticide, to be in excess of 180 times the accepted human tolerance.

FEDERAL REGULATION?

Where have our two federal regulatory agencies concerning pesticides—the Food and Drug Administration and the Department of Agriculture—been hiding during this pesticide crisis? The FDA is a typically under-budgeted and overburdened agency. Hence, less than one-tenth of one percent of all food in interstate commerce is inspected for pesticide residues. The USDA's Pesticide Regulation Division (PRD) has recently been indicted for incompetence in an amazing report by the House of Representatives Committee on Government Operations.[15] In 1953, PRD was first informed by the Public Health Service and the FDA that use of lindane vaporizers was hazardous. It took sixteen years, until 1969, for PRD to finally ban the use of vaporized lindane, but not until after an untold number of persons were needlessly exposed to this aplastic anemia-producing pesticide. Furthermore, PRD has no procedures for removing a potentially hazardous product from marketing channels after its registration has been dropped. In fact, according to the report, "in some cases hazardous products were *deliberately* allowed to remain on the market after cancellation of registrations." In another case involving the familiar yellow "no-pest strips" that are impregnated with DDVP insecticide, the investigators found that consultants to the PRD committees which were investigating the safety of DDVP were also on the payroll of the Shell Chemical Company, the manufacturer of DDVP. These are only three short examples of the many instances of USDA's "almost incredible failure" to regulate pesticides.

"El Muerte Andando"—The Walking Death

Besides the obvious hazards of DDT and the herbicides, the farm worker faces an additional problem from the organophosphates. Organophoshates are a class of chemicals originally developed by the Germans during World War II in their search for what is commonly called nerve gases. The organophosphates are among the most deadly chemicals known to man. Over 75,860,-000 pounds of organophosphates were produced in the United States during 1968. They go by names like parathion, methyl parathion, TEPP (tetraethyl pyrophosphate), azodrin, and malathion. Malathion is the allegedly safe organophosphate only because the mammalian liver renders it relatively harmless. Otherwise, the organophosphates destroy a protective body enzyme called cholinesterase. Under normal body conditions, an impulse passes from nerve to nerve with the aid of a chemical called acetylcholine. The acetylcholine is in turn destroyed by the cholinesterase. If the cholinesterase is absent, the impulses continue to flash from nerve to nerve. The movements of the whole body become uncoordinated: tremors, muscular spasms, convulsions, and death quickly result. Repeated exposures may lower the cholinesterase level in the blood until an individual reaches the brink of acute poisoning at which he may be pushed over by a very small additional exposure. But up to that point his symptoms are, unfortunately, usually taken for the flu.

For the farm workers, there are basically three modes of overexposure to organophosphates. First, in the period from 1951 to 1965, roughly 60 percent of the accidental deaths attributable to poisoning from pesticides in California were among children.

> On a large California ranch in the fall of 1965, a group of Mexican-American workers and their families were picking berries. A three-year-old girl and her four-year-old brother were playing around an unattended spray-rig next to where their mother was working. The four-year-old apparently took the cap off a gallon can of 40 percent TEPP pesticide left on the rig. The three-year-old put her finger in it and sucked it. She became unconscious, and was dead on arrival at the hospital where she was promptly taken. The estimated fatal dose of pure TEPP for an adult human is one drop orally and one drop on the skin.[16]

Second, applicators fare very badly with the organophosphates. In one instance:

> A young sprayer was found dead in the field in the tractor which had been pulling his spray-rig. He had been pouring and mixing parathion concentrate into the spray-rig tank. Parathion has an estimated fatal dose of about 9 drops orally and 32 drops dermally. In the process of mixing the concentrate, the worker contaminated his gloves inside and out. He rested his gloved hands on his trousers as he pulled the rig to apply the spray. Parathion was absorbed through the skin of his hands and thighs. He began to vomit, an early symptom of parathion poisoning. He could not remove his respirator and he aspirated the vomitus. The diagnosis of poisoning was confirmed by postmortem cholinesterase tests.[17]

The third and most insidious type of organophosphate poisoning is that from residues on the crops. The residues are usually invisible and in most states except for California, the farm worker has no idea of what has been sprayed on the crop. In California, which supposedly has the most advanced form of pesticide regulation, warning signs telling all to keep out for fifteen days must be posted following parathion spraying. However, there is little enforcement of this required posting, and a nonunionized farm worker could be fired from his crew if he protested his boss' order to go into a field too early. But sometimes even fifteen days is not enough. Near Delano, California, from May to June, 1952, three hundred acres of grapes were sprayed with 1.9 pounds of parathion per acre. *Thirty-three* days later, sixteen men came down with parathion poisoning after stripping and thinning the vines.[18] According to Mr. Edward Lester, president and director of Central California Medical Laboratories and a noted expert in the field of organophosphate poisoning, it is possible for consumers to come into contact with fruits or vegetables which still contain active residues of parathion. In another instance:

> In August of 1963, over 90 peach-pickers became sufficiently ill with parathion poisoning over a period of several days to seek medical attention. Although most of the 90 cases were mild or moderate, about one-third were hospitalized and there was one death. Of the approximately 5000 to 6000 pickers in the area, 70 were selected at random and tested during the outbreak. About half of the 70 workers showed significant reduction of blood cholinesterase levels but were either asymptomatic or had not sought medical aid for symptoms. It became obvious that the unusually heavy spraying with parathion during the spring and summer to combat the oriental fruit moth had resulted in a heavy deposit on the leaves in the orchards producing illness . . . but the amount of residue did not account sufficiently for the occurrence of poisoning. The presence of paraoxon, which is a toxic breakdown substance ten times more poisonous than its parent parathion, is strongly suspected as the cause of the poisonings.[19]

Lastly, sometimes the farm workers get as well sprayed as the target insects.

> Petra Sisneros was working in the Elmco Vineyards, tipping grape bunches, in May 1969, when four tractor-driven spray-rigs came into the field. Without any warning, one of them came right over the spot she was working in, spraying her soaking wet and blinding her to the point that she almost fell under the spray-rig. Other

women workers dragged her away from the danger of the spray-rig. Her supervisor did not take her to a doctor until she became visibly sick. Until then she had merely been told to sit in the shade under the vine. She was vomiting a great deal by this time. After she was taken to a doctor, who gave her an injection and bathed her eyes, she was returned to the vineyards where she had to wait for a ride home until her coworkers were finished for the day. She was extremely ill for the next ten days with vomiting, nausea, trembling, dizziness, headache, difficulty in breathing, tightness of the chest, and difficulty in sleeping. To this date she has received no compensation from her employer. She is still suffering from the aftereffects of this illness. When she asked her supervisor and foreman what kind of chemical she had been sprayed with, they claimed they didn't know and said it was not their fault she had been sprayed.[20]

After the summer of 1968 when several reports such as these reached the offices of the United Farm Workers, they sent their general counsel, Jerry Cohen, to the office of the Kern County agricultural commissioner to examine the pesticide application records with a view towards revealing possible violations of California pesticide regulations. The information was presumably open to the public but the commissioner denied Cohen access to the records. Two hours after his appearance at the commissioner's office, an injunction was issued by the Kern County Court barring Cohen from looking at the records. UFWOC entered a suit in the county court to overturn the injunction. Subsequently, the judge upheld the commissioner on the grounds that the records contained trade secrets. Since then the California chief deputy attorney general has filed a lawsuit to force the California State Department of Agriculture to open its files. According to Charles O'Brien, this information is "as closely guarded as the plans for our ICBM missile sites."

UFWOC has since grown more militant about the pesticide issue. In March, 1969, UFWOC filed twin suits in California and federal courts demanding that the use of DDT be halted in California and all crops sprayed with the chemical be confiscated. Further suits were filed to see the records of the county agricultural commissioners. During the brief negotiations that UFWOC had with table-grape growers early in the summer of 1969, pesticides emerged as the prime issue. The union was willing to accept virtually no increases in wages from the current level if the growers agreed to effective controls over the use of pesticides. The growers refused and the talks broke off.

Undoubtedly, Cesar Chavez's United Farm Workers Organizing Committee is an important ally for any group that is seriously interested in stopping this destructive madness on the farms. UFWOC's boycott operation, with an office in every major American city, makes it a natural link-up for localized activities as envisioned for the Environmental Teach-in on April 22, 1970. A film on the plight of the farm worker and the pesticide problem in California is now available. Entitled *By Land, Sea, and Air,* this documentary can be ordered for showings from the Oil, Chemical, and Atomic Workers International Union, 1126 Sixteenth Street, N.W., Washington, D.C. 20036.

A SAFE, BUT PERFECT APPLE?

Even with all the shortcomings of chemical pesticides, I am not advocating complete abandonment of them. The integrated control approach will have the most promise in controlling the world's pest problems after bans are placed on certain broadly disruptive or highly toxic chemicals. Integrated control means the unification of chemical, cultural, biological, and physical techniques into a smoothly working system of pest management. It is recognized that if anything is done unilaterally in the environment, this action is liable to trigger a very disruptive chain of events. Thus a pest problem in a grape vineyard or orange orchard is seen as part of the entire ecological make-up of that area. The question is asked: What factors can be brought into play to reduce the pest problem but not add to environmental disruption? Adherents to integrated control, like Dr. Robert van den Bosch, professor of entomology at the University of California at Berkeley, would never now recommend the use of broadly disruptive DDT even though, as in the case of van den Bosch, they might have been among the original supporters of the chemical.

An example of an important integrated control program is one that began in 1961 after the grape leafhopper in California became resistant to the most powerful of pesticides—the organophosphates.

One of the first things discovered was that the leafhopper was under heavy attack by a tiny wasp, *Anagrus,* during part of the season. Unfortunately, the protection afforded by the wasp did not come early enough in the season to prevent the leafhopper from causing damage to the young grape leaves. The reason for this was soon discovered. The wasps do not remain in the vineyards throughout the winter, but instead seek out blackberry vines where they attack a different leafhopper. At times the blackberries are scarce and at long distances from the grapes. Furthermore, blackberry vines are considered to be weeds and are usually killed with herbicides. In the spring when the young grape leaves are attacked by the leafhopper, the wasps are too slow getting back to the vineyards to effect good control. Experimental plantings of blackberries are now being made in vineyards and they show great promise keeping high populations of the wasp within striking distance of the leafhopper populations. At the same time new and more selective chemicals that will not interfere with this program are being evaluated for use on other grape pests.[21]

Presently there are successful integrated control programs in operation on the following crops: cotton, citrus fruits, apples and pears, tomatoes, potatoes, avocadoes, olives, corn, eggplant, lettuce, strawberries, and grapes.[22]

There is darkness and brightness in the picture ahead. Efforts on the part of the United Farm Workers and those scientists developing integrated control programs will progress and be more widely felt. On the other hand, the pesticide industry is rushing ahead with its plans to become a three-billion-dollar-a-year industry by the 1970's. And our present form of government responds best to the greatest economic power.

But in either case we have nothing to lose by beginning to act now on the quality of our environment and food supply. If we fail, we will inherit a world depleted of wildlife and breathable air, but full of sickness and disease. There is no time for mourning, only every reason for educating and organizing.

Notes

1. Rachel Carson, *Silent Spring* (Greenwich, Conn.: Fawcett Publications, 1962), p. 31.

2. *Ibid.*

3. A. Sodergren, *Oikos*, 19 (1968): 126-138; C. F. Wurster, "DDT Reduces Photosynthesis in Marine Phytoplankton," *Science*, 159 (1968): 1474-1475.

4. *New York Times*, April 30, 1969.

5. "Ecology-Pesticide into Pest," *Time*, July 11, 1969, p. 27.

6. "DDT Is Becoming a Major Menace," *Independent*, February, 1969, p. 1.

7. "Long Exposure to Pesticides Found to Disturb Workers," *New York Times*, April 8, 1969, p. 37.

8. "Swede Says Intake of DDT by Infants Is Twice Daily Limit," *New York Times*, May 6, 1969.

9. "Toxic Substances and Ecological Cycles," G. N. Woodwell, *Scientific American*, Vol. 216 No. 3 (1967), p. 24-31.

10. Taylor Pryor, "The Sea," UNESCO Conference Background Book, November 23-25, 1969, p. 3.

11. *I. F. Stone's Weekly*, December 15, 1969, p. 4.

12. Frank Mankiewicz and Tom Braden, "Sprayed Earth Policy," *New York Post*, November 4, 1969.

13. Richard Homan, "New Curbs Won't Affect Defoliation in Vietnam," *Washington Post*, October 31, 1969, p. 2.

14. "Study Challenges U.S. Policy on Tear Gas," *Washington Post*, December 6, 1969.

15. "Deficiencies in Administration of Federal Insecticide, Fungicide, and Rodenticide Act," Eleventh Report by Committee on Government Operation, House Report No. 91-637, Union Calendar No. 268, November 13, 1969, U.S. Government Printing Office: Washington.

16. Affidavit of Irma West, M.D., January, 1969, p. 2.

17. Irma West, M.D., "Occupational Disease of Farm Workers," *Archives of Environmental Health*, 9:92-98, July, 1964.

18. Quinby and Lemmon, "Parathion Residues as a Cause of Poisoning in Crop Workers," *Journal of the American Medical Association*, Vol. 166 No. 7, February 15, 1958, p. 740.

19. West, "Occupational Disease of Farm Workers," *op. cit.*

20. Statement of Cesar Chavez before Senate Committee on Migratory Labor, September 29, 1969, p. 5-6.

21. "Diminishing Returns," *Environment*, vol. 11 No. 7, September, 1969, p. 40.

22. "Water Quality Improvement Act of 1969," *Congressional Record*, October 7, 1969.

Game Ranching: An Ecologically Sensible Use of Range Lands

Maureen Shelton

Conventional cattle ranching puts stress on the environment in many ways. Cattle must be artificially provided with water and supplementary food. There must be fencing, bush control, grazing control, disease control, and reseeding. Even with these expensive ventures, there are relatively few areas in the world climatically suited to raising the present forms of domestic livestock.

By contrast, game ranching uses animals—elands, wildebeests, and other wild ungulates—indigenous to the local environment. Rather than changing the conditions to suit the animals, game ranching uses the animals which fit the conditions. These ungulates have proved to have more potential for meat production and other animal products than domestic livestock.

These conclusions come from a paper entitled, "Wild Animals as a Source of Food," by Dr. Lee M. Talbot, formerly director of the South East Asia Project of the International Union for Conservation of Nature and Natural Resources, and consultant in ecology and conservation to the United Nations Special Fund, UNESCO.

Conventional livestock—cattle, sheep, and goats—graze only on a few species of one type of food: grass. Ungulates use the available plants more efficiently. They will eat herbs, grasses, and woody plants ranging from low bushes to tall grasses.

It is not unusual to find over twenty species of ungulates inhabiting the same area. Each species seems to have a diet different from and complementary to the others. The animals will not only eat different species of food plants but also will eat different parts of the same plant.

According to Dr. Talbot:

> Red oats, although not eaten by some ungulates, are the most important single item in the diets of wildebeests, topis, and zebras. The wildebeests choose the fresh leaves of this grass until they reach about 4 inches in length. Stalks and seeds are rarely taken. Zebras feed on red-oats grass primarily when it is more mature. Most of the leaves eaten by them were over 4 inches long and also stalks and seeds were frequently taken. Zebras avoided the grass when it was dry. Topis, on the other hand, showed a marked preference for dry red-oats grass, and over 50 percent of the red oats in the stomachs of the topis examined were dry. Most of the rest were mature, about 20 percent were stalks and seeds.

The wild ungulates' use of water is more flexible than that of cattle. Cattle should be watered every day, but may be watered once every three days. The ungulates only drink every two days, even when water is available. When it is not, they are able to go without water for days, and to travel in search of water without stunting their growth rates. Some species of ungulates may go without water for months. Therefore, according to Dr. Talbot, "A large and vigorous wild ungulate population can . . . be supported yearlong on a range where a short water supply renders only a limited population of domestic livestock possible."

The meat of these wild ungulates, including the hippopotamus, when canned or prepared with care, is said to be as palatable as comparable beef. It currently sells at the same or higher prices.

Because wild ungulates function efficiently in their natural environment, they are a profitable business investment. There is little or no original outlay for stock and no cost in order to change the area to meet the conditions of the animal. The animal matures and breeds faster and more frequently than cattle. The carcass balance of ungulates when compared with domestic livestock is .3 percent fat in the wild ungulates compared to 28.4 percent fat in cattle, with 60 percent of the animal used in both cases.

The possibilities of harvesting wild ungulates are now being realized. In Southern Rhodesia, nine large cattle ranches are presently harvesting wildlife. Economic game ranching is also being carried out in many other countries.

Whereas cattle ranching must be heavily subsidized in these countries, game ranching receives no such subsidies. Says Dr. Talbot, "On the contrary, it must operate in spite of severe market restrictions due to veterinary regulations and the opposition of many cattle ranchers. In spite of these difficulties and the problems that accompany development of a new industry, game ranching has proved profitable enough to attract many cattle ranchers who state they are making a greater profit from the game, or game and cattle, than from cattle alone on the same lands."

In Southern Rhodesia at least one tame and thriving eland herd has demonstrated this profit potential. This herd is periodically put over a weigh bridge in the same manner as cattle, but they are more docile and easier to handle than cattle. They can be confined by fences and do not, when grazing free, join wild eland herds in the vicinity. They have been milked and some have been castrated, and have shown an adaption to environment and a manageability superior to that of domestic livestock.

It is true that exporting and importing wild ungulates from their native areas to areas where there is a demand for them creates certain quarantine problems.

Nevertheless, the world's growing need for food and for a future that makes ecological sense clearly indicates further use of the wild ungulates as a source of animal products.

The Economics of
the Coming Spaceship Earth

Kenneth E. Boulding

from Environmental Quality in
a Growing Economy

The closed earth of the future requires economic principles which are somewhat different from those of the open earth of the past. For the sake of picturesqueness, I am tempted to call the open economy the "cowboy economy," the cowboy being symbolic of the illimitable plains and also associated with reckless, exploitative, romantic, and violent behavior, which is characteristic of open societies. The closed economy of the future might similarly be called the "spaceman" economy, in which the earth has become a single spaceship, without unlimited reservoirs of anything, either for extraction or for pollution, and in which, therefore, man must find his place in a cyclical ecological system which is capable of continuous reproduction of material form even though it cannot escape having inputs of energy. The difference between the two types of economy becomes most apparent in the attitude towards consumption. In the cowboy economy, consumption is regarded as a good thing and production likewise; and the success of the economy is measured by the amount of the throughput from the "factors of production," a part of which, at any rate, is extracted from the reservoirs of raw materials and noneconomic objects, and another part of which is output into the reservoirs of pollution. If there are infinite reservoirs from which material can be obtained and into which effluvia can be deposited, then the throughput is at least a plausible measure of the success of the economy. The gross national product is a rough measure of this total throughput. It should be possible, however, to distinguish that part of the GNP which is derived from exhaustible and that which is derived from reproducible resources, as well as that part of consumption which represents effluvia and that which represents input into the productive system again. Nobody, as far as I know, has ever attempted to break down the GNP in this way, although it would be an interesting and extremely important exercise, which is unfortunately beyond the scope of this paper.

By contrast, in the spaceman economy, throughput is by no means a desideratum, and is indeed to be regarded as something to be minimized rather than maximized. The essential measure of the success of the economy is not production and consumption at all, but the nature, extent, qualilty, and complexity of the total capital stock, including in this the state of the human bodies and minds included in the system. In the spaceman economy, what we are primarily concerned with is stock maintenance, and any technological change which results in the maintenance of a given total stock with a lessened throughput (that is, less production and consumption) is clearly a gain. This idea that both production and consumption are bad things rather than good things is very strange to economists, who have been obsessed with the income-flow concepts to the exclusion, almost, of capital-stock concepts.

There are actually some very tricky and unsolved problems involved in the questions as to whether human welfare or well-being is to be regarded as a stock or a flow. Something of both these elements seems actually to be involved in it, and as far as I know there have been practically no studies directed towards identifying these two dimensions of human satisfaction. Is it, for instance, eating that is a good thing, or is it being well fed? Does economic welfare involve having nice clothes, fine houses, good equipment, and so on, or is it to be measured by the depreciation and the wearing out of these things? I am inclined myself to regard the stock concept as most fundamental, that is, to think of being well fed as more important than eating, and to think even of so-called services as essentially involving the restoration of a depleting psychic capital. Thus I have argued that we go to a concert in order to restore a psychic condition which might be called "just having gone to a concert," which, once established, tends to depreciate. When it depreciates beyond a certain point, we go to another concert in order to restore it. If it depreciates rapidly, we go to a lot of concerts; if it depreciates slowly, we go to few. On this view, similarly, we eat primarily to restore bodily homeostasis, that is, to maintain a condition of being well fed, and so on. On this view, there is nothing desirable in consumption at all. The less consumption we can maintain a given state with, the better off we are. If we had clothes that did not wear out, houses that did not depreciate, and even if we could maintain our bodily condition without eating, we would clearly be much better off.

It is this last consideration, perhaps, which makes one pause. Would we, for instance, really want an operation that would enable us to restore all our bodily tissues by intravenous feeding while we slept? Is there not, that is to say, a certain virtue in throughput itself, in activity itself, in production and consumption itself, in raising food and in eating it? It would certainly be rash to exclude this possibility. Further interesting problems are raised by the demand for variety. We certainly do not want a constant state to be maintained; we want fluctuations in the state. Otherwise there would be no demand for variety in food, for variety in scene, as in travel, for variety in social contact, and so on. The demand for variety can, of course, be costly, and sometimes it seems to be too costly to be tolerated or at least legitimated, as in the case of marital partners, where the maintenance of a homeostatic state in the family is usually regarded as much more desirable than the variety and excessive throughput of the libertine. There are problems here which the economics profession has neglected with astonishing singlemindedness. My own attempts to call attention to some of them, for instance, in two articles,[1] as far as I can judge, produced no response whatever; and economists continue to think and act as if production, consumption, throughput, and the GNP were the sufficient and adequate measure of economic success.

It may be said, of course, why worry about all this when the spaceman economy is still a good way off (at least beyond the lifetimes of any now living), so let us eat, drink, spend, extract and pollute, and be as merry as we can, and let posterity worry about the spaceship earth. It is always a little hard to find a convincing answer to the man who says, "What has posterity ever done for me?" and the conservationist has always had to fall back on rather vague ethical principles postulating identity of the individual with some human community or society which extends not only back into the past but forward into the future. Unless the individual identifies with some community of this kind, conservation is obviously "irrational." Why should we not maximize the welfare of this generation at the cost of posterity? *Après nous, le déluge* has been the motto of not insignificant numbers of human societies. The only answer to this, as far as I can see, is to point out that the welfare of the individual depends on the extent to which he can identify himself with others, and that the most satisfactory individual identity is that which identifies not only with a community in space but also with a community extending over time from the past into the future. If this kind of identity is recognized as desirable, then posterity has a voice, even if it does not have a vote; and in a sense, if its voice can influence votes, it has votes too. This whole problem is linked up with the much larger one of the determinants of the morale, legitimacy, and "nerve" of a society, and there is a great deal of historical evidence to suggest that a society which loses its identity with posterity and which loses its positive image of the future loses also its capacity to deal with present problems, and soon falls apart.[2]

Even if we concede that posterity is relevant to our present problems, we still face the question of time-discounting and the closely related question of uncertainty-discounting. It is a well-known phenomenon that individuals discount the future, even in their own lives. The very existence of a positive rate of interest may be taken as at least strong supporting evidence of this hypothesis. If we discount our own future, it is certainly not unreasonable to discount posterity's future even more, even if we do give posterity a vote. If we discount this at 5 percent per annum, posterity's vote or dollar halves every fourteen years as we look into the future, and after even a mere hundred years it is pretty small—only about 1½ cents on the dollar. If we add another 5 percent for uncertainty, even the vote of our grandchildren reduces almost to insignificance. We can argue, of course, that the ethical thing to do is not to discount the future at all, that time-discounting is mainly the result of myopia and perspective, and hence is an illusion which the moral man should not tolerate. It is a very popular illusion, however, and one that must certainly be taken into consideration in the formulation of policies. It explains, perhaps, why conservationist policies almost have to be sold under some other excuse which seems more urgent, and why, indeed, necessities which are visualized as urgent, such as defense, always seem to hold priority over those which involve the future.

All these considerations add some credence to the point of view which says that we should not worry about the spaceman economy at all, and that we should just go on increasing the GNP and indeed the gross world product, or GWP, in the expectation that the problems of the future can be left to the future, that when scarcities arise, whether this is of raw materials of or pollutable reservoirs, the needs of the then present will determine the solutions of the then present, and there is no use giving ourselves ulcers by worrying about problems that we really do not have to solve. There is even high ethical authority for this point of view in the New Testament, which advocates that we should take no thought for tomorrow and let the dead bury their dead. There has always been something rather refreshing in the view that we should live like the birds, and perhaps posterity is for the birds in more senses than one; so perhaps we should all call it a day and go out and pollute something cheerfully. As an old taker of thought for the morrow, however, I cannot quite accept this solution; and I would argue, furthermore, that tomorrow is not only very close, but in many respects it is already here. The shadow of the future spaceship, indeed, is already falling over our spendthrift merriment. Oddly enough, it seems to be in pollution rather than in exhaustion that the problem is first becoming salient. Los Angeles has run out of air, Lake Erie has become a cesspool, the oceans are filling up with lead and DDT, and the atmosphere may become man's major problem in another generation, at the rate at which we are filling it up with gunk. It is, of course, true that at least on a microscale, things have been worse at times in the past. The cities of today, with all their foul air and polluted waterways, are probably not as bad as the filthy cities of the pretechnical age. Nevertheless, that fouling of the nest which has been typical of man's activity in the past on a local scale now seems to be extending to the whole world society; and one certainly cannot view with equanimity the present rate of pollution of any of the natural reservoirs, whether the atmosphere, the lakes, or even the oceans.

NOTES

1. K. E. Boulding, "The Consumption Concept in Economic Theory," *American Economic Review*, 35 (May 1945):1–14; and "Income or Welfare?," *Review of Economic Studies*, 17 (1949–50): 77–86.

2. Fred L. Polak, *The Image of the Future*, Vols. I and II, translated by Elise Boulding, New York: Sythoff, Leyden and Oceana, 1961.

Economics and Ecosystems

Jon Breslaw

WASTES IN THE ECONOMY

The American economy can be best represented by the concept of a competitive market.[1] If one regards the market as a black box, then there are two processes which do not come within the market's sphere of influence—inputs and outputs. The inputs are raw materials, or resources, used in the economy—air, water, metals, minerals, and wood. The outputs are the residuals —sewage, trash, carbon dioxide and other gases released to the atmosphere, radioactive waste and so on. We shall consider the residuals first.

The environment has a certain limited capability to absorb wastes without harmful effects. Once the ambient residuals rise above a certain level, however, they become unwanted inputs to other production processes or to final consumers. The size of this residual in fact is massive. In an economy which is closed,[2] the weight of residuals ejected into the environment is about equal to the weight of input materials, plus oxygen taken from the atmosphere. This result, while obvious upon reflection, leads to the surprising and even shocking corollary that the disposal of residuals is as large an operation, in sheer tonnage, as basic materials production. This incredible volume has to be disposed of. It is at this stage that the market process breaks down.

If the functioning of the economy gave rise to incentives, such as prices, which fully reflected the costs of disposing of residuals, such incentives would be very much in point. This would be especially true if the incentives fully reflected costs to the overall society associated with the discharge of the residuals to the environment. But it is clear that, whatever other normative properties the functioning of a market economy may have, it does not reflect these costs adequately.

Market economies are effective instruments for organizing production and allocating resources, insofar as the utility functions are associated with two-party transactions. But in connection with waste disposal, the utility functions involve third parties, and the automatic market exchange process fails.

Thus the need to see man's activities as part of an ecosystem becomes clear. The outputs from the black box go through other black boxes and become inputs again. If our black box is putting out too much and overloading the system, one can only expect trouble—and that is what one gets.

If we look at a particular production process, we find that there is a flow of goods or services that consumers or businesses get whether they want it or not. An upstream river may be polluted by an industry, and the downstream user cannot usually control the quality of the water that he gets. If the polluted water wipes out a fishing industry, then there is some cost (the profit that used to be made by the fishing industry) that does not appear on the balance sheet of the upstream user. Similarly, there may be benefits involved—the upstream user may use the stream for cooling, and the hot water may support an oyster farm downstream.

The activities of an economic unit thus generate real effects that are external to it. These are called externalities. A society that relies completely on a decentralized decision-making system in which significant externalities occur, as they do in any society which contains significant concentrations of population and industrial activities, will find that certain resources are not used optimally.

The tool used by economists, and others, in determining a course of action in making social decisions is the technique of cost-benefit analysis. The basis is to list all the consequences arising from a course of action, such as building a new freeway, and to make estimates of the benefits or costs to the community of all these consequences. This is done in terms of money values and a balance is drawn up, which is compared with similar estimates of the consequences of alternative decisions, such as building a rapid transit network or doing nothing. The sensible decision is to go ahead with those projects where the benefits come out best, relative to the costs. The art of cost-benefit analysis lies in using the scanty information available to assign money values to these costs and benefits. Differences in house prices are a way of getting at noise valuation. Time is obviously worth money: how much can be esimated by looking at what people do when they have a choice between a faster and more expensive way of going from A to B and a slower but cheaper way?

Going back to our slaughtered fish, if the cost of reducing pollution by 50 percent were less than the profit that could be realized from fishing at this level of pollution, then it makes sense to spend that amount. In fact, the level of pollution should be reduced until the marginal cost of reducing pollution (the cost of reducing pollution by a very small amount) is just equal to the marginal revenue from fishing (the extra revenue that is received as a result of that amount less pollution). The question is, where there is no market, how does one get to this state of affairs?

Method One is to internalize the problem so that a single economic unit will take account of all of the costs and benefits associated with the external effects. To do this, the size of the economic unit has to be increased. A good example of this is where one has several fisheries for one limited species of fish, e.g., whales. If the fisheries operate separately, each concern takes as many as it can, regardless of the effect on the total catch. If the fisheries were to act in unison, then the maximum catch compatible with a stable population of whales would be taken, and no more—the externalities would have been internalized. Unfortunately, waste products are often so widely propagated in nature and affect so many diverse interests that the merger route is not feasible.

Method Two is the one mostly used at the moment: the use of regulations set up by government and enforceable by law. There are many examples of these: minimum net-hole size in fishing, parking regulations on busy streets, limited number of flights at airports during the night, zoning regulations as applied to land use, and certain water quality laws for industrial and municipal river users. Ideally, these regulations would take into account the different nature of the environmental difficulty, varying both over place and time, e.g., high and low flows in streams, windy days for smoke control, etc. There are two main objections to such regulations. In the first place, they are often difficult to enforce, especially if there are high monetary returns involved and the likelihood of being caught is small— flushing oil tanks in the English Channel. The other objection is more sophisticated: in a competitive market the imposition of regulations does not normally lead to the best use of resources. It is better to do this by means of pricing, since this method makes it possible to balance incremental costs and gains in a relatively precise manner. Also, regulations do not provide the funds for the construction and operation of measures of regional scope, should these prove economical.

Method Three involves the legal system and the law of nuisance. Thus when there is an oil spill on your shore and you and your property get covered in goo, then in such an obvious and easy case one would expect prompt damages—but ask the residents of Santa Barbara what they think of courts and oil companies. Thus, though in theory the courts provide a solution, in practice, they are slow and inefficient.

Method Four involves the paying of some monetary rent in order to get the practice of pollution stopped. One way is to pay a producer to stop polluting. Although such payments would be received favorably by the industries involved, the sheer size of the total payments necessary as a means of preventing pollution would put an impossible strain on any budget, and such a solution is only feasible for "special case" industrial operations. Moreover, if a steel mill is discharging its waste into a river, without charge, it is producing steel that is artificially cheap. Paying the mill to stop pollution does nothing to get the steel price back to its rightful value (i.e., when all costs are met) in the short run. In the long run, this remains true only if the assumption of a competitive market is weakened.

Another way to implement Method Four would be to charge a polluter for the pollution that he causes. Examples of such charges or taxes would be a tax on sewage effluents which is related to the quality and quantity of the discharge; or a surcharge on the price of fuels with a high sulfur content which is meant to take account of the broader cost to society external to the fuel-using enterprise. This procedure is one usually favoured by economists, since it uses economic incentives to allocate the resources (the waste assimilative capacity of the environment) similar to those generated where market mechanisms can balance costs and returns. The revenue from these charges can be used to finance other anti-pollution facilities.

The use of charges for the wasted assimilative capacity of the environment implies that you have to pay in order to put things out of the black box. Before the environment's waste assimilative capacity was overloaded, it was not used to its full capacity. A resource which is not fully utilized has a zero price; once it is utilized it receives a positive price—which is why charges now have to be imposed. From an ecological point of view this is very good, since now that one has to pay to get rid of a product, it means that this product has a value attached to it, albeit negative. The effect is to restructure industrial processes to take this into account. A society that allows waste dischargers to neglect the offsite costs of waste disposal will not only devote too few resources to the treatment of waste, but will also produce too much waste in view of the damage it causes. Or more simply, if you charge for waste disposal, industries will produce less waste, and the wastes produced will often find use in some other process—recycling. A paper-producing company using the sulphite method will find it advantageous to change to the sulphate method through increased effluent charges. In England, many firms have found profitable uses for waste products when forced to stop polluting. In a few instances, mostly in already depressed areas, plants may be capable of continuing operation only because they are able to shift all or most of that portion of production costs associated with waste disposal to other economic units. When this situation is coupled with one in which the plant is a major part of the employment base of a community, society may have an interest in assisting the plant to stay in business, while at the same time controlling the external costs it is imposing. However, these would be special cases which are used to help the adjustment to the new position of equilibrium rather than change the position of the new equilibrium.

Just such an operation has been used in the Ruhr Valley in Germany, starting in 1913. The political power of the Ruhrverband lies in the governing board made up of owners of business and other facilities in the Ruhrverband area, communities in the area, and representatives of the waterworks and other water facilities. It has built over one-hundred waste-treatment plants, oxidation lakes, and waterworks facilities. Capital came from the bond market, and operating expenses from a series of charges contingent on the amount and quality of the effluent discharged by the industries and municipalities in the region. This scheme is so successful that, though the Ruhr River flows through one of the most heavily industrialized regions of Germany, one can find ducks living on it. Shed tears for the Potomac.

NONRENEWABLE RESOURCES

The inputs to our black box consist of renewable resources, such as food and water, and nonrenewable ones such as minerals and land. In considering free resources, it was stated that in a decentralized competitive market economy such resources are not used optimally. In fact, they are overutilized—rivers are overutilized as disposal units, hence pollution; roads are utilized above their intended capacity with resultant traffic snarl-ups. The same holds true for nonrenewable resources: they are not used optimally.

Given a fixed technology, at any time in the past we would have run into a critical condition with respect to our supplies of minerals and metals. It is only changing technology, which makes for the profitable extraction of pretechnical-change unprofitable deposits, that has enabled us to manage without really bad shortages. Hence the present rate of extraction is only justifiable in the belief of future technical progress. Yet this is just the assumption that is now undergoing examination. In the past, man's technical progress was a function of man's incentive and ingenuity; now, however, he has to take into account another factor—the ability of the environment to accept his ravages.

As any child will comment, on observing the empty beer cans and discarded packets lying on the roadside and around "beauty spots," this is wrong. It is wrong because we do not put sufficient value on the natural resource—the countryside—to keep it clean. It is wrong for the same reason a second time: we do not put sufficient value on the natural resources—aluminum, plastic, paper or whatever—so that when we have used them for their original purposes, they are disposed of, as rapidly as possible. The conclusion is clear: both our renewable and nonrenewable resources are not being used optimally.

Take a specific example—oil. What are the factors that determine its price? As usual, demand is a decreasing function of price, and supply an increasing function. The point of intersection dictates the price and quantity sold. When the optimal use of oil is considered, there are two points of view that have to be taken into account.

One is the value of the oil to future generations, and the other is the social cost of the use of the oil.

In considering future generations, optimal behavior will take place in a competitive economy (with private ownership) if the private rate of return is the same as the social rate of return. In noneconomic terms, all this means is that the rate at which the future is discounted by individuals is the same as the rate at which it is discounted by society. There is dispute on this point—that is, whether the two rates are equal or not. However, even if they are, because the individual companies seek to maximize their private benefit, like in the fisheries example, the total exploration of the resources is likely to not be optimal.

At this stage, government comes into the picture. On the conservation side, a scientifically determined MER—maximum efficient rate (of oil flow)—is determined for a particular site. The main effect of this is to stop large fluctuations in the price of oil. Since half the total revenue of oil companies goes into the discovery and development of new deposits, this produces a high overhead cost. In the U. S., the aim is to produce as large a growth in the GNP as possible, subject to constraints (inflation, full employment, balance of payments, etc.). Hence the tradition of allowing industries to write off the cost of capital equipment against tax, since new capital stimulates the economy (investment) and makes for more efficient production. The oil industry felt that the same principle should apply to its capital costs—the rent it pays on oil deposits. Hence the oil depletion allowance, which allows the costs of rents to be partially offset against profits. The effect of this is to move the supply curve to the right—which results in more oil being sold at a lower price. Thus it encourages oil companies to extract more oil and find new deposits. This is great from a military point of view, but disastrous when the effect of such exploitation of the environment is considered: oil spills at sea, the probable permanent scarring of the tundra in Alaska, and smog in our cities. Yet this is exactly what is meant by social costs, the externalities which do not get considered in the market price.

If the oil depletion allowances were removed or sharply reduced,[3] the oil producing industry could not continue to function at its accustomed level of operation and maintain its accustomed price structure. Similar considerations apply to minerals (mineral depletion allowance). Yet this is only the first step. Another method that would produce the same desired results would be to make the extractor pay for the quantity of mineral or metal that he mines, just as he should pay for the right to discard his waste. This solves a whole lot of problems —by making the original substance more expensive, the demand is reduced, be it for power-using dishwashers, oil-eating automobiles, or resource-demanding economies. Moreover, these products, being more expensive, will not be discarded, but recycled, thus solving in part a pollution problem, as well as a litter problem (if they can be separated). By recycling, there will be less demand for the minerals or metals from the mining companies, since there is this new source of these materials.

To a certain extent, this view of things is recognized. In England, one of the proposals considered for solving the problem of scrapped cars around the countryside was to charge an extra twenty-five pounds on the price of each new car. This would be refundable when the vehicle was brought in for scrapping—a bit like returnable bottles. In the U.S., the use of natural gas as boiler fuel was recognized as an inferior use of an exhaustible resource. "One apparent method of preventing waste of gas is to limit the uses to which it may be put, uses for which another more abundant fuel may serve equally well" (Supreme Court, 1961). This same result could have been achieved by charging the gas producer for the quantity of gas that he took (as well as rent to the owner of the gas deposit for the right to extract gas from his property). The price that should be charged, like the prices charged for sewage disposal, vary from location to location and depend upon the characteristics of the environment. The price should be high enough to make recycling, if physically possible, both a feasible and desirable process. If the use of the resources causes some social cost—like air pollution—then this should be reflected in the price. So too should the relative scarcity of the resource, compared to substitutable alternatives, be a consideration.

If the socio-economic system fails to change quickly enough to meet changing conditions, then it is incumbent on the people to facilitate such change.

THE FUTURE

A prerequisite to any lasting solution to environmental pollution is a zero growth rate—the birth rate equaling the death rate. However, a stable population produces a difficult economic problem in an economy like that of the United States. To remain healthy (to stay the same size or grow), the economy needs a growing market, since only in a growing market can the capital goods sector remain efficient, given present technology. At first sight, then, the achievement of a stable population is linked to a recession. One might make the assumption that a growing market could still be achieved by allowing per capita consumption to increase at the same rate as the growth of the GNP. However, with restrictions on extraction industries, this will probably not provide a total solution. The slack is more likely to be made up by producing a different type of service—education at regular periods throughout one's life, the move from cities to smaller communities and the investment involved in such a move, the rebuilding (or destruction) of old cities compatible with their new uses. Put another way, the economic slack that will have to be taken up to avoid a depression gives us the opportunity to plan for the future, without worrying about providing for an expanding population.

The essential cause of environmental pollution is overpopulation, combined with an excessive population growth rate; other antipollution measures can be used temporarily, but so long as the central problem is not solved, one can expect no lasting success.

BIBLIOGRAPHY

Ayres, R., and Kneese, A. *Environmental Pollution.* Programs for the Development of Human Resources, 1968.

Day, Alan. "Value on the Quality of Life," *Observer,* 1969.

Ehrlich, Paul. *The Population Bomb.* Ballantine, 1968.

Fair, Gordon. "Pollution Abatement in the Ruhr District," in *Comparisons in Resource Management,* ed. H. Jarrett, 1961.

Hulstrunk, A. "Air Pollution," Associated Press, N. Y., 1969.

Jarrett, H., ed., *Environmental Quality in a Growing Economy.* Resources for the Future.

Kneese, A. *Economics and the Quality of the Environment.* Resources for the Future, 1968.

Kneese, A., and Bower. *Managing Water Quality, Economics, Technology, Institutions.* John Hopkins Press, 1968.

Lichtblau, J. *The Oil Depletion Issue.*

NOTES

1. The assumption is that while there is some public production and regulation, the choices concerning the use of resources are made in a decentralized decision-making system, where markets are competitive, and the individual decision makers—industries and individuals—maximize their individual private benefits. If the assumptions that the overall distribution of income is justified on ethical grounds, and that individual preference should be satisfied to the maximum extent possible, given income constraints, are accepted, and that there is open competition, then this decentralized system will produce the maximum welfare and allow the organization of production to produce what each consumer wants within the limits of his income.

2. A closed economy is one with no imports or exports, and within which there is no net accumulation of stocks (plants, equipment, inventories, consumer durables, or residential buildings).

3. This departs from the original assumption of a perfect competitive market, and from the point of view of strict economic theory there is some objection to the charge procedure described—it violates the principle of marginal cost pricing. However, methods that are less than theoretically ideal may be optimal in practice, since an important element in determining the best method for actual use is the cost of making marginal refinements. A comparatively crude method that is generally correct in principle will often realize the major share of the gains that could be achieved by more complex and conceptually more satisfying techniques.

"38 Cigarettes a Day"

Robert Rienow and Leona Train Rienow

from Moment In The Sun

A recent scientific analysis of New York City's atmosphere concluded that a New Yorker on the street took into his lungs the equivalent in toxic materials of 38 cigarettes a day. Suddenly all the scientific jargon, official warnings, reams of statistics—the overwhelming avalanche of damning facts concerning America's air pollution—took focus. Here was a reduction of the tons of soot, sulphides, monoxide, hydrocarbons, etc., into simple, understandable, personal terms.

These figures are of vital interest to two-thirds of the population, which is the percentage of Americans who already live in 212 standard metropolitan areas having only 9 per cent of the nation's land area but 99 per cent of its pollution. Some cities outdo Manhattan and on days of cloud and atmospheric inversion actually kill off small segments of their excess population (involuntarily, of course).

Smog production seems to be a cooperative effort among our great cities. "A great deal of the smoke and dirty air in New York City comes each morning from the industrial areas of New Jersey," accused former Mayor Wagner as, smiling apologetically, he testified at an October, 1964, hearing on air pollution. Then his innate fairness forced him to add: "We return the compliment each afternoon, depending on the prevailing winds, or we pass some of our smoke and gases on to our Long Island or Connecticut neighbors."

But, definitely, New York was getting the worst of everything. It is "the terminus of a 3,000-mile-long sewer of atmospheric filth starting as far away as California and growing like a dirty snowball all the way." New Jersey's champion, Chairman William Bradley of the state's pollution control commission, felt that it was New Jersey who was really behind the eight ball or, rather, dirty snowball. "We feel incapable of coping," he sighed dramatically.

What, actually, is it we are talking about when we rant about air pollution? What it is varies from city to city and from industrial complex to industrial complex. There is a conglomeration of particles—bits of metal, the metallic oxides, tar, stone, carbon, and ash, the aerosols, mists of oils, and all manner of soot.[1]

Strangely enough, Anchorage, Alaska, in the clear and pristine North, excels in this air filth, with Charleston, West Virginia, East Chicago, Phoenix, and Los Angeles treading eagerly on its heels. The electronstatic precipitator in a factory chimney or the use of a whirling water bath for smoke emissions can remove many of these solids, but such devices cost money, and money (and the treasuring thereof) is still our number one consideration.

Much more serious than filthy particles is the sulphur dioxide that comes from the combustion of all heavy fuel oils, coal, and coke. We have visual evidence that this substance eats away brick, stone, and metal bridges, but we have not taken time off to discover what it does to the human lung.[2] A derivative, sulphur trioxide, is the common sulphuric acid, which we know eats into the lungs, eyes, and skin, but again research as to how to extirpate it from the air we breathe does not add appreciably to the GNP.

Technology's contribution to the air we breathe includes—in addition to the particulates, aerosols, and sulphur oxides—a whole legion of grisly gases, among them, carbon dioxide, carbon monoxide, hydrofluoric acid, hydrochloric acid, ammonia, organic solvents, aromatic benzypyrene, deadly ozone, and perhaps another 500 or more lethal emissions (some day we shall have discovered thousands). A few years ago the oil refineries and factories were assigned most of the blame for city smog; later, incinerators took the abuse; at length it was demonstrated beyond a doubt that from 60 to 85 per cent of most city smog is caused by man's best friend, the effusive automobile.[3]

Such smog, strangely enough, has lately been discovered to be the result of the action of sunlight on the incompletely combusted automobile exhaust gases, mainly carbon monoxide, the hydrocarbons, and nitrogen oxides. An unbelievably complex and varied "mishmash" of photochemical reactions takes place all day long from dawn to dark. Out of this witches' cauldron, whose catalyst is the sunshine, emerges a whole army of killing compounds: olefins (synergetic hydrocarbons "hungry to react to something"), ketene, peroxyacetylnitrate, sulphuric acid, aldehydes, and, probably most vicious of all, ozone.[4] The automobile is a versatile chemical factory that can produce almost anything you might wish to dial. Of all these perverse and malicious agents, man knows as yet almost nothing about what they do to humans over a period of time.

Nor is there much evidence that he greatly cares.

Senator Edmund S. Muskie of Maine, who has interested himself deeply in the pure air campaign and the Clean Air Act of 1963, says that, regarding air pollution, we are as ignorant of the components and what to do about them as we were about water pollution fifty years ago. There are about eight of the possibly thousands of constituents of automobile exhaust whose presence and amounts we have documented. According to a competent study[5] the automobile emits into the atmosphere for each 1,000 gallons of gasoline consumed:

carbon monoxide	3,200 pounds
organic vapors	200–400 pounds

oxides of nitrogen	20–75	pounds
aldehydes	18	pounds
sulphur compounds	17	pounds
organic acids	2	pounds
ammonia	2	pounds
solids (zinc, metallic oxides, carbon)	.3	pounds

Now, much has been made of the sulphuric acid fumes that burn the eyes and make holes in ladies' nylons. Lately, pushed by such indomitable souls as Senator Muskie, the unburned cancer-causing hydrocarbons (organic vapors) have been getting their share of attention in the mandatory action taken in smog-bound California. Thus, it was California who led the way for the imposition, in March, 1966, of limitations on the amounts of carbon monoxide and hydrocarbons that may emerge from automobile exhaust pipes. The standards, to take effect on the 1968 models, both of domestic and imported large cars, were to raise the price tags on new models not more than $45.00.

Sighing, an industry executive admitted that the automobile manufacturers had not the ghost of a chance of evading the afterburner hassle any longer. "Politicians, it is quite clear, have come to regard this issue as they do home and mother," he said. All would seem to be set for a cleaner, more wholesome atmosphere in the cities where the automobile is king.

But now a sinister new note has been sounded that suddenly cloaks the whole campaign against the hydrocarbons and the affable acquiescence of the auto manufacturers with the faint smell of herring. Why are we so cavalierly overlooking the nitrogen oxides, perhaps the most dangerous family of all produced by internal combustion, which will not be affected by any afterburner or catalytic muffler ever made? In our first efforts to eliminate a portion of the smog problem have we actually done no more than introduce a placebo that will lull the public into a false and fatal reassurance?

Nitrogen oxides are formed in all combustion processes; the greater the pressure, the greater the amount of them. If we eliminate the hydrocarbons with which they react, what will happen? Will they then turn on us and cause even greater havoc than at present—perhaps greater havoc than the hydrocarbons and all their relatives together? We know that irritations of the mucous membranes would greatly increase. And while hydrocarbons build up in the body for the kill, nitrogen oxides like to do a faster, neater job.

Yet we are ignoring them. The truth is, the complicated and expensive accessory needed to deal with the nitrogen oxides would be almost exactly opposite to that necessary for dealing with the hydrocarbons. An automobile properly equipped to get rid of smog effectively would probably be an elaborate mess—costly, slow, and demanding of much maintenance. Coming into this new knowledge which proves so distressing—that our dearest companion, the automobile, is completely incompatible with our health and well-being—how long will we cling to it in this embrace of death?

We have noted that long after the exhaust smells have wafted away the hydrocarbons, in the presence of nitrogen oxides and that much publicized California sunlight (or anybody's less glorious, less publicized sunlight), keep on producing a veritable legion of lethal agents to inhabit the smog.

No American city is spared.[6] Two years ago in San Francisco we were driven by burning eyes to flee the city to the skyline drive high above.[7] From that height we looked down on a city swathed in a thick mustard-colored robe. This was a blanket manufactured by man himself, which he had drawn down over the once sparkling countryside and golden bay, and it was slowly smothering him to death. How long, we wondered, will man continue to sacrifice his cities, his enjoyment, his life, because of the fetid breath of a monster never built for meandering in city streets with their stops and goes and halting, jammed traffic? An ungainly, unadaptable monster whose 80 mile an hour cruising speed was geared to the long sweep of thruways and not to the bumper-bumper creep among the city's canyons?

If we would still cling to our 300-horsepower monsters in city lanes built to accommodate at most a 4-horsepower carriage, we have but two choices. Shall we choose mass poisoning in a slow fashion by the vast armies of hydrocarbon derivatives or a faster (perhaps more dashing) suicide from the nitrogen oxides? Apparently, technological difficulties so far obviate relief from both.

This small book, intent on presenting an overall view of our most pressing modern problems, does not pretend to medical authority regarding the effects of air pollution on the living community; many health authorities, specialists in the field, have performed this work with shocking competence. But one piece of medical research will be noted. As early as 1957 Dr. Paul Kotin, pathology professor of the University of Southern California, reported at Yale Medical School his findings of five years of study on laboratory animals. A group of mice exposed to the day-by-day Los Angeles air developed one and one-half times as many lung cancers as those who breathed clean air. Abnormal changes were found in the lungs of experimental animals after only a few months of this Los Angeles brew. Concluded the scientist: "Similar rapid changes can be expected in human beings, with many air pollutants combining to make the lungs more susceptible to cancer in a shorter time than previously believed."[8]

Dr. Thomas P. Manusco, industrial hygiene chief for the Ohio Health Department, told the 1958 National Conference on Air Pollution that the urban lung cancer rate "increases by the size of the city." Since these reports, studies have confirmed the findings.[9]

A man is not a mouse—usually. He has a bigger body; he may have more resistance, slower reaction. But every day the air a human breathes comes in direct contact with an area twenty-five times as great as his exposed skin area. This is the exposure surface of the tender membranes that line his lungs. Dr. Morris Cohn impressed on a New York Joint Legislative Committee on Air Pollution that while "man consumes less than ten pounds of water, fluids, and food daily, yet he requires over thirty pounds of air in the same period—and thirty pounds of air is a lot of air, 3,500 gallons of it!" It is necessary to be an alarmist to conclude that man is not immune to what affects the mouse. Indeed, physiologically, he is more like the mouse than he wants to believe.

A cartoon of a few years ago presenting the inside of a U.S. weather station of the future depicted the weatherman making the following report: "Our latest analysis of the stratosphere, Dr. Figby! . . . 21 per cent hydrogen, 7 per cent oxygen . . . and 72 per cent automobile exhaust fumes!"[10] By 1985 this cartoon will no longer amuse. Predicts sanitation expert A. C. Stern of the Taft Sanitary Engineering Center, Cincinnati: By 1985 the U.S. Weather Bureau will be issuing daily air pollution reports as well as weather forecasts. People will be "more interested in whether it will be safe to breathe than whether it will be rainy or sunny." Our only comment here is that his prediction is for ten—probably fifteen—years too late.

One more word about our shiny master, the motor-car: As motors are stepped up for higher compression, year by year, nitrogen oxides are stepped up also. And as gasoline manufacturers vie for more "pick-up" by adding new substances like tetraethyl lead and nickel to the gasoline, these extremely toxic substances are also added to our atmosphere. The insane competition for speed and power bows neither to safety nor to health.

It is unreasonable to blame the manufacturers. In the end they put out what the public demands. Indeed, some of them are ahead of public demands as a matter of company pride. Some persons claim that the industry has the know-how to combust completely the fuel within the cylinder and does not do it. But how many American buyers, when dickering for a new car, ask anything more about an engine's performance than horsepower and the fast getaway—and perhaps mileage per gallon?

True, there is the gas-turbine engine that would get rid of all the nitrogen oxides and most of the smog. It will also burn practically anything. But will Americans accept (as the Russians are now doing) conversion to an engine that gives slow starts, noisier action, a trifle less "guts"? Detroit is convinced the customer prefers the fast jump to a long and happy life.

But the Man from Mars, standing beside a super-highway as the shiny monsters hurtle by at 75 or 85 miles an hour, the drivers bent tensely over their steering wheels with riveted, lusterless eyes that see nothing but the pavement ahead, wonders what it is all about. What is this strange, strained Earth creature getting out of life? It is evident that he is not enjoying himself. And the price is high.

Air pollution in America is so varied, so complex, so changing a problem that scientists have so far only begun to scratch the surface.[11] It differs from city to city; turbulence, topography, sunlight, whether the majority of city dwellers burn coal or oil, the industries nearby, the number of automobiles and trucks—all these determine the quotient.

Typical of the great cities is the plight of Boston, described by Commissioner of Public Health Alfred L. Frechette.[12] He estimates that 2,600 tons of solid contaminants are dumped daily over the central 100 square miles of the city. A basic problem is the open burning of automobile bodies. Yet an effective city incinerator that would reduce by 85 per cent what goes into it costs about $5.00 a ton to operate, compared to the $1.50 a ton cost of open-air burning, or $3.00 a ton in a sanitary land fill operation. What shall the city fathers do?

There are two common denominators for air pollution from place to place: *first,* all air pollution is harmful, not only to people but to animals, plants, buildings, bridges, crops, and goods; and, *second,* all types are increasing everywhere at such a rate that researchers are left gasping. "Growing efforts to cope with this evil are having difficulty keeping pace with its fresh manifestations."[13]

What, ask the worried officials at the Boston Museum of Fine Arts, can they do about the black spots which have appeared all over the 300 or 400 priceless and irreplaceable bronze artworks—some of them from the first century—spots on the green patina that come, presumably, from the sulphur oxides in the Boston air? The sulphur oxides evolve from the burning of coal and fuel oil, as well as from gasoline, and their effects cannot be reversed, say officials. Or maybe the blackening comes from ozone? Nobody is quite sure what pollutant causes it, but it is decimating the Museum's treasures.

And what about the worsening air pollution in the region of the booming steel mills? Advanced science now employs oxygen streams to hurry up metal "cooking," and these cause enormous clouds of reddish-brown, acrid smoke that shuts off sunlight and air, has an evil smell, and cloaks and stains homes nearby. An electrostatic precipitator to eliminate most of the smoke and smell costs $1,000,000 per furnace, and even with greatly stepped-up steel production (and, we would assume, greatly stepped-up profits) nobody wants to pay out a million dollars each for ten or twenty furnaces in a row.

Aerial spraying of crops not only poisons rivers but may drift on winds for many miles to lodge in people's lungs. Only recently DDT has been found as a pollutant in the air far from the agricultural lands where it was employed. Nuclear explosions added the pollutants of fallout to our atmosphere, radioactive isotopes that will still be descending on us in the rains for years to come.[14]

In this connection the authors wrote in 1959 a small volume called *Our New Life with the Atom,* which raised several questions that scientists, then in the first blush of dazzling atomic predictions, were determinedly ignoring. One of these questions was: What would fallout—including radioactive iodine-131 from the multitude of Nevada tests—do to the bones and thyroids of children living nearby? The Atomic Energy Commission had been smugly assuring Americans and the entire world that the fallout it was causing was completely harmless. For example, an AEC spokesman on May 13, 1957, stated that the bomb tests would not have "the slightest possible effect" on humans.

On December 3, 1965, eight years later, an Associated Press release, originating in Salt Lake City, Utah, read as follows:

> Atomic blasts in the 1950's are suspected of affecting thyroid glands in a group of Utah children soon to be given medical tests in Salt Lake City. There are nine children to be examined at the University of Utah Medical Center. Southwestern Utah, where the children live, is crossed by winds from southern Nevada. . . . The children are 10 to 18 years old. . . . All have nodules, or small lumps, on their thyroid glands.

There is an ominous resemblance between the protestations of the "harmless fallout" experts of a few years ago and the "harmless insecticides" experts of today.

And what are we planning to do, wonders Dr. Columbus Iselin, Director of the Woods Hole Oceanographic Institution, about the possibly catastrophic effects of carbon dioxide on our weather? Modern technology is releasing great new volumes of this gas into the Earth's envelope, even while understanding that this gas is, over a period of time, a drastic climate changer. Man today is altering his environment faster than ever before, and little of it, to date, has been to the good.

Air pollution, like water pollution and all the other examples of our deteriorating conditions of living, is a by-product of too many people with too much push in the direction of economic progress and not enough in the direction of social progress. In a technology of surpassing wonders, wonders of dizzying impact, we still bear the body, psychological reactions, and evolutionary status of Cro-Magnon. Physically, we are eminently better adapted to cave living than to space living and will probably continue, if spared, in this retarded development for another million years.

Thus, in a civilization whose air may be composed of 21 per cent natural gases and 79 per cent automobile and other combustion gases, we shall be burdened with lungs that demand an outmoded mixture of some 79 per cent plain nitrogen and 21 per cent oxygen. We are trying to adapt a prehistoric physiology to an ultramodern technology and losing on every front. Paleontology tells us that unless we switch and learn to adapt our technology to our prehistoric bodies, we shall perchance pay the price of the dinosaur and the other unadaptable life species which have preceded us.[15]

The depth of our present ignorance concerning the hundreds of killer gases that we are generously releasing into our air blanket (and which, contrary to most belief, will not simply waft away out into space somewhere) remains the most incredible and awesome element of our entire way of life. Such poisons will linger in and densify ourtroposphere forever or until transformed into other substances. Their effects are therefore both acute and chronic.[16]

Crash programs to learn more about air pollution and how to ameliorate it are in progress at all governmental levels. And in this field, as in others, scientists are beginning to desert the torn standard of combat against nature, to rally around the more solid standard of learning to work with her or at least to use her help.

For example, Dr. Chauncey D. Leake, Assistant Dean of the College of Medicine at Ohio State University, has called for extensive planting of trees and other green things ("Maybe 10 trees for every automobile and 100 for every truck") to depollute the air. In this proposal he is strongly supported by Dr. Philip L. Rusden of the Bartlett Tree Research Laboratories. While humans inhale oxygen and exhale carbon dioxide, trees take in carbon dioxide and discharge oxygen, greatly helping to purify the air.

The extensive sums of money put into research by industry (including the American Petroleum Institute) throughout the nation to end pollution both of the common waters and the air are not generally known or appreciated. Leonard A. Duval, President of Hess von Bulow, Incorporated, of Cleveland, is only one of the many industrial magnates with a firm dedication toward cleaning up pollution. "Whenever I see a cloud of ugly brownish smoke pouring from a steel-mill stack," says Mr. Duval, "or when I see a stream of discolored water pouring from a plant or factory into a creek or river, I squirm a little and say to myself, 'Look at all those dollars going to waste. I'm going to get some of them.' "[17]

Already industry has learned how to recover many millions of dollars' worth of light oils, ammonia, and materials from coking coal—materials that go into drugs, plastics, chemicals, and many more products. Now Mr. Duval has dredged nearly 35,000 tons of exceptionally rich iron—washed-away mill scale—out of the Mahoning River near Warren, Ohio, for which he obtained almost $400,000. He is erecting another dredge and four-story processing plant at the cost of about $300,000 at Niles, Ohio, to work another 4,000-foot stretch of the river for a possible additional $400,000. Says Mr. Duval: "There are millions lying on the bottoms of these mill-town rivers and creeks waiting for someone to pick it up."

In like manner the massive brownish clouds of smoke that belch from modern steelmaking furnaces contain iron and zinc sulphides that persistent research will teach how to reclaim. Even the "fly-ash" emitted by coal-burning electric plants might have a use. When air and water pollutants are made truly commercial—that is, when scientists establish a cash-redemption value for each—then the nation's waters and air will be cleaned up with alacrity.

But research, like art, is long, while time continues to be fleeting. Properly, the attack on our ignorance must be spearheaded by the national government. Not only would it be sheer waste for each community or state to duplicate each other's efforts; the call now is for such highly specialized atmospheric scientists, medics, chemists, engineers, meterologists, etc., that smaller agencies of government could not easily recruit the talent called for in our emergency.

Once the facts are known and the solutions made available, the problem of applying those understandings is primarily local. As noted, one community may contend with a copper smelter, another with a chemical plant. One may suffer from atmospheric inversion demanding inflexible traffic limitations; another may have a soft coal problem. No distant official would be likely to work out the ingenious economical and effective program for trash burning, for instance, that Miami, Florida, did. There the incinerator will pay for itself by providing steam for a hospital and custom disposal for nearby Miami Beach.

There is an important role for the states, however. Enabling laws must be passed, rigid standards laid down, specialists provided for the smaller communities, and both intercommunity and interstate or regional problems attacked. The chief complaint of municipalities is that they have no "yardstick" by which to measure violations. It was partly to this end that an Air Pollution Control Board was created in New York State. And unless extensive education is carried on by all levels of government, there will not be the necessary public support to impel the large but needed outlays of money by either government or industry.

It took the Triangle Shirtwaist fire in 1911 to jar New York and then other states into enacting a labor law. It took a circus fire in Hartford to rouse us to more action. It took the near calamity of drought in the East to start pulling in the pollution violators for court hearings. We have already had some wholesale executions by air pollution in London, Los Angeles, and New York City on occasions of atmospheric inversion that hugged the smog close to the earth for a few days at a time. How big must the slaughter be to get real action?

Certainly what we need most is deglomeration of people.[18] Excessive pollution of air as well as of water can deglomerate, even decimate, cities unhealthily crowded with men and cars. But there must be more pleasant ways.

One way less unpleasant than mass biocide by gas asphyxiation would be to lean a trifle harder on that phase of research seeking to produce a combustion engine that completely combusts its fuel and emits a minimum of poisons. Our present combustion engines waste oceans of fuel every year. Can the gas turbine engine be perfected? Chrysler's directional turbine nozzle is a smart advance in fuel efficiency and is hopeful. But why, ask the automobile industry's Members of the Board behind closed doors, throw in a wrench when you've got such a good thing going? No reason at all.[19]

But the White House has given out a hint that a reason may be made. The President's Science Advisory Committee, newly alarmed about the leads and additives that have pushed air pollution to critically high levels, has been mumbling (not too indistinctly) about tighter federal controls under a sort of Food and Drug Administration type setup. They are going so far as to suggest that the time is coming "when it will be necessary to get rid of the present engine and fuels altogether." They have asked automakers seriously to "mull the idea of scrapping present engines and powering cars with non-toxic fuel cells instead."

This is no small request. Fuel cells, while they would completely do away with auto smog and all its train of miseries, are rather far from perfection; indeed, they are far from any practical application. The fact is, the condition of our cities' air is so bad we cannot afford to wait for them. What, then?

Since most families have two cars already it is suggested that one of them be a small electric cart for city driving and the other a high-powered machine for the road. No, the electric cart will not leap forward like a rocket at the green light, but consider this: No more poisonous vapors, odors, smoke clouds, corrosion, gluey oils, inflammatory gasoline; accidents cut to a tenth, less noise, easier parking, the innovation of a relaxed kind of driving (not to mention the cut in incidence of lung cancer, bronchitis, heart conditions, and smarting eyes).

There are, in all, from 8,000 to 10,000 tons of gases, vapors, and solids being thrown into a large city's air every day—a generous two-thirds of it from the automobile—to saturate the lungs of roughly two-thirds of the nation's population. Years ago former Surgeon General Leroy T. Burney declared categorically that there is a "definite association between community air pollution and high mortality rates," a fact that is today universally accepted.

While cars get faster and longer, lives get slower and shorter. While Chrysler competes with Buick for the getaway, cancer competes with emphysema for the layaway. This generation is indeed going to have to choose between humans and the automobile. Perhaps most families have too many of both.

NOTES

1. See A. W. Breidenbach, "Pesticide Residues in Air and Water," *Archives of Environmental Health,* June, 1965, pp. 827–30.
2. The technical literature is developing with articles such as M. B. Gardner's "Biological Effects of Air Pollution: Lung Tumors in Mice," *Archives of Environmental Health,* Mar., 1966, pp. 305–13; and R. B. W. Smith, "Tokyo-Yokohama Asthma: An Area Specific Air Pollution Disease," *Ibid.,* June, 1964, pp. 805–17; T. M. Gocke "What Is the Role of Air Pollution as a Cause of Disease?" *American Journal of Public Health,* Jan., 1964, pp. 71–78.
3. C. W. Griffen, Jr., "America's Airborne Garbage," *Saturday Review,* May 22, 1965, pp. 32ff.
4. See *The Breath of Life* by Donald E. Carr (New York: Norton, 1965), Chapter 7, p. 91.
5. John T. Middleton and Diana Clarkson, "Motor Vehicle Pollution Control," *Traffic Quarterly,* Apr., 1961, pp. 306–17. See also N. Kendall, "Atmospheric Pollution: Reducing Pollution from Motor Vehicles," *Automobile Engineer,* Nov., 1965, pp. 485–87.
6. Dr. Reid O. Bryson of the University of Wisconsin's Center for Climatic Research speculates that man with his dust and pollution may have affected the climate. (*New York Times,* Mar. 15, 1966, p. 19.)
7. See the report of the Air Conservation Commission of the American Association for the Advancement of Science entitled *Air Conservation* and published by the Association, Washington, D.C., in 1965.

A report on what industry is doing to combat smog may be found in *Chemical and Engineering News* of Oct. 10, 1966, p. 33.

8. *Science News Letter*, May 25, 1957, p. 325.

9. *Knickerbocker News* (Albany, New York), Nov. 19, 1958.

10. *Lichty*, "Grin and Bear It," New York *Journal-American*, Aug. 4, 1957.

11. The seventh annual air pollution research conference papers appeared in the *Archives of Environmental Health*, Feb., 1965, pp. 141–388. In Great Britain, the National Society of Clean Air held its thirty-first conference October 20–23, 1965, reported in *Chemistry and Industry*, Nov. 21, 1964, p. 1947.

12. "Neglected Assets . . . Clean Air and Water," *Current Municipal Problems*, Nov., 1963, pp. 103–09.

13. Walter Sullivan's "Polluted Air Said to Raise Death Rates," (*New York Times*, Nov. 13, 1963), capsuling report by Division of Air Pollution of U.S. Public Health Service is recommended. Consult L. D. Neidberg, J. J. Schueneman, P. A. Humphrey, and R. A. Prindle, "Air Pollution and Health: General Description of a Study in Nashville, Tenn.," *Journal, Air Pollution Control Assn.*, June, 1961, pp. 289–97.

14. A thoroughgoing study by Dr. Malcolm L. Peterson called "Environmental Contamination from Nuclear Reactors" appears in *Scientist and Citizen*, Nov., 1965, a publication of the St. Louis Citizens' Committee for Nuclear Information.

15. U.S. Senate Air Pollution Study under Ron M. Linton, staff director of the Senate Public Works Committee, as reported in the *New York Times*, Oct. 25, 1963, p. 62.

16. Lung cancer, once almost unknown, reached a new high of 4,000 deaths in 1935. Today about 43,000 Americans die each year from this one cause, reported the U.S. Public Health Service in 1966.

17. Mr. Duval speaking to George R. Reiss in an exclusive interview for the *Christian Science Monitor*, June 22, 1964.

18. Dr. James P. Lodge of the National Center for Atmospheric Research is reported to have observed that what man does to pollute the air and similar problems can only be met by population control. (*New York Times*, Mar. 15, 1966, p. 19.)

19. Donald E. Carr (*op. cit.*) presents the case for and against the gas turbine engine (Chapter 11, p. 139).

Education and Ecology

Garrett De Bell

Education, particularly higher education, is critically important to solving our ecological crisis. At present, universities do much of the specialized research which develops the technology that is raping the earth and threatening our survival. They do this job devastatingly well. Yet the knowledge and wisdom to apply technology wisely is neglected. The whole direction and purpose and thrust of our culture is toward greater production, greater exploitation. In many, if not in most of our universities, there is little criticism of the basic assumptions and value judgments that underline our current priorities. The university is quite capable of developing an automated machine to harvest almost any crop, but it is unable to evaluate the long-term social costs of such a development. Do farm workers want to be forced out of work and into the cities? Is it desirable to replace people with machines whenever it is feasible? Does this use of machines increase the crop, or just the profit? Some of these machines use gamma radiation to determine if the crop is ripe. Is this a safe and desirable practice? Special strains of crops are developed by plant-breeding programs to meet the needs of the machine system—strains with synchronous ripening, uniform size, tough skins, and long storage life. Does this selection have a detrimental effect on food value? Use of machines makes us more dependent on high technology and the energy needed to make and run the machines. Should we continue to replace labor by energy-using machines when petroleum reserves are sufficient for only a few more generations and energy use pollutes the environment? These are the kinds of questions that go unasked.

The universities are characterized by increasingly narrow specialization in all fields. For instance, ecology as a field emphasizing interrelationships—the study of the total impact of man and other animals on the balance of nature. Yet only a few professional ecologists are willing to brave the disapproval of their narrowly professional colleagues by pursuing the broad spectrum that ecology implies. Some of their names are houshold words—the late Rachael Carson, Paul Ehrlich, Kenneth Watt, Barry Commoner, Lamont Cole, and Garrett Hardin. The rest do very specialized studies that appear in journals such as *Ecology, Ecological Monographs,* and the *Journal of Animal Ecology.*

The biological and social sciences are trying to emulate the elegant work of a few nuclear physicists and molecular biologists and are learning more and more about increasingly trivial subjects.

Very little research is aimed at developing alternatives to our present disastrous pattern of existence with excessive production—waste; conspicuous consumption; manipulative advertising; growth for its own sake; poverty in the midst of plenty; and destruction of the air, water, soil, and organisms that are the basis of the life-support system. One reason that we don't get the right answers is that we aren't asking the right questions.

Probably most important is that we are not providing the kind of education that will allow the electorate to evaluate the choices that are, or will be, available to them.

Our system is, in a word, geared to diplomas, not education. What is to be done? A statement of Paul Goodman's is appropriate:

Today, because of the proved incompetence of our adult institutions and the hyprocrisy of most professionals, university students have a right to a large say in what goes on. . . . Professors will, of course, teach what they please. My advice to students is that given by Prince

Kropotkin, in "A Letter to the Young": "Ask what kind of world do you want to live in? What are you good at and want to work at to build that world? What do you need to know? Demand that your teachers teach you that." Serious teachers would be delighted by this approach.

A recent report to the President's Environmental Quality Council (OST 1969)[1] recognized many of the barriers to effective multidisciplinary education on the campus and makes specific suggestions for reform. It recognizes both the need for people trained much more broadly than the present overspecialized Ph.D. and the resistance within the faculty to truly interdisciplinary work. It found that only separate institutes that had control of the faculty-reward structure (raises, tenure, hiring, and firing) and that had complete "freedom to be innovative in introducing course material, educational programs, work study programs, and curriculum requirements for degrees were successfully achieving meaningful multidisciplinary teaching and research." They found many students coming to these programs after lapses of many years in their schooling, because they felt their earlier education was inadequate for interdisciplinary work. They also found students eager to work in programs aimed at finding workable solutions to our environmental problems.

At least, good ideas on education have been presented to the federal government. Since these ideas will require real changes by the people who control the universities, the trustees, the department heads and deans, there will be vigorous opposition to implementing the proposals. If you are interested in education reform, get hold of the report and press for change on your campus.

It will be a challenging task to make our education system both uplifting and truly relevant to our environment. There is a chance to revitalize the system around the central theme of survival and ecology as suggested in John Fischer's article on page 134. In their calls for a relevant education, students have shown tremendous enthusiasm for study that relates to solving the social and ecological problems that are threatening our existence. They would respond very favorably to efforts by faculty and administration to devote more of the universities' teaching and research to important environmental problems on all levels, especially where they could get directly involved, as through work-study programs. Real inquiry may rescue the university from the sterile degree-and-diploma game it has become.

SUGGESTIONS FOR ACTION

Examine the course content, curriculum, and research of your university or college to see if there is a reasonable balance between pure and applied research; between teaching and research that perpetuates present trends and that which questions trends and suggests alternatives.

How can you make your field relevant to serving our environment? Take surveys of graduate students to see how many are pursuing relevant theses and how many would like to. If the numbers differ significantly, ask questions about the reasons they have not chosen relevant topics.

Check into faculty salaries, fellowships, and grants in different fields and subfields to see where the main priorities are in federal and campus programs. Are these priorities good? See how your local representatives at state and federal levels feel about these priorities and then volunteer to campaign for them or for their opponents depending on their answers. Check the voting record against their answers to be sure.

Set up an experimental college with faculty controlled by students to get some open discussion and fresh ideas. Hire graduate students, uncredentialed people with experience in the real world, politicians, or anyone else you feel could get out of the overspecialized, study-problems-to-death academic syndrome. One dollar per student per quarter at U.C.-Berkeley could provide $108,000 for this purpose. This could provide ten full-time faculty appointments. You might choose to bring in people for a quarter or shorter periods to get more variety. Appointments could be made by the student senate, if it is representative of the general student body on your campus. Provision might be made to ensure that small interest groups were able to have an influence. The purpose of the experimental college would be to counter the university's resistance to change. There are a great number of vested interests in the faculty and administration that resist any change that might alter their power. Students don't have the same vested interests and are more willing to experiment.

NOTES

1. OST 1969: Office of Science and Technology, Executive Office of the President, *The Universities and Environmental Quality—Commitment to Problem Focused Education,* a report to the President's Enviromental Quality Council by John S. Steinhart and Stacie Cherniack, September 1969. For sale by the Supt. of Documents, U.S. Government Printing Office, Washington, D.C. 20402, price 70 cents.

Survival U: Prospectus for a Really Relevant University

John Fischer

from Harper's

It gets pretty depressing to watch what is going on in the world and realize that your education is not equipping you to do anything about it.
> —From a letter by a University
> of California senior

She is not a radical, and has never taken part in any demonstration. She will graduate with honors, and profound disillusionment. From listening to her—and a good many like-minded students at California and East Coast campuses—I think I am beginning to understand what they mean when they say that a liberal-arts education isn't relevant.

They mean it is incoherent. It doesn't cohere. It consists of bits and pieces which don't stick together, and have no common purpose. One of our leading Negro educators, Arthur Lewis of Princeton, recently summed it up better than I can. America is the only country, he said, where youngsters are required "to fritter away their precious years in meaningless peregrination from subject to subject . . . spending twelve weeks getting some tidbits of religion, twelve weeks learning French, twelve weeks seeing whether the history professor is stimulating, twelve weeks seeking entertainment from the economics professor, twelve weeks confirming that one is not going to be able to master calculus."

These fragments are meaningless because they are not

134

organized around any central purpose, or vision of the world. The typical liberal-arts college has no clearly defined goals. It merely offers a smorgasbord of courses, in hopes that if a student nibbles at a few dishes from the humanities table, plus a snack of science, and a garnish of art or anthropolgy, he may emerge as "a cultivated man"—whatever that means. Except for a few surviving church schools, no university even pretends to have a unifying philosophy. Individual teachers may have personal ideologies—but since they are likely to range, on any given campus, from Marxism to worship of the scientific method to exaltation of the irrational (à la Norman O. Brown), they don't cohere either. They often leave a student convinced at the end of four years that any given idea is probably about as valid as any other—and that none of them has much relationship to the others, or to the decisions he is going to have to make the day after graduation.

Education was not always like that. The earliest European universities had a precise purpose: to train an elite for the service of the Church. Everything they taught was focused to that end. Thomas Aquinas had spelled it all out: what subjects had to be mastered, how each connected with every other, and what meaning they had for man and God.

Later, for a span of several centuries, Oxford and Cambridge had an equally clear function: to train administrators to run an empire. So too did Harvard and Yale at the time they were founded; their job was to produce the clergymen, lawyers, and doctors that a new country needed. In each case, the curriculum was rigidly prescribed. A student learned what he needed, to prepare himself to be a competent priest, district officer, or surgeon. He had no doubts about the relevance of his courses—and no time to fret about expanding his consciousness or currying his sensual awareness.

This is still true of our professional schools. I have yet to hear an engineering or medical student complain that his education is meaningless. Only in the liberal-arts colleges—which boast that "we are not trade schools"—do the youngsters get that feeling that they are drowning in a cloud of feathers.

For a long while some of our less complacent academics have been trying to restore coherence to American education. When Robert Hutchins was at Chicago, he tried to use the Great Books to build a comprehensible framework for the main ideas of civilized man. His experiment is still being carried on, with some modifications, at St. John's—but it has not proved irresistibly contagious. Sure, the thoughts of Plato and Machiavelli are still pertinent, so far as they go—but somehow they don't seem quite enough armor for a world beset with splitting atoms, urban guerrillas, nineteen varieties of psychotherapists, amplified guitars, napalm, computers, astronauts, and an atmosphere polluted simultaneously with auto exhaust and TV commercials.

Another strategy for linking together the bits-and-pieces has been attempted at Harvard and at a number of other universities. They require their students to take at least two years of survey courses, known variously as core studies, general education, or world civilization. These too have been something less than triumphantly successful. Most faculty members don't like to teach them, regarding them as superficial and synthetic. (And right they are, since no survey course that I know of has a strong unifying concept to give it focus.) Moreover, the senior professors shun such courses in favor of their own narrow specialties. Consequently, the core studies which are meant to place all human experience—well, at least the brightest nuggets—into One Big Picture usually end up in the perfunctory hands of resentful junior teachers. Naturally the undergraduates don't take them seriously either.

Any successful reform of American education, I am now convinced, will have to be far more revolutionary than anything yet attempted. At a minimum, it should be:

1. Founded on a single guiding concept—an idea capable of knotting together all strands of study, thus giving them both coherence and visible purpose.

2. Capable of equipping young people to do something about "what is going on in the world"—notably the things which bother them most, including war, injustice, racial conflict, and the quality of life.

Maybe it isn't possible. Perhaps knowledge is proliferating so fast, and in so many directions, that it can never again be ordered into a coherent whole, so that molecular biology, Robert Lowell's poetry, and highway engineering will seem relevant to each other and to the lives of ordinary people. Quite possibly the knowledge explosion, as Peter F. Drucker has called it, dooms us to scholarship which grows steadily more specialized, fragmented, and incomprehensible.

The Soviet experience is hardly encouraging. Russian education is built on what is meant to be a unifying ideology: Marxism-Leninism. In theory, it provides an organizing principle for all scholarly activity—whether history, literature, genetics, or military science. Its purpose is explicit: to train a Communist elite for the greater power and glory of the Soviet state, just as the medieval universities trained a priesthood to serve the Church.

Yet according to all accounts that I have seen, it doesn't work very well. Soviet intellectuals apparently are almost as restless and unhappy as our own. Increasing numbers of them are finding Marxism-Leninism too simplistic, too narrowly doctrinaire, too oppressive; the bravest are risking prison in order to pursue their own heretical visions of reality.

Is it conceivable, then, that we might hit upon another idea which could serve as the organizing principle for many fields of scholarly inquiry; which is relevant to the urgent needs of our time; and which would not, on the other hand, impose an ideological strait jacket, as both ecclesiastical and Marxist education attempted to do?

Just possibly it could be done. For the last two or

three years I have been probing around among professors, college administrators, and students—and so far I have come up with only one idea which might fit the specifications. It is simply the idea of survival.

For the first time in history, the future of the human race is now in serious question. This fact is hard to believe, or even think about—yet it is the message which a growing number of scientists are trying, almost frantically, to get across to us. Listen, for example, to Professor Richard A. Falk of Princeton and of the Center for Advanced Study in the Behavioral Sciences:

> The planet and mankind are in grave danger of irreversible catastrophe. . . . Man may be skeptical about following the flight of the dodo into extinction, but the evidence points increasingly to just such a pursuit. . . . There are four interconnected threats to the planet—wars of mass destruction, overpopulation, pollution, and the depletion of resources. They have a cumulative effect. A problem in one area renders it more difficult to solve the problems in any other area. . . . The basis of all four problems is the inadequacy of the sovereign states to manage the affairs of mankind in the twentieth century.

Similar warnings could be quoted from a long list of other social scientists, biologists, and physicists, among them such distinguished thinkers as Rene Dubos, Buckminster Fuller, Loren Eiseley, George Wald, and Barry Commoner. They are not hopeless. Most of them believe that we still have a chance to bring our weapons, our population growth, and the destruction of our environment under control before it is too late. But the time is short, and so far there is no evidence that enough people are taking them seriously.

That would be the prime aim of the experimental university I'm suggesting here: to look seriously at the interlinking threats to human existence, and to learn what we can do to fight them off.

Let's call it Survival U. It will not be a multiversity, offering courses in every conceivable field. Its motto—

emblazoned on a life jacket rampant—will be: "What must we do to be saved?" If a course does not help to answer that question, it will not be taught here. Students interested in musicology, junk sculpture, the Theater of the Absurd, and the literary *dicta* of Leslie Fiedler can go somewhere else.

Neither will our professors be detached, dispassionate scholars. To get hired, each will have to demonstrate an emotional commitment to our cause. Moreover, he will be expected to be a moralist; for this generation of students, like no other in my lifetime, is hungering and thirsting after righteousness. What it wants is a moral system it can believe in—and that is what our university will try to provide. In every class it will preach the primordial ethic of survival.

The biology department, for example, will point out that it is sinful for anybody to have more than two children. It has long since become glaringly evident that unless the earth's cancerous growth of population can be halted, all other problems—poverty, war, racial strife, uninhabitable cities, and the rest—are beyond solution. So the department naturally will teach all known methods of birth control, and much of its research will be aimed at perfecting cheaper and better ones.

Its second lesson in biological morality will be: "Nobody has a right to poison the environment we live in." This maxim will be illustrated by a list of public enemies. At the top will stand the politicians, scientists, and military men—of whatever country—who make and deploy atomic weapons; for if these are ever used, even in so-called defensive systems like the ABM, the atmosphere will be so contaminated with strontium 90 and other radioactive isotopes that human survival seems most unlikely. Also on the list will be anybody who makes or tests chemical and biological weapons—or who even attempts to get rid of obsolete nerve gas, as our Army recently proposed, by dumping the stuff in the sea.

Only slightly less wicked, our biology profs will indicate, is the farmer who drenches his land with DDT. Such insecticides remain virulent indefinitely, and as they wash into the streams and oceans they poison fish, water fowl, and eventually the people who eat them. Worse yet—as John Hay noted in his recently published *In Defense of Nature*—"The original small, diluted concentrations of these chemicals tend to build up in a food chain so as to end in a concentration that may be thousands of times as strong." It is rapidly spreading throughout the globe. DDT already has been found in the tissues of Eskimos and of Antarctic penguins, so it seems probable that similar deposits are gradually building up in your body and mine. The minimum fatal dosage is still unknown.

Before he finishes this course, a student may begin to feel twinges of conscience himself. Is his motorcycle exhaust adding carbon monoxide to the smog we breathe? Is his sewage polluting the nearest river? If so, he will be reminded of two proverbs. From Jesus: "Let him who is without sin among you cast the first stone." From Pogo: "We have met the enemy and he is us."

In like fashion, our engineering students will learn not only how to build dams and highways, but where *not* to build them. Unless they understand that it is immoral to flood the Grand Canyon or destroy the Everglades with a jetport, they will never pass the final exam. Indeed, our engineering graduates will be trained to ask a key question about every contract offered them: "What will be its effect on human life?" That obviously will lead to other questions which every engineer ought to comprehend as thoroughly as his slide rule. Is this new highway really necessary? Would it be wiser to use the money for mass transit—or to decongest traffic by building a new city somewhere else? Is an offshore oil well really a good idea, in view of what happened to Santa Barbara?

Our engineering faculty also will specialize in training men for a new growth industry: garbage disposal. Americans already are spending $4.5 billion a year to collect and get rid of the garbage which we produce more profusely than any other people (more than five pounds a day for each of us). But unless we are resigned to stifling in our own trash, we are going to have to come up with at least an additional $835 million a year.* Any industry with a growth rate of 18 percent offers obvious attractions to a bright young man—and if he can figure out a new way to get rid of our offal, his fortune will be unlimited.

Because the old ways no longer work. Every big city in the United States is running out of dumping grounds. Burning won't do either, since the air is dangerously polluted already—and in any case, 75 percent of the incinerators in use are inadequate. For some 150 years Californians happily piled their garbage into San Francisco Bay, but they can't much longer. Dump-and-fill operations already have reduced it to half its original size, and in a few more decades it would be possible to walk dry-shod from Oakland to the Embarcadero. Consequently San Francisco is now planning to ship garbage 375 miles to the yet-uncluttered deserts of Lassen County by special train—known locally as "The Twentieth Stenchery Limited" and "The Excess Express." The city may actually get away with this scheme, since hardly anybody lives in Lassen County except Indians, and who cares about them? But what is the answer for the metropolis that doesn't have an unspoiled desert handy?

A few ingenious notions are cropping up here and there. The Japanese are experimenting with a machine which compacts garbage, under great heat and pressure, into building blocks. A New York businessman is thinking of building a garbage mountain somewhere upstate, and equipping it with ski runs to amortize the cost. An aluminum company plans to collect and reprocess used aluminum cans—which, unlike the old-fashioned tin can, will not rust away. Our engineering department will try to Think Big along these lines. That way lies not only new careers, but salvation.

Survival U's Department of Earth Sciences will be

* According to Richard D. Vaughn, chief of the Solid Wastes Program of HEW, in his recent horror story entitled "1968 Survey of Community Solid Waste Practices."

headed—if we are lucky—by Dr. Charles F. Park, Jr., now professor of geology and mineral engineering at Stanford. He knows as well as anybody how fast mankind is using up the world's supply of raw materials. In a paper written for the American Geographical Society he punctured one of America's most engaging (and pernicious) myths: our belief than an ever-expanding economy can keep living standards rising indefinitely.

It won't happen; because, as Dr. Park demonstrates, the tonnage of metal in the earth's crust won't last indefinitely. Already we are running short of silver, mercury, tin, and cobalt—all in growing demand by the high-technology industries. Even the commoner metals may soon be in short supply. The United States alone is consuming one ton of iron and eighteen pounds of copper every year, for each of its inhabitants. Poorer countries, struggling to industrialize, hope to raise their consumption of these two key materials to something like that level. If they should succeed—and if the globe's population doubles in the next forty years, as it will at present growth rates—then the world will have to produce, somehow, *twelve times* as much iron and copper every year as it does now. Dr. Parks sees little hope that such production levels can ever be reached, much less sustained indefinitely. The same thing, of course—doubled in spades—goes for other raw materials: timber, oil, natural gas, and water, to note only a few.

Survival U, therefore, will prepare its students to consume less. This does not necessarily mean an immediate drop in living standards—perhaps only a change in the yardstick by which we measure them. Conceivably Americans might be happier with fewer automobiles, neon signs, beer cans, supersonic jets, barbecue grills, and similar metallic fluff. But happy or not, our students had better learn how to live The Simpler Life, because that is what most of them are likely to have before they reach middle age.

To help them understand how very precious resources really are, our mathematics department will teach a new kind of bookkeeping: social accounting. It will train people to analyze budgets—both government and corporate—with an eye not merely to immediate dollar costs, but to the long-range costs to society.

By conventional bookkeeping methods, for example, the coal companies strip-mining away the hillsides of Kentucky and West Virginia show a handsome profit. Their ledgers, however, show only a fraction of the true cost of their operations. They take no account of destroyed land which can never bear another crop; of rivers poisoned by mud and seeping acid from the spoil banks; of floods which sweep over farms and towns downstream, because the ravaged slopes can no longer hold the rainfall. Although these costs are not borne by the mining firms, they are nevertheless real. They fall mostly on the taxpayers, who have to pay for disaster relief, flood-control levees, and the resettlement of Appalachian farm families forced off the land. As soon as our students (the taxpayers of tomorrow) learn to read a social balance sheet, they obviously will throw the strip miners into bankruptcy.

Another case study will analyze the proposal of the Inhuman Real Estate Corporation to build a fifty-story skyscraper in the most congested area of midtown Manhattan. If 90 percent of the office space can be rented at $12 per square foot, it looks like a sound investment, according to antique accounting methods. To uncover the true facts, however, our students will investigate the cost of moving 12,000 additional workers in and out of midtown during rush hours. The first (and least) item is $8 million worth of new city buses. When they are crammed into the already clogged avenues, the daily loss of man-hours in traffic jams may run to a couple of million more. The fumes from their diesel engines will cause an estimated 9 percent increase in New York's incidence of emphysema and lung cancer: this requires the construction of three new hospitals. To supply them, plus the new building, with water—already perilously short in the city—a new reservoir has to be built on the headwaters of the Delaware River, 140 miles away. Some of the dairy farmers pushed out of the drowned valley will move promptly into the Bronx and go on relief. The subtraction of their milk output from the city's supply leads to a price increase of two cents a quart. For a Harlem mother with seven hungry children, that is the last straw. She summons her neighbors to join her in riot, seven blocks go up in flames, and the Mayor demands higher taxes to hire more police. . . .

Instead of a sound investment, Inhuman Towers now looks like criminal folly, which would be forbidden by any sensible government. Our students will keep that in mind when they walk across campus to their government class.

Its main goal will be to discover why our institutions have done so badly in their efforts (as Dr. Falk put it) "to manage the affairs of mankind in the twentieth century." This will be a compulsory course for all freshmen, taught by professors who are capable of looking critically at every political artifact, from the Constitution to the local county council. They will start by pointing out that we are living in a state of near-anarchy, because we have no government capable of dealing effectively with public problems.

Instead we have a hodgepodge of 80,000 local governments—villages, townships, counties, cities, port authorities, sewer districts, and special purpose agencies. Their authority is so limited, and their jurisdictions so confused and overlapping, that most of them are virtually impotent. The states, which in theory could put this mess into some sort of order, usually have shown little interest and less competence. When Washington is called to help out—as it increasingly has been for the last thirty-five years—it often has proved ham-handed and entangled in its own archaic bureaucracy. The end result is that nobody in authority has been able to take care of the country's mounting needs. Our welfare rolls keep growing, our air and water get dirtier, housing gets scarcer, airports jam up, road traffic clots, railways fall apart, prices rise, ghettos burn, schools turn out more losing confidence in American institutions. In their present state, they don't deserve much confidence.

The advanced students of government at Survival U will try to find out whether these institutions can be renewed and rebuilt. They will take a hard look at the few places—Jacksonville, Minnesota, Nashville, Appalachia—which are creating new forms of government. Will these work any better, and if so, how can they be duplicated elsewhere? Can the states be brought to life, or should we start thinking about an entirely different kind of arrangement? Ten regional prefectures, perhaps, to replace the fifty states? Or should we take seriously Norman Mailer's suggestion for a new kind of city-state to govern our great metropolises? (He merely called for New York City to secede from its state; but that isn't radical enough. To be truly governable, the new Republic of New York City ought to include chunks of New Jersey and Connecticut as well.) Alternatively, can we find some way to break up Megalopolis, and spread our population into smaller and more livable communities throughout the continent? Why should we keep 70 percent of our people crowded into less than 2 percent of our land area, anyway?

Looking beyond our borders, our students will be encouraged to ask even harder questions. Are nation-states actually feasible, now that they have power to destroy each other in a single afternoon? Can we agree on something else to take their place, before the balance of terror becomes unstable? What price would most people be willing to pay for a more durable kind of human organization—more taxes, giving up national flags, perhaps the sacrifice of some of our hard-won liberties?

All these courses (and everything else taught at Survival U) are really branches of a single science. Human ecology is one of the youngest disciplines, and probably the most important. It is the study of the relationship between man and his environment, both natural and technological. It teaches us to understand the consequences of our actions—how sulfur-laden fuel oil burned in England produces an acid rain that damages the forests of Scandinavia, why a well-meant farm subsidy can force millions of Negro tenants off the land and lead to Watts and Hough. A graduate who comprehends ecology will know how to look at "what is going on in the world," and he will be equipped to do something about it. Whether he ends up as a city planner, a politician, an enlightened engineer, a teacher, or a reporter, he will have had a relevant education. All of its parts will hang together in a coherent whole.

And if we can get enough such graduates, man and his environment may survive a while longer, against all the odds.

Wilderness

Kenneth Brower

Wilderness, and the problem of preserving it, has been on the American mind for some time. "A world from which solitude has been extirpated is a very poor ideal," wrote John Stuart Mill. "What is the use of a house if you haven't got a tolerable planet to put it on?" Thoreau wondered. "It is the love of country that has lighted and that keeps glowing the holy fire of patriotism. And this love is excited, primarily, by the beauty of the country," J. Horace McFarland said, in 1908. Joseph Wood Krutch agrees.

The desire to experience the reality of the great poem Thoreau wrote about, the great terrestrial poem before its best pages were ripped out and thrown away, is the desire, Krutch feels, that brought the best people to America's shores. Solitude, wildness, and beauty of earth are at their most solitary, wild, and beautiful in wilderness. Wilderness is a citadel for the forces that bore on us during the formative years of our national consciousness, the forces that brought the best to our shores. And wilderness is more, of course. If man destroys wilderness, Dr. J. A. Rush writes, he will have repudiated more than an American tradition—he will have repudiated the tradition that put him on the planet, and will find himself terribly alone.

As Nancy Newhall observes, wilderness has answers to questions that man has not learned how to ask. Why is it, for example, that of all mammals in creation only the wolverine is free of arthritis? The wolverine requires

147

a sizable wilderness to range about in, and that wilderness holds the answer. How many discoveries, like quinine, or the antibiotic virtues of abalone blood, or paper, even, remain undiscovered in wilderness? How much more do we need to learn about evolutionary processes there? What was it that enabled Eskimo shamen, their minds a product of the taiga, tundra, and sea ice, to travel on spirit journeys under the ocean and to talk with the fishes and the potent beings who lived on the bottom? How did the shamen develop the hypnotic power they employed in their seances? What can we learn from the shamen who survive about thought transference and ESP? The answers are in the arctic wilderness still left to us.

Wilderness is a bench mark, a touchstone. In wilderness we can see where we have come from, where we are going, how far we've gone. In wilderness is the only unsullied earth sample of the forces generally at work in the universe.

New perspectives come out of the wilderness. Jesus, Zoroaster, Moses, and Mohammed went to the wilderness and came back with messages. It was from the wilderness, and the people who knew wilderness, that the first concern about pollution and environmental decay came. Men and women who knew how water should taste, air should breathe, and grass should grow, were the first to detect when these things were happening wrong. This handbook, and the teach-in it serves, have their beginnings in wilderness.

More important, perhaps, than its value as a place for research and a place to touch home—more than its value to mankind—is the value of wilderness to individual men, its value as balm, quiet, solitude; as a place to catch a breath, to connect consecutive thoughts, to sleep early, to wake to the light, dry, aromatic air of uncultivated places that Willa Cather wrote about. Recreation, in the real sense of the word, happens best in wilderness.

Wilderness is important as an idea. For Aldo Leopold, the most interesting part of a map was the blank places.

They were spots he might explore some day, and he made imaginary use of them. Wilderness, Wallace Stegner wrote, developing the idea, is part of the Geography of Hope. It's a commodity we make use of even when we aren't in it; its existence makes New York City or Oakland more tolerable, because we know that there is something else. What comes out of the wilderness can become a possession of the entire race, John Collier writes. Scott died in the Antarctic wilderness but his journal survived to challenge mankind forever, Collier notes. *Green Mansions* came from the Patagonian desert (and W. H. Hudson). It's not hard to add to Collier's list. *Moby Dick* came from the contiguous wildernesses of the sea and Herman Melville's mind. Most of the best of American writers, even modern ones like Twain, Steinbeck, Hemingway, set their stories against the land. The American earth is the source of our great wealth in more than a commercial way.

All of the preceding defenses of wilderness are sound, I think, but they come a little too easily to me. I am the son of an eloquent conservationist, and I grew up in the years that he was developing his eloquence. All the wilderness arguments were old when I was still very young. Children need to find their own causes. I became a ten-year-old expert on injustices against the American Indian and an historian of Western Indian wars.

But lately I have been rereading my father's arguments. I began casually, just to see what the old man had been up to. I was struck first by how well he wrote, after all, then by the number of references he made to us, his children. He wrote a lot of children and sons, of our children's children, of each generation's obligation to generations yet unborn, but just as often he wrote of us by name. I remember once thinking that this must be a rhetorical device, or perhaps a way of apologizing to us for all the times his work kept him away. I knew our father loved us, but I also knew how intensely he worked at conservation, and it was hard for me to imagine that he thought much about us when he was gone. Now, closer to being a father myself, hearing the distant patter of little feet, I think I understand better.

"Thomas Jefferson," my father wrote, "long ago, said that one generation could not bind another; each had the right to set its own course. Go out across this land and try to find someone to argue that he was wrong. You won't find a taker. It is the national consensus that we don't have this right.

"But deeds are not matching words. This generation is speedily using up, beyond recall, a very important right that belongs to future generations—the right to have wilderness in their civilization, even as we have it in ours; the right to find solitude somewhere; the right to see, and enjoy, and be inspired and renewed, somewhere, by those places where the hand of God has not been obscured by the industry of man.

"Our decisions today will determine the fate of that right, so far as people of our time can pass opportunity along to our sons. Apathy here can mean that we pass them a dead torch. Or we can keep it aflame, knowing that this is a very special torch that man cannot light again."

I can understand that sentiment, though with its flaming torch it sounds a bit like J. Horace McFarland. I prefer my father's introduction to his Manual of Ski Mountaineering, which took the form of a series of winter suggestions to my brother and me, suggestions he would have liked to give us, he wrote, but refrained because we were teen-agers and would not have listened:

Finally I would have tried to explain to them what ski mountaineering had meant to me; about the peaks I had made first ascents of, for the most part on skis; of the high snow camps I had known and what it was like to be up on top in early winter morning and evening, when the world is painted with a very special light; of the kind of competence and even braveness, maybe, that one picks up from good friends and challenging peaks, up there when the storms hit and the snow pelts the fabric all through the night; of the kind of exhilaration we got when, after two winter struggles, the third put us on top of a fourteen-thousander and we were first to be there in winter and see how magnificently winter treats a high land we already knew well in summer but in a lesser beauty; of the long vibrant moments when we were back on our skis, skimming down the uncrevassed glacier on just the right depth of new powder, letting our skis go, finding that every turn worked, hearing the vigorous flapping of our ski pants even though the wind was singing in our ears and stinging our faces, sensing how rapidly the peaks climbed above us, those peaks that had dropped so reluctantly to our level in all the slow day's climb; of the care we had to take after night found us out and we sideslipped and sidestepped down into the tortuous little basins and then into the hummocky forest floor that lay in darkness between us and camp; I would have described that hot cup of soup I cuddled in my hand in exhaustion, sipping slowly to absorb its warmth and its energy at a retainable rate; and I would speak of the morning after and, not its hangover, but its glow as I looked back up to the rocky palisade above the glacier and was just pleased as hell to have got there at last—pleased with the weather, the companions, and the luck —and also forgivably pleased a little that I could do it.

In writing of my little brother, who saw his first moose when he was three, yet knew instantly and cried "moose!" three years later when he saw his second, my father wrote, "The image fixed well, as wild images do, on that perfectly sensitized but almost totally unexposed film of his mind."

My own first memories are of the wilderness of the Sierra Nevada. I remember the people. There was Tommy Jefferson, a packer, a full-blooded Mono Indian— Tommy Jefferson and his full Indian face, strong back and short Indian legs, his boots and levis, sprinting in delight after a bronco mule that was throwing its load, jumping on the mule and biting its ear until the mule calmed itself. There was Tommy's boss Bruce Morgan, owner of Mt. Whitney Pack Trains, with his two white riding mules and the .45 pistol in case one of his pack animals broke its leg. There was my father, the campfire speaker, the singer, the rock climber, the man with more alpine medals on his hat than anyone else.

But mostly I remember me in the mountains. I remember walking over Army Pass in the hailstorm, the lightning striking so close that a blue light shone ahead of us, the hailstones dancing on the rocks around us. I remember wild onions, and the long descent from the High Sierra down to the desert of the Owens Valley. I remember how in elementary school, every year about spring, I would begin to long for the mountains. The mountains were something I had, like a disguised prince his secret.

My own son should have the same memories, or the chance to have them. For me, the atavistic joy in first intimations of fatherhood are mixing with the determination that there be wilderness left for my son to ramble in. My father's passion is creeping up on me.

I hope he stays in good shape, so the three of us can go together.

A Future That Makes Ecological Sense

Garrett De Bell

For the last few years I've noticed two trends in literature about the future. Journals like *Audubon Magazine, Sierra Club Bulletin,* and *Cry California* are generally concerned about imminent ecological disaster —the death of canyons and valleys, the end of whales, big cats, eagles, falcons, pelicans, and even man. The magazines popularizing science, such as *Popular Science* and *Popular Mechanics,* speak of the technological Utopia of the future—a television screen attached to every telephone, a helicopter on every rooftop, and sleek supersonic transports for the fortunate few within them who cannot hear their sonic boom. The two kinds of journal seem oblivious of each other and mutually exclusive. Yet there is a connection: The more we strive to reach the popular science future, the more likely we are to achieve the ecological disaster.

The production, use and disposal of technologically sophisticated gadgets is a big part of our ecological problem. The solution to the problem is not found in a simple banning of billboards and non-returnable bottles, nor in the promotion of anti-litter campaigns and highway beautification. Some of our best polluters encourage such useful activities with advertising that professes deep concern about environment. This kind of effort is at worst cynical and at best misguided. Dealing with our ecological crises in population, water and air pollution, pesticides, transportation and the quality of life requires more than mere palliatives. It requires the restructuring of many aspects of society.

We need first to halt growth of the world's population and then work toward reducing the current three and a half billion people to something less than one billion people. This number, perhaps, could be supported at a standard of living roughly similar to that of countries such as Norway and the Netherlands at the present time. The absurdly affluent and destructive standard of living in a country like the United States could not be sustained for very long for a population of more than three or four hundred million people all over the world.

One of the main purposes of the teach-in and the whole ecological movement in this country today is to direct attention to a new kind of thinking about our environmental problems, a search for options so that we can decide the goals and the directions to take to provide for a future that makes ecological sense. What might such a future be like? Imagine your own.

You can imagine hearing someone say, "Remember the subdivision that used to be where that orange grove is?" You can see a web of parks throughout the cities replacing the freeways and streets that once dominated. You can see agriculture become diversified again, with a great variety of crops grown together, replacing the old reliance on mass-produced single crop operations that are highly dependent on pesticides, machines, and cheap farm labor. The traditional American values of rural life come back, and many more people grow their own food on smaller holdings and with a better quality of existence for the farm workers—and for everyone else.

More fruits and vegetables have insects on them instead of poisons. They can be brushed off or swallowed accidentally without harm. They are not mutagenic. They eat very little themselves, and because there is no monocrop, they can't wipe it out.

We see an end to some of the contradictions in American life. Where we once burned fossil fuels and polluted the air to provide electricity to run the escalators and other labor-saving devices that fattened us and sent us to the electric exercise machines and calorie-free soft drinks, we can rediscover walking. Where we overheated or overconditioned our air, we rely again on the human adaptability to stress that shaped us and gave us our physical integrity over a million years of living. Although the small labor-saving devices did not use much power, their aggregate use increased the demand for electricity, and with it the need for more dams, more oxidizing of fossil fuel, and more proliferation of nuclear power plants and their radionuclides. We find that diminishing dependence upon electric devices diminishes the need to build dams on wild rivers, pollute the air and sea with fossil fuels, and poison the ecosphere with dispersing nuclear waste.

With conspicuous consumption eliminated, we have more leisure time and a shorter work week. There are fewer automobiles, less reliance upon wasteful packaging, and less need for the labor saving devices that exploited natural resources in order to save time to spend with little reward in our overdepleted world. We produce what we need and not a surplus. We allocate limited resources. New economists adjust economic sights to accommodate the requirements of our spaceship Earth, limited closed system that it is. The economists rethink about growth and know that "growth for the sake of growth is the ideology of the cancer cell," as Edward Abbey pointed out.

There is less spectator sport and more participating. The American people, once a nation of watchers, are "do-it-yourself people" again. They ski where the snowmobiles took them, walk where trail bikes crudded the wilderness and swim where motorboats droned over lakes they oiled. The people buy less music and make more of their own. There is a world quiet enough to hear it in.

People are healthier. Fewer coronaries strike them because walking and bicycling and swimming keep them fitter. There are fewer people in hospitals because the old murderous automobile-oriented transportation system has been brought under control. Even the former automobile manufacturers, salesmen, and service people live longer, better lives. One major change is that every product we buy includes in its price the cost of its ultimate disposal. The many products that once were cheap because they were dumped at will have become so expensive that they no longer end up cluttering the environment.

Many of the people who were producing automobiles have been shifted into the housing or building industry. Their main job is restructuring the urban wastes to planned cities, restoring land to good agricultural use, building high-quality clustered dwellings at the edges of the good agricultural land, using recycled material from the old buildings. People ride the short distance to their work and have a chance to farm a little in the sun. There are legs and arms and abdomens where the flab was, and the air is once again transparent.

The idea that a steady state works is commonplace. The population is declining slowly toward a balance between man and the other living things upon which his own life depends. The need for, and number of, schools, doctors, highways, roads, public parks, recreational facilities, swimming pools, and other facilities is roughly the same from year to year. People work enough to service equipment and to replace things that wear out. They devote energy to increasing the quality of life rather than to providing more and more possessions. The job of the garbage man and junk man is elevated to the stature of recycling engineer, looping systems in such a way that materials cause no environmental deterioration. Many power plants and dams are dismantled as the amount of energy needed each year declines and people develop sensible ways of living that require much less power, pollution, and environmental disruption. There is decentralization of many basic services. Ecologically sound food stores prosper, offering pesticide-free produce in returnable containers.

Advertising serves to inform, not to overstimulate, and is believable again. Wilderness areas are no longer under attack, and retread wilderness increases substantially each year; less land is needed for commercial timber production because of effective recycling of wood products, reduction of conspicuous consumption and the lessening of need as the population drops. Poisoning of the ecosystem by the leaded automobile gasoline has ceased because engine redesign eliminates the need for lead additives.

Emphysema and lung cancer caused by smog are eliminated and the smog goes. People learn how to garden again, and allow the recovery to take place of the natural forms of "pest" control instead of heavy doses of pesticides.

People are learning progressively more about relying less on gadgets. They have long since refused to buy ten cents worth of food in a T.V. dinner on an aluminum platter that will outlast the food for generations.

Many of the things built in the past in the name of conservation are being unbuilt. The Army Corps of Engineers is spending its time undoing the damage it has done over the past decades. Cities no longer ask the Corps to build a dam to prevent flooding of houses unwisely built on a flood plain. Instead, they ask the Corps to restore the flood plain to a vegetative cover that accommodates floods—good creative work for engineers.

And that technological mistake, the supersonic transport, has long since been a strange delusion, the few that were built having been dismantled and forgotten.

So much for one view of the future—more Utopian than likely, unless people want it that way. Many believe we cannot solve the environmental problems because of the powerful influence of vested interests. Obviously we can't solve these problems unless we meet these interests directly in the political arena and demonstrate that survival—theirs and ours—requires continuing change. The massive grass-roots political movement which we now see growing can bring this about. One of the major changes of the decade can come from an ecological-political movement that bridges the gap between Left and Right and young and old. This movement will get people together behind candidates who press for a healthy environment and will turn out of office those who only pretend to do so.

The thing people must realize above all is that the solution to our environmental crises involves simple, small measures by many people in accelerating sequence. The changes needed will require a conversion like that required to win World War II and then to reconvert to peace. The reward is worth this kind of effort. Consider the alternative.

Many projections of a tenable future are possible and feasible. FRIENDS OF THE EARTH welcomes yours Perhaps you can suggest one here, detach it, and send it in to:

FRIENDS OF THE EARTH

30 East 42nd Street, New York, New York 10017.

Eco-Catastrophe!

Paul R. Ehrlich

from Ramparts

In the following scenario, Dr. Paul Ehrlich predicts what our world will be like in ten years if the present course of environmental destruction is allowed to continue. Dr. Ehrlich is a prominent ecologist, a professor of biology at Stanford University, and author of The Population Bomb (*Ballantine*).

The end of the ocean came late in the summer of 1979, and it came even more rapidly than the biologists had expected. There had been signs for more than a decade, commencing with the discovery in 1968 that DDT slows down photosynthesis in marine plant life. It was announced in a short paper in the technical journal, *Science,* but to ecologists it smacked of doomsday. They knew that all life in the sea depends on photosynthesis, the chemical process by which green plants bind the sun's energy and make it available to living things. And they knew that DDT and similar chlorinated hydrocarbons had polluted the entire surface of the earth, including the sea.

But that was only the first of many signs. There had been the final gasp of the whaling industry in 1973, and the end of the Peruvian anchovy fishery in 1975. Indeed, a score of other fisheries had disappeared quietly from overexploitation and various eco-catastrophes by 1977. The term "eco-catastrophe" was coined by a California ecologist in 1969 to describe the most spectacular of man's attacks on the systems which sustain his life. He drew his inspiration from the Santa Barbara offshore oil disaster of that year, and from the news which spread among naturalists that virtually all of the Golden State's seashore bird life was doomed because of chlorinated hydrocarbon interference with its reproduction. Eco-catastrophes in the sea became increasingly common in the early 1970's. Mysterious "blooms" of previously rare microoragnisms began to appear in offshore waters. Red tides—killer outbreaks of a minute single-celled plant —returned to the Florida Gulf coast and were sometimes accompanied by tides of other exotic hues.

It was clear by 1975 that the entire ecology of the ocean was changing. A few types of phytoplankton were becoming resistant to chlorinated hydrocarbons and were gaining the upper hand. Changes in the phytoplankton community led inevitably to changes in the community of zooplankton, the tiny animals which eat the phyto-plankton. These changes were passed on up the chains of life in the ocean to the herring, plaice, cod and tuna. As the diversity of life in the ocean diminished, its sta-bility also decreased.

Other changes had taken place by 1975. Most ocean fishes that returned to freshwater to breed, like the salmon, had become extinct, their breeding streams so damned up and polluted that their powerful homing instinct only resulted in suicide. Many fishes and shell-fishes that bred in restricted areas along the coasts fol-lowed them as onshore pollution escalated.

By 1977 the annual yield of fish from the sea was down to 30 million metric tons, less than one-half the per capita catch of a decade earlier. This helped mal-nutrition to escalate sharply in a world where an esti-mated 50 million people per year were already dying of starvation. The United Nations attempted to get all chlorinated hydrocarbon insecticides banned on a world-wide basis, but the move was defeated by the United States. This opposition was generated primarily by the American petrochemical industry, operating hand in glove with its subsidiary, the United States Department of Agriculture. Together they persuaded the government to oppose the U.N. move—which was not difficult since most Americans believed that Russia and China were more in need of fish products than was the United States. The United Nations also attempted to get fishing nations to adopt strict and enforced catch limits to preserve dwindling stocks. This move was blocked by Russia, who, with the most modern electronic equipment, was in the best position to glean what was left in the sea. It was, curiously, on the very day in 1977 when the Soviet Union announced its refusal that another ominous article appeared in *Science*. It announced that incident solar radiation had been so reduced by worldwide air pollution that serious effects on the world's vegetation could be expected.

Apparently it was a combination of ecosystem destabilization, sunlight reduction, and a rapid escalation in chlorinated hydrocarbon pollution from massive Thanodrin applications which triggered the ultimate catastrophe. Seventeen huge Soviet-financed Thanodrin plants were operating in underdeveloped countries by 1978. They had been part of a massive Russian "aid offensive" designed to fill the gap caused by the collapse of America's ballyhooed 'Green Revolution."

It became apparent in the early '70s that the "Green Revolution" was more talk than substance. Distribution of high yield "miracle" grain seeds had caused temporary local spurts in agricultural production. Simultaneously, excellent weather had produced record harvests. The combination permitted bureaucrats, especially in the United States Department of Agriculture and the Agency for International Development (AID), to reverse their previous pessimism and indulge in an outburst of optimistic propaganda about staving off famine. They raved about the approaching transformation of agriculture in the underdeveloped countries (UDCs). The reason for the propaganda reversal was never made clear. Most historians agree that a combination of utter ignorance of ecology, a desire to justify past errors, and pressure from agro-industry (which was eager to sell pesticides, fertilizers, and farm machinery to the UDCs and agencies helping the UDCs) was behind the campaign. Whatever the motivation, the results were clear. Many concerned people, lacking the expertise to see through the Green Revolution drivel, relaxed. The population-food crisis was "solved."

But reality was not long in showing itself. Local famine persisted in northern India even after good weather brought an end to the ghastly Bihar famine of the mid-'60s. East Pakistan was next, followed by a resurgence of general famine in northern India. Other foci of famine rapidly developed in Indonesia, the Philippines, Malawi, the Congo, Egypt, Colombia, Ecuador, Honduras, the Dominican Republic, and Mexico.

Everywhere hard realities destroyed the illusion of the Green Revolution. Yields dropped as the progressive farmers who had first accepted the new seeds found that their higher yields brought lower prices—effective demand (hunger plus cash) was not sufficient in poor countries to keep prices up. Less progressive farmers, observing this, refused to make the extra effort required to cultivate the "miracle" grains. Transport systems proved inadequate to bring the necessary fertilizer to the fields where the new and extremely fertilizer-sensitive grains were being grown. The same systems were also inadequate to move produce to markets. Fertilizer plants were not built fast enough, and most of the underdeveloped countries could not scrape together funds to purchase supplies, even on concessional terms. Finally, the inevitable happened, and pests began to reduce yields in even the most carefully cultivated fields. Among the first were the famous "miracle rats" which invaded Philippine "miracle rice" fields early in 1969. They were quickly followed by many insects and viruses, thriving on the relatively pest-susceptible new grains, encouraged by the vast and dense plantings, and rapidly acquiring resistance to the chemicals used against them. As chaos spread until even the most obtuse agriculturists and economists realized that the Green Revolution had turned brown, the Russians stepped in.

In retrospect it seems incredible that the Russians, with the American mistakes known to them, could launch an even more incompetent program of aid to the underdeveloped world. Indeed, in the early 1970's there were cynics in the United States who claimed that outdoing the stupidity of American foreign aid would be physically impossible. Those critics were, however, obviously unaware that the Russians had been busily destroying their own environment for many years. The virtual disappearance of sturgeon from Russian rivers caused a great shortage of caviar by 1970. A standard joke among Russian scientists at that time was that they had created an artificial caviar which was indistinguishable from the real thing—except by taste. At any rate the Soviet Union, observing with interest the progressive deterioration of relations between the UDCs and the United States, came up with a solution. It had recently developed what it claimed was the ideal insecticide, a highly lethal chlorinated hydorcarbon complexed with a special agent for penetrating the external skeletal armor of insects. Announcing that the new pesticide, called Thanodrin, would truly produce a Green Revolution, the Soviets entered into negotiations with various UDCs for the construction of massive Thanodrin factories. The USSR would bear all the costs; all it wanted in return were certain trade and military concessions.

It is interesting now, with the perspective of years, to examine in some detail the reasons why the UDCs welcomed the Thanodrin plan with such open arms. Government officials in these countries ignored the protests of their own scientists that Thanodrin would not solve the problems which plagued them. The governments now knew that the basic cause of their problems was overpopulation, and that these problems had been exacerbated by the dullness, daydreaming, and cupidity endemic to all governments. They knew that only population control and limited development aimed primarily at agriculture could have spared them the horrors they now faced. They knew it, but they were not about to admit it. How much easier it was simply to accuse the

Americans of failing to give them proper aid; how much simpler to accept the Russian panacea.

And then there was the general worsening of relations between the United States and the UDCs. Many things had contributed to this. The situation in America in the first half of the 1970's deserves our close scrutiny. Being more dependent on imports for raw materials than the Soviet Union, the United States had, in the early 1970's, adopted more and more heavy-handed policies in order to insure continuing supplies. Military adventures in Asia and Latin America had further lessened the international credibility of the United States as a great defender of freedom—an image which had begun to deteriorate rapidly during the pointless and fruitless Viet Nam conflict. At home, acceptance of the carefully manufactured image lessened dramatically, as even the more romantic and chauvinistic citizens began to understand the role of the military and the industrial system in what John Kenneth Galbraith had aptly named "The New Industrial State."

At home in the USA the early '70s were traumatic times. Racial violence grew and the habitability of the cities diminished, as nothing substantial was done to ameliorate either racial inequities or urban blight. Welfare rolls grew as automation and general technological progress forced more and more people into the category of "unemployable." Simultaneously a taxpayers' revolt occurred. Although there was not enough money to build the schools, roads, water systems, sewage systems, jails, hospitals, urban transit lines, and all the other amenities needed to support a burgeoning population, Americans refused to tax themselves more heavily. Starting in Youngstown, Ohio, in 1969 and followed closely by Richmond, California, community after community was forced to close its schools or curtail educational operations for lack of funds. Water supplies, already marginal in quality and quantity in many places by 1970, deteriorated quickly. Water rationing occurred in 1,723 municipalities in the summer of 1974, and hepatitis and epidemic dysentery rates climbed about 500 percent between 1970 and 1974.

Air pollution continued to be the most obvious manifestation of environmental deterioration. It was, by 1972, quite literally in the eyes of all Americans. The year 1973 saw not only the New York and Los Angeles smog disasters, but also the publication of the surgeon general's massive report on air pollution and health. The public had been partially prepared for the worst by the publicity given to the U.N. pollution conference held in 1972. Deaths in the late '60s caused by smog were well known to scientists, but the public had ignored them because they mostly involved the early demise of the old and sick rather than people dropping dead on the freeways. But suddenly our citizens were faced with nearly 200,000 corpses and massive documentation that they could be the next to die from respiratory disease. They were not ready for that scale of disaster. After all, the U.N. conference had not predicted that accumulated air pollution would make the planet uninhabitable until almost 1990. The population was terrorized as TV screens became filled with scenes of horror from the disaster areas. Especially vivid was NBC's coverage of hundreds of unattended people choking out their lives outside of New York's hospitals. Terms like nitrogen oxide, acute bronchitis and cardiac arrest began to have real meaning for most Americans.

The ultimate horror was the announcement that chlorinated hydrocarbons were now a major constituent of air pollution in all American cities. Autopsies of smog disaster victims revealed an average chlorinated hydrocarbon load in fatty tissue equivalent to 26 parts per million of DDT. In October, 1973, the Department of Health, Education and Welfare announced studies which showed unequivocally that increasing death rates from hypertension, cirrhosis of the liver, liver cancer and a series of other diseases had resulted from the chlorinated hydrocarbon load. They estimated that Americans born since 1946 (when DDT usage began) now had a life expectancy of only 49 years, and predicted that if current patterns continued, this expectancy would reach 42 years by 1980, when it might level out. Plunging insurance stocks triggered a stock market panic. The president of Velsicol, Inc., a major pesticide producer, went on television to "publicly eat a teaspoonful of DDT" (it was really powdered milk) and announce that HEW had been infiltrated by Communists. Other giants of the petro-chemical industry, attempting to dispute the indisputable evidence, launched a massive pressure campaign on Congress to force HEW to "get out of agriculture's business." They were aided by the agro-chemical journals, which had decades of experience in misleading the public about the benefits and dangers of pesticides. But by now the public realized that it had been duped. The Nobel Prize for medicine and physiology was given to Drs. J. L. Radomski and W. B. Deichmann, who in the late 1960's had pioneered in the documentation of the long-term lethal effects of chlorinated hydrocarbons. A presidential commission with unimpeachable credentials directly accused the agrochemical complex of "condemning many millions of Americans to an early death." The year 1973 was the year in which Americans finally came to understand the direct threat to their existence posed by environmental deterioration.

And 1973 was also the year in which most people finally comprehended the indirect threat. Even the president of Union Oil Company and several other industrialists publicly stated their concern over the reduction of bird populations which had resulted from pollution by DDT and other chlorinated hydrocarbons. Insect populations boomed because they were resistant to most pesticides and had been freed, by the incompetent use of those pesticides, from most of their natural enemies. Rodents swarmed over crops, multiplying rapidly in the absence of predatory birds. The effect of pests on the wheat crop was especially disastrous in the summer of 1973, since that was also the year of the great drought. Most of us can remember the shock which greeted the announcement by atmospheric physicists that the shift of the jet stream which had caused the drought was probably permanent. It signalled the birth of the Midwestern desert. Man's air-polluting activities had by then caused gross changes in climatic patterns. The news, of course, played hell with commodity and stock markets. Food prices skyrocketed, as savings were poured into hoarded canned goods. Official assurances that food supplies would remain ample fell on deaf ears, and even the government showed signs of nervousness when California migrant field workers went out on strike again in protest against the continued use of pesticides by growers. The strike burgeoned into farm burning and riots. The workers, calling themselves "The Walking Dead," demanded immediate compensation for their shortened lives, and crash research programs to attempt to lengthen them.

It was in the same speech in which President Edward Kennedy, after much delay, finally declared a national emergency and called out the National Guard to harvest California's crops, that the first mention of population control was made. Kennedy pointed out that the United States would no longer be able to offer any food aid to other nations and was likely to suffer food shortages herself. He suggested that, in view of the manifest failure of the Green Revolution, the only hope of the UDCs lay in population control. His statement, you will recall, created an uproar in the underdeveloped countries. Newspaper editorials accused the United States of wishing to prevent small countries from becoming large nations and thus threatening American hegemony. Politicians asserted that President Kennedy was a "creature of the giant drug combine" that wished to shove its pills down every woman's throat.

Among Americans, religious opposition to population control was very slight. Industry in general also backed the idea. Increasing poverty in the UDCs was both destroying markets and threatening supplies of raw materials. The seriousness of the raw material situation had been brought home during the congressional hard resources hearings in 1971. The exposure of the ignorance

of the cornucopian economists had been quite a spectacle
—a spectacle brought into virtually every American's
home in living color. Few would forget the distinguished
geologist from the University of California who suggested that economists be legally required to learn at
least the most elementary facts of geology. Fewer still
would forget that an equally distinguished Harvard economist added that they might be required to learn some
economics, too. The overall message was clear: America's resource situation was bad and bound to get worse.
The hearings had led to a bill requiring the Departments
of State, Interior, and Commerce to set up a joint resource procurement council with the express purpose of
"insuring that proper consideration of American resource
needs be an integral part of American foreign policy."

Suddenly the United States discovered that it had a
national consensus: population control was the only
possible salvation of the underdeveloped world. But that
same consensus led to heated debate. How could the
UDCs be persuaded to limit their populations, and
should not the United States lead the way by limiting
its own? Members of the intellectual community wanted
America to set an example. They pointed out that the
United States was in the midst of a new baby boom:
her birth rate, well over 20 per thousand per year, and
her growth rate of over one percent per annum were
among the very highest of the developed countries. They
detailed the deterioration of the American physical and
psychic environments, the growing health threats, the
impending food shortages, and the insufficiency of funds
for desperately needed public works. They contended
that the nation was clearly unable or unwilling to properly care for the people it already had. What possible
reason could there be, they queried, for adding any
more? Besides, who would listen to requests by the
United States for population control when that nation
did not control her own profligate reproduction?

Those who opposed population controls for the U.S.
were equally vociferous. The military-industrial complex,

with its all-too-human mixture of ignorance and avarice, still saw strength and prosperity in numbers. Baby food magnates, already worried by the growing nitrate pollution of their products, saw their market disappearing. Steel manufacturers saw a decrease in aggregate demand and slippage for that holy of holies, the Gross National Product. And military men saw, in the growing population-food-environment crisis, a serious threat to their carefully nurtured Cold War. In the end, of course, economic arguments held sway, and the "inalienable right of every American couple to determine the size of its family," a freedom invented for the occasion in the early '70s, was not compromised.

The population control bill, which was passed by Congress early in 1974, was quite a document, nevertheless. On the domestic front, it authorized an increase from 100 to 150 million dollars in funds for "family planning" activities. This was made possible by a general feeling in the country that the growing army on welfare needed family planning. But the gist of the bill was a series of measures designed to impress the need for population control on the UDCs. All American aid to countries with overpopulation problems was required by law to consist in part of population control assistance. In order to receive any assistance each nation was required not only to accept the population control aid, but also to match it according to a complex formula. "Overpopulation" itself was defined by a formula based on U.N. statistics, and the UDCs were required not only to accept aid, but also to show progress in reducing birth rates. Every five years the status of the aid program for each nation was to be re-evaluated.

The reaction to the announcement of this program dwarfed the response to President Kennedy's speech. A coalition of UDCs attempted to get the U.N. General Assembly to condemn the United States as a "genetic aggressor." Most damaging of all to the American cause was the famous "25 Indians and a dog" speech by Mr. Shankarnarayan, Indian Ambassador to the U.N. Shankarnarayan pointed out that for several decades the

United States, with less than six percent of the people of the world, had consumed roughly 50 percent of the raw materials used every year. He described vividly America's contribution to worldwide environmental deterioration, and he scathingly denounced the miserly record of United States foreign aid as "unworthy of a fourth-rate power, let alone the most powerful nation on earth."

It was the climax of his speech, however, which most historians claim once and for all destroyed the image of the United States. Shankarnarayan informed the assembly that the average American family dog was fed more animal protein per week than the average Indian got in a month. "How do you justify taking fish from protein-starved Peruvians and feeding them to your animals?" he asked. "I contend," he concluded, "that the birth of an American baby is a greater disaster for the world than that of 25 Indian babies." When the applause had died away, Mr. Sorensen, the American representative, made a speech which said essentially that "other countries look after their own self-interest, too." When the vote came, the United States was condemned.

This condemnation set the tone of U.S.-UDC relations at the time the Russian Thanodrin proposal was made. The proposal seemed to offer the masses in the UDCs an opportunity to save themselves and humiliate the United States at the same time; and in human affairs, as we all know, biological realities could never interfere with such an opportunity. The scientists were silenced, the politicians said yes, the Thanodrin plants were built, and the results were what any beginning ecology student could have predicted. At first Thanodrin seemed to offer excellent control of many pests. True, there was a rash of human fatalities from improper use of the lethal chemical, but, as Russian technical advisors were prone to note, these were more than compensated for by increased yields. Thanodrin use skyrocketed throughout the underdeveloped world. The Mikoyan design group developed a dependable, cheap agricultural aircraft which the Soviets donated to the effort in large numbers.

MIG sprayers became even more common in UDCs than MIG interceptors.

Then the troubles began. Insect strains with cuticles resistant to Thanodrin penetration began to appear. And as streams, rivers, fish culture ponds and onshore waters became rich in Thanodrin, more fisheries began to disappear. Bird populations were decimated. The sequence of events was standard for broadcast use of a synthetic pesticide: great success at first, followed by removal of natural enemies and development of resistance by the pest. Populations of crop-eating insects in areas treated with Thanodrin made steady comebacks and soon became more abundant than ever. Yields plunged, while farmers in their desperation increased the Thanodrin dose and shortened the time between treatments. Death from Thanodrin poisoning became common. The first violent incident occurred in the Canete Valley of Peru, where farmers had suffered a similar chlorinated hydrocarbon disaster in the mid-'50s. A Russian advisor serving as an agricultural pilot was assaulted and killed by a mob of enraged farmers in January, 1978. Trouble spread rapidly during 1978, especially after the word got out that two years earlier Russia herself had banned the use of Thanodrin at home because of its serious effects on ecological systems. Suddenly Russia, and not the United States, was the *bête noir* in the UDCs. "Thanodrin parties" became epidemic, with farmers, in their ignorance, dumping carloads of Thanodrin concentrate into the sea. Russian advisors fled, and four of the Thanodrin plants were leveled to the ground. Destruction of the plants in Rio and Calcutta led to hundreds of thousands of gallons of Thanodrin concentrate being dumped directly into the sea.

Mr. Shankarnarayan again rose to address the U.N., but this time it was Mr. Potemkin, representative of the Soviet Union, who was on the hot seat. Mr. Potemkin heard his nation described as the greatest mass killer of all time as Shankarnarayan predicted at least 30 million deaths from crop failures due to overdependence on Thanodrin. Russia was accused of "chemical aggression," and the General Assembly, after a weak reply by Potemkin, passed a vote of censure.

It was in January, 1979, that huge blooms of a previously unknown variety of diatom were reported off the coast of Peru. The blooms were accompanied by a massive die-off of sea life and of the pathetic remainder of the birds which had once feasted on the anchovies of the area. Almost immediately another huge bloom was reported in the Indian Ocean, centering around the Seychelles, and then a third in the South Atlantic off the African coast. Both of these were accompanied by spectacular die-offs of marine animals. Even more ominous were growing reports of fish and bird kills at oceanic points where there were no spectacular blooms. Biologists were soon able to explain the phenomenon: the diatom had evolved an enzyme which broke down Thanodrin; that enzyme also produced a breakdown product which interfered with the transmission of nerve impulses, and was therefore lethal to animals. Unfortunately, the biologists could suggest no way of repressing the poisonous diatom bloom in time. By September, 1979, all important animal life in the sea was extinct. Large areas of coastline had to be evacuated, as windrows of dead fish created a monumental stench.

But stench was the least of man's problems. Japan and China were faced with almost instant starvation from a total loss of the seafood on which they were so dependent. Both blamed Russia for their situation and demanded immediate mass shipments of food. Russia had none to send. On October 13, Chinese armies attacked Russia on a broad front. . . .

A pretty grim scenario. Unfortunately, we're a long way into it already. Everything mentioned as happening before 1970 has actually occurred; much of the rest is based on projections of trends already appearing. Evidence that pesticides have long-term lethal effects on human beings has started to accumulate, and recently Robert Finch, Secretary of the Department of Health, Education and Welfare, expressed his extreme apprehension about the pesticide situation. Simultaneously the petrochemical industry continues its unconscionable poison-peddling. For instance, Shell Chemical has been carrying on a high-pressure campaign to sell the insecticide Azodrin to farmers as a killer of cotton pests. They continue their program even though they know that Azodrin is not only ineffective, but often *increases* the pest density. They've covered themselves nicely in an advertisement which states, "Even if an overpowering migration [*sic*] develops, the flexibility of Azodrin lets you regain control fast. Just increase the dosage according to label recommendations." It's a great game—get people to apply the poison and kill the natural enemies of the pests. Then blame the increased pests on "migration" and sell even more pesticide!

Right now fisheries are being wiped out by over-exploitation, made easy by modern electronic equipment. The companies producing the equipment know this. They even boast in advertising that only their equipment will keep fishermen in business until the final kill. Profits must obviously be maximized in the short run. Indeed, Western society is in the process of completing the rape and murder of the planet for economic gain. And, sadly, most of the rest of the world is eager for the opportunity to emulate our behavior. But the underdeveloped peoples will be denied that opportunity—the days of plunder are drawing inexorably to a close.

Most of the people who are going to die in the greatest cataclysm in the history of man have already been born. More than three and a half billion people already populate our moribund globe, and about half of them are hungry. Some 10 to 20 million will starve to death *this year*. In spite of this, the population of the earth will have increased by 70 million in 1969. For mankind has artificially lowered the death rate of the human population, while in general, birth rates have remained high. With the input side of the population system in high gear and the output side slowed down, our fragile planet has filled with people at an incredible rate. It took several million years for the population to reach a total of two billion people in 1930, while a *second two billion will have been added by 1975!* By that time some experts feel that food shortages will have escalated the present level of world hunger and starvation into famines of unbelievable proportions. Other experts, more optimistic, think the ultimate food-population collision will not occur until the decade of the 1980's. Of course more massive famine may be avoided if other events cause a prior rise in the human death rate.

Both worldwide plague and thermonuclear war are made more probable as population growth continues. These, along with famine, make up the trio of potential "death rate solutions" to the population problem—solutions in which the birth rate-death rate imbalance is redressed by a rise in the death rate rather than by a lowering of the birth rate. Make no mistake about it, *the imbalance will be redressed.* The shape of the population-growth curve is one familiar to the biologist. It is the outbreak part of an outbreak-crash sequence. A population grows rapidly in the presence of abundant resources, finally runs out of food or some other necessity, and crashes to a low level or extinction. Man is not only running out of food, he is also destroying the life support systems of the Spaceship Earth. The situation was recently summarized very succinctly: "It is the top of the ninth inning. Man, always a threat at the plate, has been hitting Nature hard. It is important to remember, however, that NATURE BATS LAST."

The SST

Brenn Stilley

The supersonic transport (SST) summarizes, in one project, our society's demented priorities. It is a virtual catalog of the reasons why the United States is ailing in the midst of its affluence—nationalistic vanity, pandering to corporate profit, the worship of technology, and the deteriorating human environment.

It is scarcely possible to make out a case for building the SST on the grounds that it will make life better. At best, it will result in a meager saving of time for an infinistesimal percentage of the world's population at a huge financial, physiological, and psychological cost to the rest.

Flying at 1800 m.p.h. instead of the 600 m.p.h. of present jetliners, the SST should, in theory, be able to transport its passengers between a traffic jam in New York and a traffic jam in London in one-third of the time now required. Taking into account delays on highways en route to and from airports, waiting at the airport, and the plane's wait to take off and land, the actual saving in time will be considerably less. It is estimated that the total door-to-door travel time on a transatlantic flight would be about 8 hours as opposed to 11 hours by conventional jet, a mere 27 percent reduction. Who needs it? Why this insane passion for speed at any cost? Is life *that* short? not so long ago, transatlantic travelers spent 5 days making the voyage by ship; strangely enough, many enjoyed it.

Other arguments for the SST are all economic or

political. It is claimed that sales of the SSTs to foreign airlines would improve the country's balance of payments. But if the passengers are mostly American businessmen and tourists, the fares paid to the foreign airlines and the money they spend overseas might well equal or exceed the cost of the plane. Another argument claims that the manufacture of 500 to 1200 American SSTs—and there is no assurance that anything remotely approaching that number would ever be ordered—would create 50,000 jobs. Many, however, would simply be transfers from jobs on other types of airplanes. Moreover, the great need is for jobs for less-skilled workers, not the highly skilled groups who would build SSTs.

Other countries are building SSTs: The French and British Concorde, the Russian Tu-144. Our "prestige" supposedly will suffer if we don't build an SST as well. But what pride can we take in the degradation of our own environment? What if the United States is *not* first among nations producing SSTs? Italians, Norwegians, New Zealanders, and many others manage to live out their lives knowing that their countries are not always going to be first in everything. Why can't we?

In a sense, it is pointless to try to refute the official case for the SST. Aside from nationalism, the real reason that the SST is being built is the reason that most things are done in America—profit. Boeing (to whom the government awarded the SST development contract) and its subcontractor stand to make a mint. It is difficult to say how much will eventually be spent on the SST, since initial cost estimates for such projects are notoriously prone to be revised upwards. It will certainly be at least $1 billion; the Federal Aviation Agency itself, sponsor of the project, estimates about $2.5 billion; other estimates range as high as $3.5 billion. The taxpayers will foot most of the bill, as they have so far. In October, 1969, President Nixon requested from Congress $662 million to support the program in the next five year period. Donald F. Anthrop, writing in the *Bulletin of Atomic Scientists,* May, 1969, put the issue

bluntly: "The whole SST program is an economic boon-
doggle, the prime beneficiary of which is the aircraft
manufacturing industry."

Ironically, the SST may well turn out to be a financial
failure. At least 300 Boeing SSTs must be sold (at $40
million each) if the undertaking is to be an economic
success. So far, airlines have placed tentative orders for
122, with no additions in the last two years. The Institute for Defense Analysis, in a painstaking two-
volume study, concluded that if supersonic travel is to be
restricted to overwater flight, only 120 to 200 planes
would be sold.

The amount that the government is asked to spend
on the SST is, of course, insignificant compared with the
billions which the people's representatives dole out each
year to the "defense" industries. But it seems inconceivable that, at a time when many are calling for vast
increases in spending for environmental improvement,
we should with the other hand subsidize a project which
will cause further damage to the environment.

Supersonic transport flights will produce shock waves,
called sonic booms, in a roughly 50-mile-wide area below the plane's flight path during the entire time it is
flying above the speed of sound. During a 2500-mile
trip, of which about 2000 miles would be supersonic,
the area struck by the sonic boom would be 50 miles
times 2000 miles, or 100,000 square miles, equal to
about 10 times the area of Massachusetts.

There is extensive evidence of the damage which
sonic booms can cause. The U.S. government has conducted several series of tests of the effects of sonic booms
over cities. In St. Louis, in 1961 and 1962, 150 supersonic flights resulted in 5000 complaints, 1,624 damage
claims, and $58,648 in damage payments. A more
extensive test series over Oklahoma City in 1964, involving 1,254 flights, caused 15,000 complaints, 4,901
damage claims, and over $100,000 in damages awarded
so far—many claims are still pending. This, despite a
massive pro-SST publicity campaign and the fact that
Oklahoma City's economy is largely dependent on avia-

tion. Only 49 flights over Chicago in 1965 produced 6,116 complaints, 2,964 damage claims, and $114,763 paid for damages.

SST booms were found to crack and shatter glass windows, to crack plaster, masonry, tiles, building foundations, and fragile antiques and art objects. They shook shelves, causing dishes and other objects to fall and break. They have also triggered rock slides. In 1966 a boom from an Air Force plane caused 80,000 tons of rock to fall on ancient cliff-dwellings in the Canyon de Chelly National Monument in Arizona, causing irreparable damage. A similar incident occurred in 1968 when a sonic boom loosened 66,000 tons of rock in Mesa Verde National Park.

Psychological and physiological damage is harder to estimate. At best, sonic booms are annoying; 27 percent of the people polled in Oklahoma City said that they could "never learn to live with the boom." Sonic booms are loud, sounding like an explosion or a titanic door slamming, and they occur without warning. They excite in human beings the typical "startle reaction," and prolonged exposure to them can result in harmful cardiovascular, glandular, and respiratory effects. Light sleepers would be continually awakened by them. A woman in England has been awarded damages for permanent loss of hearing from sonic booms. The high noise level of modern life, often called "sound pollution," is now recognized as a major environmental problems. The SST would make it infinitely worse.

The adverse effects of the booms are so clear that it would seem inconceivable that SSTs could be flown over cities. But there are no guarantees that they would not be flown over land, and economic considerations make it likely that the pressure to allow SST routes over sparsely populated land areas will be tremendous. What this means is that all those who have escaped to the country to find peace will have their tranquillity shattered by teeth-rattling sonic booms, and there will be hardly a place left on earth free from the less desirable aspects of modern civilization. Even in the unlikely event that SSTs are restricted to overwater flights, people on boats would be affected. Are fishermen and mariners second-class citizens? Should they have to endure what city dwellers can't tolerate?

The SST will pour out vast amounts of carbon dioxide and water vapor into the atmosphere above the level of effective wind circulation. As with many environmental questions, the possible effects of this are not yet certain, but they may include a blanketing effect which will alter the climate.

There is no *need* for the SST. The new "jumbo" jets, such as the Boeing 747, can carry more passengers (more than 400 *vs.* 280) over a longer range (6300 miles *vs.* 4000 miles) at fares lower than those at present (while SST fares are expected to be 15 to 25 percent higher). At subsonic speeds, they will produce no sonic booms. The problems of air travel today include overcrowded air lanes, overburdened air traffic control systems, delays in passenger processing, and excessive noise around airports. The SST would solve none of these, and make most of them worse.

By renouncing the intention of building an SST, the United States could make it clear to the world that we value the wishes of a few jet-setters and our corporations less than the need of everyone for a quiet and peaceful environment. Will we do it?

The Highway and the City

Lewis Mumford

from The Highway and the City

When the American people, through their Congress, voted a little while ago (1957) for a twenty-six-billion-dollar highway program, the most charitable thing to assume about this action is that they hadn't the faintest notion of what they were doing. Within the next fifteen years they will doubtless find out; but by that time it will be too late to correct all the damage to our cities and our countryside, not least to the efficient organization of industry and transportation, that this ill-conceived and preposterously unbalanced program will have wrought.

Yet if someone had foretold these consequences before this vast sum of money was pushed through Congress, under the specious, indeed flagrantly dishonest, guise of a national defense measure, it is doubtful whether our countrymen would have listened long enough to understand; or would even have been able to change their minds if they did understand. For the current American way of life is founded not just on motor transportation but on the religion of the motorcar, and the sacrifices that people are prepared to make for this religion stand outside the realm of rational criticism. Perhaps the only thing that could bring Americans to their senses would be a clear demonstration of the fact that their highway program will, eventually, wipe out the very area of freedom that the private motorcar promised to retain for them.

As long as motorcars were few in number, he who had one was a king: he could go where he pleased and halt where he pleased; and this machine itself appeared as a compensatory device for enlarging an ego which had been shrunken by our very success in mechanization. That sense of freedom and power remains a fact today only in low-density areas, in the open country; the popularity of this method of escape has ruined the promise it once held forth. In using the car to flee from the metropolis the motorist finds that he has merely transferred congestion to the highway and thereby doubled it. When he reaches his destination, in a distant suburb, he finds that the countryside he sought has disappeared: beyond him, thanks to the motorway, lies only another suburb, just as dull as his own. To have a minimum amount of communication and sociability in this spread-out life, his wife becomes a taxi driver by daily occupation, and the sum of money it costs to keep this whole system running leaves him with shamefully overtaxed schools, inadequate police, poorly staffed hospitals, overcrowded recreation areas, ill-supported libraries.

In short, the American has sacrificed his life as a whole to the motorcar, like someone who, demented with passion, wrecks his home in order to lavish his income on a capricious mistress who promises delights he can only occasionally enjoy.

For most Americans, progress means accepting what is new because it is new, and discarding what is old because it is old. This may be good for a rapid turnover in business, but it is bad for continuity and stability in life. Progress, in an organic sense, should be cumulative, and though a certain amount of rubbish-clearing is always necessary, we lose part of the gain offered by a new invention if we automatically discard all the still valuable inventions that preceded it.

In transportation, unfortunately, the old-fashioned linear notion of progress prevails. Now that motorcars are becoming universal, many people take for granted that pedestrian movement will disappear and that the railroad system will in time be abandoned; in fact, many of the proponents of highway building talk as if that day were already here, or if not, they have every intention of making it dawn quickly. The result is that we have actually crippled the motorcar, by placing on this single means of transportation the burden for every kind of travel. Neither our cars nor our highways can take such a load. This overconcentration, moreover, is rapidly destroying our cities, without leaving anything half as good in their place.

What's transportation for? This is a question that highway engineers apparently never ask themselves: probably because they take for granted the belief that transportation exists for the purpose of providing suitable outlets for the motorcar industry. To increase the number of cars, to enable motorists to go longer distances, to more places, at higher speeds, has become an end in itself. Does this overemployment of the motorcar not consume ever larger quantities of gas, oil, concrete, rubber, and steel, and so provide the very groundwork for an expanding economy? Certainly, but none of these make up the essential purpose of transportation. The purpose of transportation is to bring people or goods to places where they are needed, and to concentrate the greatest variety of goods and people within a limited area, in order to widen the possibility of choice without making it necessary to travel. A good transportation system minimizes unnecessary transportation; and in any event, it offers a change of speed and mode to fit a diversity of human purposes.

Diffusion and concentration are the two poles of transportation: the first demands a closely articulated network of roads—ranging from a footpath to a six-lane expressway and a transcontinental railroad system. The second demands a city. Our major highway systems are conceived, in the interests of speed, as linear organizations, that is to say as arteries. That conception would be a sound one, provided the major arteries were not overdeveloped to the exclusion of all the minor elements of transportation. Highway planners have yet to realize that these arteries must not be thrust into the delicate tissue of our cities; the blood they circulate must rather enter through an elaborate network of minor blood vessels and capillaries. As early as 1929 Benton MacKaye worked out the rationale of sound highway development, in his conception of the Townless Highway; and this had as its corollary the Highwayless Town. In the quarter century since, all the elements of MacKaye's conception have been carried out, except the last—certainly not the least.

In many ways, our highways are not merely masterpieces of engineering, but consummate works of art: a few of them, like the Taconic State Parkway in New York, stand on a par with our highest creations in other fields. Not every highway, it is true, runs through country that offer such superb opportunities to an imaginative highway builder as this does; but then not every engineer rises to his opportunities as the planners of this highway did, routing the well-separated roads along the ridgeways, following the contours, and thus, by this single stratagem, both avoiding towns and villages and opening up great views across country, enhanced by a lavish planting of flowering bushes along the borders. If this standard of comeliness and beauty were kept generally in view, highway engineers would not so often lapse into the brutal assaults against the landscape and against urban order that they actually give way to when they aim solely at speed and volume of traffic, and bulldoze and blast their way across country to shorten their route by a few miles without making the total journey any less depressing.

Perhaps our age will be known to the future historian as the age of the bulldozer and the exterminator; and in many parts of the country the building of a highway has about the same result upon vegetation and human structures as the passage of a tornado or the blast of an atom bomb. Nowhere is this bulldozing habit of mind so disastrous as in the approach to the city. Since the engineer regards his own work as more important than the other human functions it serves, he does not hesitate to lay waste to woods, streams, parks, and human neighborhoods in order to carry his roads straight to their supposed destination.

The fatal mistake we have been making is to sacrifice every other form of transportation to the private motor-car—and to offer, as the only long-distance alternative, the airplane. But the fact is that each type of transportation has its special use; and a good transportation policy must seek to improve each type and make the most of it. This cannot be achieved by aiming at high speed or continuous flow alone. If you wish casual opportunities for meeting your neighbors, and for profiting by chance contacts with acquaintances and colleagues, a stroll at two miles an hour in a concentrated area, free from needless vehicles, will alone meet your need. But if you wish to rush a surgeon to a patient a thousand miles away, the fastest motorway is too slow. And again, if you wish to be sure to keep a lecture engagement in winter, railroad transportation offers surer speed and better insurance against being held up than the airplane. There is no one ideal mode or speed: human purpose should govern the choice of the means of transportation. That is why we need a better transportation *system,* not just more highways. The projectors of our national highway program plainly had little interest in transportation. In their fanatical zeal to expand our highways, the very allocation of funds indicates that they are ready to liquidate all other forms of land and water transportation. The result is a crudely over-simplified and inefficient method of mono-transportation: a regression from the complex many-sided transportation system we once boasted.

In order to overcome the fatal stagnation of traffic in and around our cities, our highway engineers have come up with a remedy that actually expands the evil it is meant to overcome. They create new expressways to serve cities that are already overcrowded within, thus tempting people who had been using public transportation to reach the urban centers to use these new private facilities. Almost before the first day's tolls on these expressways have been counted, the new roads themselves are overcrowded. So a clamor arises to create other similar arteries and to provide more parking garages in the center of our metropolises; and the generous provision of these facilities expands the cycle of congestion, without any promise of relief until that terminal point when all the business and industry that originally gave rise to the congestion move out of the city, to escape strangulation, leaving a waste of expressways and garages behind them. This is pyramid building with a vengeance: a tomb of concrete roads and ramps covering the dead corpse of a city.

But before our cities reach this terminal point, they will suffer, as they do now, from a continued erosion of their social facilities: an erosion that might have been avoided if engineers had understood MacKaye's point that a motorway, properly planned, is another form of railroad for private use. Unfortunately, highway engineers, if one is to judge by their usual performance, lack both historic insight and social memory: accordingly, they have been repeating, with the audacity of confident ignorance, all the mistakes in urban planning committed by their predecessors who designed our railroads. The wide swaths of land devoted to cloverleaves, and even more complicated multi-level interchanges, to expressways, parking lots, and parking garages, in the very heart of the city, butcher up precious urban space in exactly the same way that freight yards and marshalling yards did when the railroads dumped their passengers and freight inside the city. These new arteries choke off the natural routes of circulation and limit the use of abutting properties, while at the points where they disgorge their traffic they create inevitable clots of congestion, which effectively cancel out such speed as they achieve in approaching these bottlenecks.

Today the highway engineers have no excuse for invading the city with their regional and transcontinental trunk systems: the change from the major artery to the local artery can now be achieved without breaking the bulk of goods or replacing the vehicle: that is precisely the advantage of the motorcar. Arterial roads, ideally speaking, should engirdle the metropolitan area and define where its greenbelt begins; and since American cities are still too impoverished and too improvident to acquire greenbelts, they should be planned to go through the zone where relatively high-density building gives way to low-density building. On this perimeter, through traffic will bypass the city, while cars that are headed for the center will drop off at the point closest to their destination.

Since I don't know a city whose highways have been planned on this basis, let me give as an exact parallel the new semicircular railroad line, with its suburban stations, that bypasses Amsterdam. That is good railroad planning, and it would be good highway planning, too, as the Dutch architect H. Th. Wijdeveld long ago pointed out. It is on relatively cheap land, on the edge of the city, that we should be building parking areas and garages: with free parking privileges to tempt the commuter to leave his car and finish his daily journey on the public transportation system. The public officials who have been planning our highway system on just the opposite principle are likewise planning to make the central areas of our cities unworkable and uninhabitable. Route 128 in Boston might seem a belated effort to provide such a circular feeder highway; but actually it is a classic example of how the specialized highway engineer, with his own concerns solely in mind, can defeat sound urban design.

Now it happens that the theory of the insulated, high-speed motorway, detached from local street and road systems, immune to the clutter of roadside "developments," was first worked out, not by highway engineers, but by Benton MacKaye, the regional planner who conceived the the Appalachian Trail. He not merely put together its essential features, but identified its principal characteristic: the fact that to achieve speed it must bypass towns. He called it in fact the Townless Highway. (See *The New Republic,* March 30, 1930.) Long before the highway engineers came through with Route 128, MacKaye pointed out the necessity for a motor bypass around the ring of suburbs that encircle Boston, in order to make every part of the metropolitan area accessible, and yet to provide a swift bypass route for through traffic.

MacKaye, not being a one-eyed specialist, visualized this circuit in all its potential dimensions and developments: he conceived accordingly a metropolitan recreation belt with a northbound motor road forming an arc on the inner flank and a southbound road on the outer flank—the two roads separated by a wide band of usable parkland, with footpaths and bicycle paths for recreation. In reducing MacKaye's conception to Route 128, without the greenbelt and without public control of the areas adjacent to the highway, the "experts" reduced the multi-purpose Bay Circuit to the typical "successful" expressway: so successful in attracting industry and business from the center of the city that it already ceases to perform even its own limited functions of fast transportation, except during hours of the day when ordinary highways would serve almost as well. This, in contrast to MacKaye's scheme, is a classic example of how not to do it.

Just as highway engineers know too little about city planning to correct the mistakes made in introducing the early railroad systems into our cities, so, too, they have curiously forgotten our experience with the elevated railroad—and unfortunately most municipal authorities have been equally forgetful. In the middle of the nineteenth century the elevated seemed the most facile and up-to-date method of introducing a new kind of rapid transportation system into the city; and in America, New York led the way in creating four such lines on Manhattan Island alone. The noise of the trains and the overshadowing of the structure lowered the value of the abutting properties even for commercial purposes; and the supporting columns constituted a dangerous obstacle to surface transportation. So unsatisfactory was elevated transportation even in cities like Berlin, where the structures were, in contrast to New York, Philadelphia, and Chicago, rather handsome works of engineering, that by popular consent subway building replaced elevated railroad building in all big cities, even though no one could pretend that riding in a tunnel was nearly as pleasant to the rider as was travel in the open air. The destruction of the old elevated railroads in New York was, ironically, hailed as a triumph of progress precisely at the moment that a new series of elevated highways was being built, to repeat on a more colossal scale the same errors.

Like the railroad, again, the motorway has repeatedly taken possession of the most valuable recreation space the city possesses, not merely by thieving land once dedicated to park uses, but by cutting off easy access to the waterfront parks, and lowering their value for refreshment and repose by introducing the roar of traffic and the bad odor of exhausts, though both noise and carbon monoxide are inimical to health. Witness the shocking spoilage of the Charles River basin parks in Boston, the arterial blocking off of the Lake Front in Chicago (after the removal of the original usurpers, the railroads), the barbarous sacrifice of large areas of Fairmount Park in Philadelphia, the partial defacement of the San Francisco waterfront, even in Paris the ruin of the Left Bank of the Seine.

One may match all these social crimes with a hundred other examples of barefaced highway robbery in every other metropolitan area. Even when the people who submit to the annexations and spoliations are dimly aware of what they are losing, they submit without more than a murmur of protest. What they do not understand is that they are trading a permanent good for a very temporary advantage, since until we subordinate highway expansion to the more permanent requirements of regional planning, the flood of motor traffic will clog new channels. What they further fail to realize is that the vast sums of money that go into such enterprises drain necessary public monies from other functions of the city, and make it socially if not financially bankrupt.

Neither the highway engineer nor the urban planner can, beyond a certain point, plan his facilities to accommodate an expanding population. On the over-all problem of population pressure, regional and national policies must be developed for throwing open, within our country, new regions of settlement, if this pressure, which appeared so suddenly, does not in fact abate just as unexpectedly and just as suddenly. But there can be no sound planning anywhere until we understand the necessity for erecting norms, or ideal limits, for density of population. Most of our congested metropolises need a lower density of population, with more parks and open spaces, if they are to be attractive enough physically to retain even a portion of their population for day-and-night living; but most of our suburban and exurban communities must replan large areas at perhaps double their present densities in order to have the social, educational, recreational, and industrial facilities they need closer at hand. Both suburb and metropolis need a regional form of government, working in private organizations as well as public forms, to reapportion their resources and facilities, so as to benefit the whole area.

To say this is to say that both metropolitan congestion and suburban scattering are obsolete. This means that good planning must work to produce a radically new pattern for urban growth. On this matter, public policy in the United States is both contradictory and self-defeating. Instead of lowering central area densities, most urban renewal schemes, not least those aimed at housing the groups that must be subsidized, either maintain old levels of congestion or create higher levels than existed in the slums they replaced. But the Home Loan agencies, federal and private, on the other hand, have been subsidizing the wasteful, ill-planned, single-family house, on cheap land, ever remoter from the center of our cities; a policy that has done as much to promote the suburban drift as the ubiquitous motorcar.

In order to cement these errors in the most solid way possible, our highway policy maximizes congestion at the center and expands the area of suburban dispersion —what one might call the metropolitan "fall-out." The three public agencies concerned have no official connections with each other: but the total result of their efforts proves, once again, that chaos does not have to be planned.

Motorcar manufacturers look forward confidently to the time when every family will have two, if not three, cars. I would not deny them that hope, though I remember that it was first voiced in 1929, just before the fatal crash of our economic system, too enamored of high profits even to save itself by temporarily lowering prices. But if they don't want the motorcar to paralyze urban life, they must abandon their fantastic commitment to the indecently tumescent organs they have been putting on the market. For long-distance travel, a roomy car, if not artfully elongated, of course has many advantages; but for town use, let us insist upon a car that fits the city's needs: it is absurd to make over the city to fit the swollen imaginations of Detroit. The Isetta and the Goggomobil have already pointed the way; but what we need is an even smaller vehicle, powered by electricity, delivered by a powerful storage cell, yet to be invented: the exact opposite of our insolent chariots.

Maneuverability and parkability are the prime urban virtues in cars; and the simplest way to achieve this is by designing smaller cars. These virtues are lacking in all but one of our current American models. But why should our cities be destroyed just so that Detroit's infantile fantasies should remain unchallenged and unchanged?

If we want to make the most of our New Highway program, we must keep most of the proposed expressways in abeyance until we have done two other things. We must replan the inner city for pedestrian circulation, and we must rebuild and extend our public forms of mass transportation. In our entrancement with the motorcar, we have forgotten how much more efficient and how much more flexible the footwalker is. Before there was any public transportation in London, something like fifty thousand people an hour used to pass over London Bridge on their way to work: a single artery. Railroad transportation can bring from forty to sixty thousand people per hour, along a single route, whereas our best expressways, using far more space, cannot move more than four to six thousand cars: even if the average occupancy were more than one and a half passengers, as at present, this is obviously the most costly and inefficient means of handling the peak hours of traffic. As for the pedestrian, one could move a hundred thousand people, by the existing streets, from, say, downtown Boston to the Common, in something like half an hour, and find plenty of room for them to stand. But how many weary hours would it take to move them in cars over these same streets? And what would one do with the cars after they had reached the Common? Or where, for that matter, could one assemble these cars in the first place? For open spaces, long distances, and low population densities, the car is now essential; for urban space, short distances, and high densities, the pedestrian.

Every urban transportation plan should, accordingly, put the pedestrian at the center of all its proposals, if only to facilitate wheeled traffic. But to bring the pedestrian back into the picture, one must treat him with the respect and honor we now accord only to the automobile: we should provide him with pleasant walks, insulated from traffic, to take him to his destination, once he enters a business precinct or residential quarter. Every city should heed the example of Rotterdam in creating the Lijnbaan, or of Coventry in creating its new shopping area. It is nonsense to say that this cannot be done in America, because no one wants to walk.

Where walking is exciting and visually stimulating, whether it is in a Detroit shopping center or along Fifth Avenue, Americans are perfectly ready to walk. The legs will come into their own again, as the ideal means of neighborhood transportation, once some provision is made for their exercise, as Philadelphia is now doing, both in its Independence Hall area, and in Penn Center. But if we are to make walking attractive, we must not only provide trees and wide pavements and benches, beds of flowers and outdoor cafés, as they do in Rotterdam: we must also scrap the monotonous uniformities of American zoning practice, which turns vast areas, too spread out for pedestrian movement, into single-district zones, for commerce, industry, or residential purposes. (And as a result, only the mixed zones are architecturally interesting today despite their disorder.)

Why should anyone have to take a car and drive a couple of miles to get a package of cigarettes or a loaf of bread, as one must often do in a suburb? Why, on the other hand, should a growing minority of people not be able again to walk to work, by living in the interior of the city, or, for that matter, be able to walk home from the theatre or the concert hall? Where urban facilities are compact, walking still delights the American: does he not travel many thousands of miles just to enjoy this privilege in the historic urban cores of Europe? And do not people now travel for miles, of an evening, from the outskirts of Pittsburgh, just for the pleasure of a stroll in Mellon Square? Nothing would do more to give life back to our blighted urban cores than to reinstate the pedestrian, in malls and pleasances designed to make circulation a delight. And what an opportunity for architecture!

While federal funds and subsidies pour without stint into highway improvements, the two most important modes of transportation for cities—the railroad for long distances and mass transportation, and the subway for shorter journeys—are permitted to languish and even to disappear. This is very much like what has happened to our postal system. While the time needed to deliver a letter across the continent has been reduced, the time needed for local delivery has been multiplied. What used to take two hours now sometimes takes two days. As a whole our postal system has been degraded to a level that would have been regarded as intolerable even thirty years ago. In both cases, an efficient system has been sacrificed to an overfavored new industry, motorcars, telephones, airplanes; whereas, if the integrity of the system itself had been respected, each of these new inventions could have added enormously to the efficiency of the existing network.

If we could overcome the irrational drives that are now at work, promoting shortsighted decisions, the rational case for rebuilding the mass transportation system in our cities would be overwhelming. The current objection to mass transportation comes chiefly from the fact that it has been allowed to decay: this lapse itself reflects the general blight of the central areas. In order to maintain profits, or in many cases to reduce deficits, rates have been raised, services have decreased, and equipment has become obsolete, without being replaced and improved. Yet mass transportation, with far less acreage in roadbeds and rights of way, can deliver at least ten times more people per hour than the private motorcar. This means that if such means were allowed to lapse in our metropolitan centers—as the inter-urban electric trolley system, that complete and efficient network, was allowed to disappear in the nineteen-twenties—we should require probably five to ten times the existing number of arterial highways to bring the present number of commuters into the city, and at least ten times the existing parking space to accommodate them. In that tangled mass of highways, interchanges, and parking lots, the city would be nowhere: a mechanized nonentity ground under an endless procession of wheels.

That plain fact reduces a one-dimensional transportation system, by motorcar alone, to a calamitous absurdity, as far as urban development goes, even if the number of vehicles and the population count were not increasing year by year. Now it happens that the population of the core of our big cities has remained stable in recent years: in many cases the decline which set in as early as 1910 in New York seems to have ceased. This means that it is now possible to set an upper limit for the daily inflow of workers, and to work out a permanent mass transportation system that will get them in and out again as pleasantly and efficiently as possible.

In time, if urban renewal projects become sufficient

in number to permit the design of a system of minor urban throughways, at ground level, that will bypass the neighborhood, even circulation by motorcar may play a valuable part in the total scheme—provided, of course, that minuscule-sized town cars take the place of the long-tailed dinosaurs that now lumber about our metropolitan swamps. But the notion that the private motorcar can be substituted for mass transportation should be put forward only by those who desire to see the city itself disappear, and with it the complex, many-sided civilization that the city makes possible.

There is no purely local engineering solution to the problems of transportation in our age: nothing like a stable solution is possible without giving due weight to all the necessary elements in transportation—private motorcars, railroads, airplanes, and helicopters, mass transportation services by trolley and bus, even ferry-boats, and finally, not least, the pedestrian. To achieve the necessary over-all pattern, not merely must there be effective city and regional planning, before new routes or services are planned; we also need eventually—and the sooner the better—an adequate system of federated urban government on a regional scale.

Until these necessary tools of control have been cre-ated, most of our planning will be empirical and blunder-ing; and the more we do, on our present premises, the more disastrous will be the results. In short we cannot have an efficient form for our transportation system until we can envisage a better permanent structure for our cities. And the first lesson we have to learn is that a city exists, not for the constant passage of motorcars, but for the care and culture of men.

Warning: The Automobile Is Dangerous to Earth, Air, Fire, Water, Mind and Body

Kenneth P. Cantor

Chuck Herrick was cofounder of Ecology Action in Berkeley more than two years ago, when few had heard the word "ecology" and fewer were doing anything about it. Chuck was killed in an automobile crash on the way to a Peace and Freedom party convention in Ann Arbor in May, 1968.

He joined over 50,000 Americans who that year sacrificed their lives to the great god of American culture, the Private Motorcar. Over 2 million more were injured, many of them permanently. Only war can claim to surpass this number of premature deaths and injury; the death rate from automobiles is greater than the combined death rate from falls, burnings, drownings, railroads, firearms, and poisonous gases. Since 1963 more than ten times as many Americans have been killed on the roads and highways of the United States than have been killed in Vietnam. The death and destruction we wage on ourselves is, for some reason, less visible than our barbarous and inexcusable conduct in the Vietnamese war.

The automobile and the American public are locked in a life and death struggle. The car is robbing the American people of their land, air, minds, and their very lives. It is becoming increasingly clear that solution of the transportation-automobile problem is of high priority if we are to come to terms with the environment, and with ourselves.

The recent record of public transportation in the United States is appalling. Once we had choices. For local transport we could decide to use streetcars, ferries, buses, trolleys, cars, or rapid transit. For travel over longer distances there were trains, buses, cars, ships, or planes. The range of alternatives has rapidly been diminishing, and increasingly we are left with the two most wasteful and destructive forms of travel—the private automobile and the plane.

Since 1950, the railroad track used for passenger service decreased from 150,000 to 68,000 miles, electric railway track fell from 9,600 to 790 miles; many ferry routes were eliminated; the last American-flag passenger liner crossed the Atlantic—the list goes on. Requests by railroads to the Interstate Commerce Commission to decrease or curtail passenger service have been commonplace. During the same period, streets and highways increased by almost 400,000 miles—from 3.3 million to 3.7 million miles.

It is not clear that this trend accurately represents the preference of most travelers. The Metroliner, a new high-speed train between New York and Washington, has been quite successful. The number of daily trips has been tripled since service began in the beginning of 1969. In the words of public relations men, "there has been a great public acceptance of this mode of transport"—which is to say that people dig it. They'd rather go to Pennsylvania Station in downtown Manhattan and get on a fast train which will leave on time rather than take a taxi or limousine to the airport (a half-hour trip), wait in the air terminal (fifteen to forty-five minutes), etc. If they also knew that the train burned less fuel, used less land, and created less air pollution—and understood what these facts mean in their own lives and those of their children—air travel between New York and

Washington, and by extension between all cities separated by less than five hundred miles, would become an historical curiosity.

The technology to operate 150-mile-per-hour trains is presently available. (It is being used in Japan.) We in the United States have not seen it because, under a curious system of priorities, federal transportation funds are going to the supersonic transport and the federal highway system. In December, 1969, President Nixon proudly signed a bill assigning $300 million to the Department of Transportation for grants toward development and construction of rapid transit and other public transportation facilities. (The new San Francisco Bay Area rapid transit system alone cost $1.2 billion.) Through the sixties, an average of more than $3 billion annually was spent by the federal government on highway construction—ten times the amount now belatedly being spent on public transport. Large sums are being pumped into wasteful, inefficient, and destructive modes of transportation while environmentally sound systems are allowed to languish and atrophy. This pattern must be reversed if we are to survive.

MIND AND BODY

The automobile is polluting not only the earth we (sometimes) walk on and the air we breathe. In the literal as well as figurative sense, it is destroying our minds and bodies. The following is excerpted from "Cities and Culture," from *The Hidden Dimension* by Edward T. Hall.

Automobiles insulate man not only from the environment but from human contact as well. They permit only most limited types of interaction, usually competitive, aggressive, and destructive. If people are to be brought together again, given a chance to get acquainted with each other and involved in nature, some fundamental solutions must be found to the problems posed by the automobile.

EARTH

Each mode of transportation uses a larger or smaller portion of the earth's surface:

Auto: A transportation corridor one highway lane (12 feet) wide can carry a maximum of 3,600 passengers per hour.[1]

Bus: Half-filled buses can carry 60,000 people per hour—17 times as many as the car.[2]

Train: Trains, half-filled, will transport 42,000 passengers per hour—12 times the number handled by the auto.[3]

Bicycle: A highway lane can comfortably hold two bicycle lanes, allowing passage of 10,600 people per hour—almost 3 times as many as cars.[4]

Walking: A path the width of a highway lane can accommodate 6,300 walkers per hour—1.7 as many as automobile passengers.[5]

Mode	Number of passengers per hour	Efficiency relative to auto
Auto	3,600	1
Bus	60,000	17
Train	42,000	12
Bicycle	10,000	2.8
Walk	6,300	1.7

LAND USE

Berkeley, California is a moderate-sized city, neither truly urban nor suburban in nature, lying somewhere in the middle ground which characterizes many cities close to large metropoli. In Berkeley, each citizen has 28.1 square feet of parks. Each automobile has 968 square feet of roads.

A full quarter of the city's land is devoted to the automobile—17 percent for roadways and an additional 9 percent for driveways, garages, parking lots, service stations, car washes, and so on. By contrast, Berkeley's park system, reasonably good compared to most cities, uses only 1.2 percent of the city's acreage.[6] The city of Berkeley, California is not unusual in its use of land.

Suburban Sprawl. Ubiquitous use of th... made possible the extensive suburban s[...] of today's American landscape, sometime[...] countryside of rich agricultural lands, an[...] ways creating a monolithic and oppressive hu[...] [...]oi-tat. Low-density suburban development, in t[...]n, has made necessary the use of the automobile. The suburb and the private motorcar are locked in an embrace of destruction. We must start thinking about phasing out both of them. Higher density living arrangements, such as cluster developments, leave large areas of open space and agricultural lands untouched. In addition to many other benefits, they allow for rational transportation alternatives. Within the human habitat, the foot, the bicycle, perhaps the minibus, for greater distances, the train or bus.

Recycling. Each year, almost one million broken-down autos are abandoned along roadsides, in fields, and on city streets. They are creating immense problems, both aesthetic and ecological. Automobile hulks may be re-cycled—they can be melted down and used in the manufacture of new steel. This process, not a new one by any means, is increasingly impractical as the cost of transporting abandoned vehicles becomes greater than the scrap value itself. This problem could be solved by providing a subsidy or tax relief to salvage (recycling) companies, with funds to come from a "disposal fee," to be added to the selling price of each new automobile. The cost of automobile disposal should be borne by the owner-user, not by society as a whole.

All forms of power production requiring the burning of fossil fuels, be it in a generating plant or in an internal combustion engine, create "air pollution," which is to say that they add substances to the atmosphere which weren't there previously. Sixty percent of all pollutants added to the air in the United States come from the

...ernal combustion engine. (In 1967, 87.4 percent of the 14,000 tons per day added to the air above Los Angeles came from gasoline-powered motor vehicles.) The atmosphere around us has truly become a garbage dump.

"Air pollution" has been placed in quotes because many different types of foreign matter are added to the air through combustion. Different sources contribute different amounts of these substances and even the same source adds different amounts of the various materials at different times, depending on the season and local weather conditions. There are seven major types of air pollutants: lead, organic compounds, carbon monoxide, nitrogen oxides, particulates, sulfur oxides, and carbon dioxide. All of these, with the exception of carbon dioxide (in the amounts normally produced by engines), are hazardous to human health. Organic compounds and nitrogen oxides, reacting chemically with atmospheric oxygen in sunlight, are the major constitutents of the brown photochemical smog typical of the Los Angeles basin. Sulfur oxides combine with water vapor in the atmosphere to form sulfuric and other acids. This is the pollutant most responsible for pitting of certain metallic surfaces and discoloration of paints. "Particulates" is jargon for airborne dirt.

In comparing the pollution produced by various forms of transportation, it is most convenient to express pollutant production in units (grams, for example) per passenger mile of travel. Thus, for a bus carrying an average of 25 passengers, the amount of pollutant produced in a mile is measured and then divided by 25. The automobile produces more lead, organic compounds, carbon monoxide, and nitrogen oxides per passenger mile than does the helicopter, the commercial passenger plane (Boeing 707), the bus, the train, the motorcycle, or the steam car. Of these modes of transportation, only the bus produces more sulfur oxides than the automobile; all others produce less. Only the helicopter produces more carbon dioxide than the automobile; the steam car produces the same amount; all others produce less. The gasoline-driven internal combustion engine (of the automobile and motorcycle) is the only source of airborne lead among the various means of transport, and is by far the major overall producer of this extremely dangerous pollutant of the earth's atmosphere. We need not comment on the air pollution caused by bicycles and walking. The following chart summarizes the information above. It gives the amounts of various pollutants, relative to the automobile, produced by four alternative means of transportation.

Air pollution control devices currently being installed in gasoline-burning motor vehicles reduce emission of organics compounds and carbon monoxide to between one-fourth and one-half the uncontrolled output. Even *with* these control devices, automobiles produce more pollutants per passenger mile than buses or trains with uncontrolled engines (control devices for these are now being installed as well).

As long ago as 1949, air pollution in Los Angeles County caused damage to crops amounting to almost half a million dollars. Its most serious effects were on leafy greens such as lettuce and spinach. Estimates of the 1961 crop loss in California were eight million dollars, quite a bit of food. There is little available current information on the subject, but we can be sure that today's losses are far above those of nine years ago. Today, spinach and a few other vegetables *cannot be grown* in the Los Angeles basin, and many of those which can are stunted and unhealthy because of the air pollution. A recent survey shows that smog is killing 100,000 acres of Ponderosa and Jeffrey pine trees in the San Bernardino National Forest sixty miles away from Los Angeles proper, on the eastern rim of the basin. According to the study, "smog oxidants destroy the leaf tissues which carry on the vital processes of photosynthesis" by which the trees are nourished. This problem is not confined to the West Coast. Eastern White pines have been similarly affected. The life of the very vegetation covering the earth's surface is being threatened by the internal combustion engine! As the amount of gaseous and par-

	Lead	Organic compounds	Carbon monoxide	Nitrogen oxides	Particulates	Sulfur oxides	Carbon dioxide
Car	1	1	1	1	1	1	1
Bus	0	$\frac{1}{19}$	$\frac{1}{214}$	$\frac{2}{15}$	1* $\frac{2}{2}$	1* $\frac{1}{15}$	$\frac{1}{5}$
Train	0	$\frac{1}{37}$	$\frac{1}{410}$	$\frac{2}{29}$	1* $\frac{1}{3}$	$\frac{8}{15}$	$\frac{1}{11}$
Walking	0	0	0	0	0	0	$\frac{1}{5}$
Bicycle	0	0	0	0	0	0	$\frac{1}{26}$

The amount of several pollutants, relative to the automobile, produced per passenger mile by four alternative means of transportation. In each case, the production of pollutants by the car is "1," and pollutants for alternatives are expressed as fractions of that produced by autos. Most of the information used in compiling this chart comes from Driesbach, *Handbook of the San Francisco Region* (1969).

* The bus and train produce more dirt (particulates) per passenger mile than the auto. The bus produces more sulfur oxides.

ticulate junk we dump into "our" atmospheric garbage can grows from years to year, we can be sure that damage to agricultural crops and other vegetation is also increasing.

Although few specific diseases have been attributed to air pollution, there is no doubt that continual breathing of polluted air is injurious to health. The rate of lung cancer and emphysema among nonsmoking city dwellers is several times that of their rural counterparts who breathe cleaner air. In central Los Angeles, about 10,000 persons per year are advised by their doctors to move from the city for reasons of health. By order of the Los Angeles Board of Education and County Medical Association, the school children of Los Angeles are not allowed to "run, skip, or jump" inside or outside on smog-alert days, of which there were several during 1969.

Lead is one of the most pernicious of all pollutants emitted by automobiles. People with more than about 0.5 parts per million of lead in their blood show visible signs of lead poisoning: constipation, headaches, anemia, and emaciation at low levels of exposure; paralysis, blindness, insanity, and finally death at higher levels. In addition, lead can cause sterility, miscarriage, stillbirths, infant mortality, and mental retardation of offspring. There are no obvious effects of lead when it is present in the blood at concentrations less than 0.5 parts per million; but there are undoubtedly small yet important effects due to low-level exposure. Little medical research has been performed on these subthreshold exposures, so we really don't know the extent of the danger over long periods. The concentration of lead in the air we breathe has increased several fold in the last three decades, as the use of gasoline-powered motor vehicles has grown. The average city dweller in the United States now has 0.17 parts per million of lead in his blood. The amount is increasing yearly. (It is now believed that the collapse of the Roman Empire was in part due to lead poisoning of the upper classes who consumed wine prepared in lead-lined pots.)

Lead as an air pollutant is totally unnecessary. Lead compounds are added to gasoline to cheaply and artificially improve octane rating. For approximately 2 cents per gallon (for the average driver, $14 per year) increase in the price of gasoline, the petroleum industry could modify refining techniques to increase the octane rating, thereby removing the necessity for lead additives. How many people will suffer from lead poisoning before this occurs?

In keeping with our present practice of labelling cigarette packs, all automobiles should have written on their dashboards and above their exhaust pipes in large letters: "Caution: air pollution produced by this vehicle is damaging to health and may result in premature death from lung cancer, cardiovascular disease, emphysema, or other causes." Service stations, automobile sales agencies, and used-car lots should be required to carry similar warnings: "The combustion of fuel sold in this service station produces air pollution which is damaging." Or "vehicles sold by this agency produce air pollution which is damaging."

FIRE

In its use of fuel the automobile is the most wasteful and destructive form of land transportation known to man. The private motorcar, which on the average carries 1.5 people, consumes 4.4 gallons per 100 passenger miles. (The airplane and the helicopter are more wasteful than the automobile, using 5.5 (Boeing 707) and 13 gallons per 100 passenger miles respectively.) Motorcycles are about 3 times less wasteful. Public ground-transportation uses far less fuel—the bus 0.8 gallons and the train 0.36 gallons per 100 passenger miles. The bus is 5 times as efficient as the car; the train 12 times as efficient.

In 1967, motor vehicles in the United States consumed 80 billion gallons of fuel. One half of the world's 200 million motor vehicles are in the United States. If all human beings used as much petroleum for transportation as do Americans, the estimated 100 billion barrels of oil in the Prudhoe Bay, Alaska, field—the largest ever discovered in the United States—would last for 3 or 4 years. We are irresponsibly depleting the world's nonrenewable resources of fossil fuel as rapidly as possible—all in the name of progress. Carbon dioxide production from combustion of fossil fuels, with its attendant effects on the earth's climate, is another negative aspect of our excessive use of private motor vehicles.

The message which must guide action is clear. We should minimize as much as possible our burning of fossil fuels, be it in the internal combustion engine, in the steam engine, or in electrical power generators. Present levels of fuel consumption must be reduced. In the realm of transportation, we should place emphasis on those forms which are least wasteful of fossil fuels—the train, the bus, the bicycle, and finally, but not least, the human foot. We must design our cities and guide our personal lives so that living, working, and recreation areas are proximally located to, among other reasons, minimize the amount of fuel-consuming travel in our lives.

WATER

Transportation by private automobile uses almost one-half the crude petroleum production in the United States. Supplying this vast amount of fuel, amounting to 80 billion gallons yearly, takes equipment of gigantic proportions and entails great risks. The latest in oil transportation, other than the 800-mile, 40-inch trans-Alaskan pipeline, are new supertankers whose size boggles the imagination. The *Torrey Canyon,* which in 1967 ran aground on well-charted rocks in broad daylight, was in the smaller-size class of the new ships. When it broke apart, it released some 105,000 tons of oil (18 million gallons) to eventually cover the beaches of Southern England and Northern France. In December, 1969, the 207-000-ton *Marpessa* exploded

.and sank 80 miles off the west coast of Africa. Luckily, the ship was empty. "There would have been a hell of a lot of oil on the coast of Africa if the Marpessa had been loaded," according to a delegate to an international conference on prevention and control of oil slicks.

There are now 180 tankers with a carrying capacity of 100,000 tons. In addition, 310 supertankers are on the drawing boards (as of December, 1969), many of which will carry more than 200,000 tons. Some will fall in the 300,000-ton class. In view of the past safety record of oil tankers, the future looks dismal indeed. The 488 American tankers of 30,000 tons or more registered with American Bureau of Shipping have been involved in 553 collisions over the past 10 years. Oil spillage was a possibility in 43 of the accidents. Even with "safeguards," we can expect major tanker disasters, to say nothing of minor accidents, to occur with increasing frequency in the future. Such is the price of "progress." How convenient for the petroleum industry if it were no longer compelled to drill wells and such for petroleum, but could simply skim oil from the ocean's surface!

A visit to Santa Barbara—February, 1969: Oil, Oil on birds. Oil on docks. Oil on boats. Oil on beaches. No open flames or smoking in the harbor area. A stench extending for miles. Thousands of bales of hay spread over the water and on beaches to absorb oil. A sunny weekend day. No one using boats. Black death in the intertidal zone. A new kind of plague. Along the docks and piers, salesmen for every chemical company peddling the latest in oil-dispersing agents. Some giving demonstrations. Getting pretty dirty! Union Oil's bird "rescue" station at Carpenteria State Beach—a few miles down the coast. Butter is shoved down avian gullets to cleanse digestive tracts of oil. Oil, along with natural waterproofing waxes, being washed with detergents from the feathers of gulls, cormorants, western grebes, many other species. Dying birds. A dead bird is carried off in a plastic bag. I try to take a picture of it. Its guardian shields it from my lens. Birds are now no longer waterproof. Must be kept until they moult and have new, waxy feathers. Most die. Somehow, millions of years of evolution haven't prepared them for a six-month incarceration in sheds at the Ventura County Fairgrounds. How unkind nature has been to Union Oil.

Oil is still being pumped from the platforms in the Santa Barbara Channel. Put that in your gas tank and burn it! (See "The Black Tide" by Julian McCaull in November, 1969 *Environment*. Also "Alaska: The Ecology of Oil" by Barry Weisberg in January, 1970 *Ramparts*.)

THE TRUE PRICE

When we choose to travel by automobile instead of by another means, our decision is influenced in part by the amount of money we must individually spend, and in part by the relative convenience and freedom (or increasingly, the lack thereof) afforded by operating our own private motor vehicle. We rarely consider our contribution to air pollution and its injurious effects on human health and agriculture, our wasteful use of the land, our depletion of irreplaceable fossil fuels, our influence on the earth's climate through addition of carbon dioxide. The murders and maimings on our highways are buried deep in our minds, as is the *Torrey Canyon's* ruination of British and French seashores, the 1969 disaster at Santa Barbara, the ravaging of Alaska for its underground "wealth," and criminal acts made possible through the use of the automobile. We don't pay directly for all these things. They are social costs, and are borne by elements of society often far removed from those who benefit most from the use of the automobile. These costs should be internalized in the operation of the private motor vehicle, instead of being moved to other segments of society or to future generations. Beyond internalization of costs, there are many possible actions.

COMING TO TERMS—SUGGESTIONS FOR ACTION

The most difficult aspect of coming to an ecological understanding of the world is in changing one's own life style to conform to the new comprehension. Many of the values in the United States are in direct conflict with the dictates of ecology, and so, as Americans, the task is all the more difficult for us. The values of America are rooted in consumption (using more than what is truly needed), growth (dis-equilibrium), and competition (the antithesis of traspecific cooperation). The kinds of change necessary to make American society ecologically and humanly sane are truly gargantuan. But they begin in one place and in one form—in our own heads and in our own day-to-day actions. We can only change bit by bit—perhaps one day putting garbage in a compost heap rather than into a garbage can; on another, using an extra blanket rather than an electric one; on another, walking the few blocks to the store instead of riding in a car. The following list contains suggestions for action—individual, local, and national—in the area of transportation. It is by no means complete. We would insist only on the first one. Otherwise, do what comes most naturally to you.

Individual. Read. Learn what the issues are and what the facts are. Acquaint yourself with the ideas of imaginative thinkers. Uninformed action is often destructive.

Buy and use a bicycle for trips of five miles or less. In a city, you will probably save time.

Hitch-hike.

If you must drive, pick up hitchhikers.

If a car is an absolute necessity (as it often is in our poorly equipped and designed cities) and you are about to purchase one, get a small, efficient model. If cars in the U.S. averaged 28 miles per gallon, America would consume one-half as much petroleum for transportation as at present. If buying a car, insist on having detailed information on its pollution production. If the dealer refuses, move on. Word will travel.

Walk in areas you've never been before—enjoy yourself and the scenery.

Plant a tree so walking will be more pleasant.

Find out about the patterns of land-use in your city or town. How is land used? How much land area do automobiles take? How much living space does the average person have? You can take our analysis of Berkeley as a model for a similar local study of your own—or do your own thing.

If you see, read, or hear a misleading advertisement ("the pollution-free gasoline"), let the medium (TV station, radio station, newspaper) as well as the manufacturer know you're on to them—remind them of their responsibility.

Patronize local public-transportation facilities. Insist on frequent scheduling and well-designed vehicles.

Action is often easier if your friends are with you, in body and/or spirit. Let them know what's up.

Local (groups). Public transportation agencies might be willing to devote some advertising space on buses, subway cars, etc., to "public service announcements" carrying the truth about automobiles. Get together in defeating public abominations such as new freeways and highway bridges. Both San Francisco and New York City have recently defeated plans for new freeways.

See that city government takes bicycles into account when designing for traffic flow, building parks, one-way streets, and other related projects.

Sponsor happenings, parades, and festivals with ecological themes. Ecology Action in Berkeley had a successful "smog-free locomotion parade" recently. People joined in with a steam car, bicycles, roller skates, feet, unicycles, and a homemade electrically powered vehicle. Festivals culminating in the ceremonial burying of internal combustion engines have also been held.

Campaign for pledges from people never to fly on an SST. Airports might be good places to start getting signatures.

City councils, planning commissions, park departments, and other organs of city government are often quite interested in working with citizen groups and individuals. Try them out. If you make a presentation before any governmental body, get your facts together. Make sure your opinions have a firm foundation in fact and try to make practical and workable suggestions.

National. (federal priorities and programs). Population programs, with the aim of achieving zero domestic population growth by 1975, must receive the highest priority.

All subsidies and other support of the SST must be stopped immediately.

Programs aimed at reduction of automobile usage to one-tenth of the present levels must receive high priority.

Place a disposal tax on the sale of all new automobiles to fund the recycling of all old car hulks (after the usable parts have been removed).

While federal highways are still being built, law should require that each highway be provided with bicycle paths.

Federal gas taxes go into a highway trust fund. The law should be changed so that transportation is treated in an integrated way, allowing gasoline taxes to be used for support of other transportation programs.

Rapidly phase out the federal highway program, while vastly increasing support of research and development of rapid transit systems, reinstating railroad passenger service, etc.

Take steps, such as tax relief and subsidies, to make passenger railroad-service, especially on all intercity routes of less than five hundred miles, competitive with other forms of transportation. Among other programs, encourage the purchase of new, fast equipment to make railroad travel attractive to potential customers.

Establish statutory requirements for all automobiles, service stations, dealers, and used-car lots to carry warnings such as those outlined at the end of the "AIR" section above.

NOTES

1. Sixty-five m.p.h., 140-foot spacing (recommended for this speed), 1.5 people per car (the average number from many studies).

2. Sixty-five m.p.h., 140-foot spacing.

3. One per minute. The right-of-way for a train track is about the same width as a highway lane.

4. Fifteen m.p.h., 10-foot spacing.

5. Three m.p.h., 4 columns of walkers, 10-foot spacing.

6. Berkeley's land area is 6,500 acres. There are 229.1 miles of public roads, with average width of 40 feet; these roads take 1,110 acres. The driveways, garages, and other auxiliaries take 570 acres. There are 50,000 autos in Berkeley. The park system comprises 77.3 acres.

Recycling

Garrett De Bell

America has been described as a nation knee-deep in garbage, firing rockets to the moon. This phrase aptly points out the misguided priorities of the American government as well as the magnitude of the solid-waste crisis. Many solutions to the solid-waste, or trash, problem have been proposed—sanitary land fill, dumping waste into old mines, compressing it into building blocks, incineration, and dumping at sea. Even the best of these methods waste materials. The principle of recycling is to regard wastes as raw materials to be utilized; this is the only ecologically sensible long term solution to the solid-waste problem.

Recycling is a major part of the solution of many environmental problems. It is important to air and water pollution and to wilderness preservation. The environmental crisis has come into the public consciousness so recently that the word "recycle" doesn't even appear in most dictionaries. The core of its meaning is that resources be used over and over again and cycled through human economic-production systems in a way that is analagous to the cycles of elements (carbon, nitrogen, phosphorus, etc.) in natural eco-systems. This is directly contrary to the present produce and discard production system with its one-way flow of materials from the mine or farm through the household and into the garbage dumps, air, and water.

The benefits of reuse of materials (recycling) in our overcrowded world are obvious. Each ton of paper, aluminum, or iron reclaimed from waste is a ton less needed from our forests and mines, and a ton less solid waste in our environment. Recycling of many important materials is now technically feasible and major corporations are devoting some attention to it.

Aluminum is very easy to recycle because it need only be melted down for reuse. Because of aluminum's very high value, large-scale recycling operations are now feasible. Currently, scrap aluminum brings $200 per ton where scrap newspaper brings only $5 per ton. Reynolds Aluminum has been running ads stressing its interest in recycling aluminum cans; plants to accept used cans for recycling are now being built.

Paper and cardboard can also be recycled. Remember the paper drives of past years? The price is now so low that scrap paper is not economical to reuse unless it is delivered to the mill in large quantities by very cheap labor. But demands on our forests have become so great that there is now pressure for more intense management of timber to increase annual production. Those of us who prefer wilderness and maximum areas of unmanaged forests would prefer that the demand for timber be reduced by increasing the percentage that is recycled. Current research on improving the techniques is being done by U.S. Forest Products Laboratories. More recycling of paper means less pressure for increased cutting in the forests.

At present, however, the reuse or recycling of solid wastes is not economically feasible for most materials. Since it is ecologically necessary to start recycling our solid wastes, our approach is to find ways to make recycling economical.

Suitable legislation can go a long way toward doing this. At the state or federal level, legislation should incorporate the cost of disposal of each product in its price in the form of a tax. By giving a competitive advantage to products with a lower tax, this tax would encourage the use of simple bio-degradable or easily recycled containers, such as those made out of paper, cardboard, and aluminum, and also reusable bottles and containers. It would discourage the use of plastic containers of types that cannot be recycled and of containers made of a mix of materials that are very difficult or impossible to recycle, such as paper and plastic laminated together or foil-covered cardboard.

The tax can be collected either at the factory or at time of purchase depending on the circumstances. The revenues gained from this tax would go into a fund to subsidize recycling of products. The amount of tax would be determined by the subsidy needed to make recycling economically feasible. For example, aluminum, being economically recyclable, would require no subsidy. Paper, if its recycling required a two-cent-per-pound subsidy, would carry a two-cent tax. Products that could not be recycled at all would carry a tax equal to the full direct and social costs of ultimate disposal after use.

To properly recycle our wastes will require an industry perhaps as large as the present automobile industry. Recycling-plants can provide people with socially useful jobs, increase the resource base, and improve the quality of life for everyone.

There are two major barriers to recycling wastes. The first is the problem of transporting the wastes to the site of the recycling. This is an economic problem which the subsidy will solve. The second is getting wastes sorted. The subsidy can be high enough to pay for this, or each city might establish a dual set of garbage rates, which people could choose between freely. One rate would be for unsorted garbage. The other rate would be for garbage separated into organic wastes, glass, and metal, and into plastic, paper, and cardboard. The difference in the two rates would simply be the cost to the municipality of sorting the garbage. There may be objection to having to sort or pay, but it is time to realize that this is one of the costs we have to pay for a decent environment.

This legislation represents a specific application of the economic theory of externalities. Instead of the usual practice of including only the cost of production in the price of a product, we also include any additional social cost—such as the cost in environmental deterioration—in the price of the product. This removes the incentive to industries to follow practices which save them money in the short run but produce environmental destruction in the long run.

WHAT INDIVIDUALS CAN DO TO PROMOTE RECYCLING

Supermarkets should be made to minimize packaging and/or use returnable, reusable containers. You can bring pressure on your supermarket. On the day of the Environmental Teach-In get everyone in your neighborhood to return packaging and containers accumulated from purchases over the preceding week to the supermarket and make it *their* problem to dispose of them. To make this demonstration even more effective, make arrangements with scrap dealers handling paper, aluminum, glass, ferrous metals, and other materials to pick up the accumulated trash and recycle it. This would demonstrate both the magnitude of the solid waste crisis and the possibility of recycling wastes.

Don't accept hangers from laundries. Take your clothes off the hanger and leave them. If you accumulate hangers at home, take them back to the cleaners. Boycott laundries that won't reuse hangers. Follow the same practice with other products that are generally used once and thrown away, but could be reused many times. Don't buy products that come in unreusable containers.

COMPOSTING

Recycle your own vegetable wastes by starting a compost pile. All kinds of vegetable matter—everything from coffee grounds and banana peels to dead leaves, straw and sawdust—can be mixed together, piled up, and left for a couple of months to decompose to make a fine soil conditioner and fertilizer for your garden. Any vegetable wastes from your kitchen are good for composting, but don't use bones or other animal wastes, as they may attract rodents. Eggshells, seaweed, and ashes are good, but not in large quantities, as they may add too much salt or alkalinity. Don't use eucalyptus leaves. Sheep, horse, or cow manure, or small amounts of chicken manure, make an excellent addition.

"Turn" or move your pile every couple of weeks, or when it is getting too hot in the center. Take the top part of the pile and put it on the bottom, then put the bottom part on top. This prevents spontaneous combustion from starting as the result of the accumulated heat of decomposition in the center of the pile, and also helps the compost to decompose evenly. Keep the pile covered with dirt to prevent any odor. Some dirt mixed into the organic material helps it to decompose, since it contains decomposing bacteria. The compost will "work" faster if it is kept damp.

When your pile is big enough—maybe three to six feet high—stop adding to it (start a second pile), continue turning it when necessary, and wait until it is well decomposed and is no longer noticeably warm in the center. Then it is ready to use as a soil conditioner, fertilizer, or mulch in your garden.

BEYOND THE RECYCLE PRINCIPLE

Normally the recycling concept means reuse of materials. Additional steps outside this concept can be taken to reduce the rates of solid-waste production and resource depletion. In general, both legislation and citizens in their private lives can stress maintenance and repair of existing products rather than planned obsolescence. This will create less jobs on the assembly line, but more jobs for repairmen and renovators.

Too Many People

Paul R. Ehrlich

from The Population Bomb

Americans are beginning to realize that the undeveloped countries of the world face an inevitable population-food crisis. Each year food production in undeveloped countries falls a bit further behind burgeoning population growth, and people go to bed a little bit hungrier. While there are temporary or local reversals of this trend, it now seems inevitable that it will continue to its logical conclusion: mass starvation. The rich are going to get richer, but the more numerous poor are going to get poorer. Of these poor, a minimum of three and one-half million will starve to death this year, mostly children. But this is a mere handful compared to the numbers that will be starving in a decade or so. And it is now too late to take action to save many of those people.

In a book about population there is a temptation to stun the reader with an avalanche of statistics. I'll spare you most, but not all, of that. After all, no matter how you slice it, population is a numbers game. Perhaps the best way to impress you with numbers is to tell you about the "doubling time"—the time necessary for the population to double in size.

It has been estimated that the human population of 6000 B.C. was about five million people, taking perhaps one million years to get there from two and a half million. The population did not reach 500 million until almost 8,000 years later—about 1650 A.D. This means it doubled roughly once every thousand years or so. It reached a billion people around 1850, doubling in some 200 years. It took only 80 years or so for the next doubling, as the population reached two billion around 1930. We have not completed the next doubling to four billion yet, but we now have well over three billion people. The doubling time at present seems to be about 37 years.[1] Quite a reduction in doubling times: 1,000,000 years, 1,000 years, 200 years, 80 years, 37 years. Perhaps the meaning of a doubling time of around 37 years is best brought home by a theoretical exercise. Let's examine what might happen on the absurd assumption that the population continued to double every 37 years into the indefinite future.

If growth continued at that rate for about 900 years, there would be some 60,000,000,000,000,000 people on the face of the earth. Sixty million billion people. This is about 100 persons for each square yard of the Earth's surface, land and sea. A British physicist, J. H. Fremlin,[2] guessed that such a multitude might be housed in a continuous 2,000-story building covering our entire planet. The upper 1,000 stories would contain only the apparatus for running this gigantic warren. Ducts, pipes, wires, elevator shafts, etc., would occupy about half of the space in the bottom 1,000 stories. This would leave three or four yards of floor space for each person. I will leave to your imagination the physical details of existence in this ant heap, except to point out that all would not be black. Probably each person would be limited in his travel. Perhaps he could take elevators through all 1,000 residential stories but could travel only within a circle of a few hundred yards' radius on any floor. This would permit, however, each person to choose his friends from among some ten million people! And, as Fremlin points out, entertainment on the worldwide TV should be excellent, for at any time "one could expect some ten million Shakespeares and rather more Beatles to be alive.

Could growth of the human population of the Earth continue beyond that point? Not according to Fremlin. We would have reached a "heat limit." People themselves, as well as their activities, convert other forms of energy into heat which must be dissipated. In order to permit this excess heat to radiate directly from the top of the "world building" directly into space, the atmosphere would have been pumped into flasks under the sea well before the limiting population size was reached. The precise limit would depend on the technology of the day. At a population size of one billion billion people, the temperature of the "world roof" would be kept around the melting point of iron to radiate away the human heat generated.

But, you say, surely Science (with a capital "S") will find a way for us to occupy the other planets of our solar system and eventually of other stars before we get all that crowded. Skip for a moment the virtual certainty that those planets are uninhabitable. Forget also the insurmountable logistic problems of moving billions of people off the Earth. Fremlin has made some interesting calculations on how much time we could buy by occupying the planets of the solar system. For instance, at any given time it would take only about 50 years to populate Venus, Mercury, Mars, the moon, and the moons of Jupiter and Saturn to the same population density as Earth.[8]

What if the fantastic problems of reaching and colonizing the other planets of the solar system, such as Jupiter and Uranus, can be solved? It would take only about 200 years to fill them "Earth-full." So we could perhaps gain 250 years of time for population growth in the solar system after we had reached an absolute limit on Earth. What then? We can't ship our surplus to the stars. Professor Garrett Hardin[4] of the University of California at Santa Barbara has dealt effectively with this fantasy. Using extremely optimistic assumptions, he has calculated that Americans, by cutting their standard of living down to 18% of its present level, could in *one year* set aside enough capital to finance the exportation to the stars of *one day's* increase in the population of the world.

Interstellar transport for surplus people presents an

amusing prospect. Since the ships would take generations to reach most stars, the only people who could
be transported would be those willing to exercise strict
birth control. Population explosions on space ships
would be disastrous. Thus we would have to export our
responsible people, leaving the irresponsible at home on
Earth to breed.

Enough of fantasy. Hopefully, you are convinced that
the population will have to stop growing sooner or later
and that the extremely remote possibility of expanding
into outer space offers no escape from the laws of population growth. If you still want to hope for the stars, just
remember that, at the current growth rate, in a few
thousand years everything in the visible universe would
be converted into people, and the ball of people would
be expanding with the speed of light![5] Unfortunately,
even 900 years is much too far in the future for those
of us concerned with the population explosion. As you
shall see, the next *nine* years will probably tell the story.

Of course, population growth is not occurring uni-
formly over the face of the Earth. Indeed, countries
are divided rather neatly into two groups: those with
rapid growth rates, and those with relatively slow growth
rates. The first group, making up about two-thirds of
the world population, coincides closely with what are
known as the "undeveloped countries" (UDCs). The
UDCs are not industrialized, tend to have inefficient
agriculture, very small gross national products, high
illiteracy rates and related problems. That's what UDCs
are technically, but a short definition of undeveloped is
"starving." Most Latin American, African, and Asian
countries fall into this category. The second group consists, in essence, of the "developed countries" (DCs).
DCs are modern, industrial nations, such as the United
States, Canada, most European countries, Israel, Russia,
Japan, and Australia. Most people in these countries are
adequately nourished.

Doubling times in the UDCs range around 20 to
35 years. Examples of these times (from the 1968
figures just released by the Population Reference

Bureau) are Kenya, 24 years; Nigeria, 28; Turkey, 24; Indonesia, 31; Philippines, 20; Brazil, 22; Costa Rica, 20; and El Salvador, 19. Think of what it means for the population of a country to double in 25 years. In order just to keep living standards at the present inadequate level, the food available for the people must be doubled. Every structure and road must be duplicated. The amount of power must be doubled. The capacity of the transport system must be doubled. The number of trained doctors, nurses, teachers, and administrators must be doubled. This would be a fantastically difficult job in the United States—a rich country with a fine agricultural system, immense industries, and rich natural resources. Think of what it means to a country with none of these.

Remember also that in virtually all UDCs, people have gotten the word about the better life it is possible to have. They have seen colored pictures in magazines of the miracles of Western technology. They have seen automobiles and airplanes. They have seen American and European movies. Many have seen refrigerators, tractors, and even TV sets. Almost all have heard transistor radios. They *know* that a better life is possible. They have what we like to call "rising expectations." If twice as many people are to be happy, the miracle of doubling what they now have will not be enough. It will only maintain today's standard of living. There will have to be a tripling or better. Needless to say, they are not going to be happy.

Doubling times for the populations of the DCs tend to be in the 50-to-200-year range. Examples of 1968 doubling times are the United States, 63 years; Austria, 175; Denmark, 88; Norway, 88; United Kingdom, 140; Poland, 88; Russia, 63; Italy, 117; Spain, 88; and Japan, 63. These are industrialized countries that have undergone the so-called demographic transition—a transition from high to low growth rate. As industrialization progressed, children became less important to parents as extra hands to work on the farm and as support in old age. At the same time they became a financial drag—expensive to raise and educate. Presumably these are the reasons for a slowing of population growth after industrialization. They boil down to a simple fact—people just want to have fewer children.

This is not to say, however, that population is not a problem for the DCs. First of all, most of them are overpopulated. They are overpopulated by the simple criterion that they are not able to produce enough food to feed their populations. It is true that they have the money to buy food, but when food is no longer available for sale they will find the money rather indigestible. Then, too, they share with the UDCs a serious problem of population distribution. Their urban centers are getting more and more crowded relative to the countryside. This problem is not as severe as it is in the UDCs (if current trends should continue, which they cannot, Calcutta could have 66 million inhabitants in the year 2000). As you are well aware, however, urban concentrations are creating serious problems even in America. In the United States, one of the more rapidly growing DCs, we hear constantly of the headaches caused by growing population: not just garbage in our environment, but overcrowded highways, burgeoning slums, deteriorating school systems, rising crime rates, riots, and other related problems.

From the point of view of a demographer, the whole problem is quite simple. A population will continue to grow as long as the birth rate exceeds the death rate —if immigration and emigration are not occurring. It is, of course, the balance between birth rate and death rate that is critical. The birth rate is the number of births per thousand people per year in the population. The death rate is the number of deaths per thousand people per year.[6] Subtracting the death rate from the birth rate, and ignoring migration, gives the rate of increase. If the birth rate is 30 per thousand per year, and the death rate is 10 per thousand per year, then the rate of increase is 20 per thousand per year $(30 - 10 = 20)$. Expressed as a percent (rate per hundred people), the rate of 20 per thousand becomes 2%. If the rate of increase is 2%, then the doubling time will be 35 years. Note that if you simply added 20 people per thousand per year to the population, it would take 50 years to add a second thousand people $(20 \times 50 = 1,000)$. But the doubling time is actually much less because populations grow at compound interest rates. Just as interest dollars themselves earn interest, so people added to populations produce more people. It's growing at compound interest that makes populations double so much more rapidly than seems possible. Look at the relationship between the annual percent increase (interest rate) and the doubling time of the population (time for your money to double):

Annual percent increase	Doubling time
1.0	70
2.0	35
3.0	24
4.0	17

Those are all the calculations—I promise. If you are interested in more details on how demographic figuring is done, you may enjoy reading Thompson and Lewis's excellent book, *Population Problems.*[7]

There are some professional optimists around who like to greet every sign of dropping birth rates with wild pronouncements about the end of the population explosion. They are a little like a person who, after a low temperature of five below zero on December 21, interprets a low of only three below zero on December 22 as a cheery sign of approaching spring. First of all, birth rates, along with all demographic statistics, show short-term fluctuations caused by many factors. For instance, the birth rate depends rather heavily on the number of women at reproductive age. In the United States the current low birth rates soon will be replaced by higher rates as more post World War II "baby boom" children move into their reproductive years. In Japan, 1966, the Year of the Fire Horse, was a year of very low birth rates. There is widespread belief that girls born in the

Year of the Fire Horse make poor wives, and Japanese couples try to avoid giving birth in that year because they are afraid of having daughters.

But, I repeat, it is the relationship between birth rate and death rate that is most critical. Indonesia, Laos, and Haiti all had birth rates around 46 per thousand in 1966. Costa Rica's birth rate was 41 per thousand. Good for Costa Rica? Unfortunately, not very. Costa Rica's death rate was less than nine per thousand, while the other countries all had death rates above 20 per thousand. The population of Costa Rica in 1966 was doubling every 17 years, while the doubling times of Indonesia, Laos, and Haiti were all above 30 years. Ah, but, you say, it was good for Costa Rica—fewer people per thousand were dying each year. Fine for a few years perhaps, but what then? Some 50% of the people in Costa Rica are under 15 years old. As they get older, they will need more and more food in a world with less and less. In 1983 they will have twice as many mouths to feed as they had in 1966, if the 1966 trend continues. Where will the food come from? Today the death rate in Costa Rica is low in part because they have a large number of physicians in proportion to their population. How do you suppose those physicians will keep the death rate down when there's not enough food to keep people alive?

One of the most ominous facts of the current situation is that roughly 40% of the population of the undeveloped world is made up of people *under 15 years old*. As that mass of young people moves into its reproductive years during the next decade, we're going to see the greatest baby boom of all time. Those youngsters are the reason for all the ominous predictions for the year 2000. They are the gunpowder for the population explosion.

How did we get into this bind? It all happened a long time ago, and the story involves the process of natural selection, the development of culture, and man's swollen head. The essence of success in evolution is reproduction. Indeed, natural selection is simply defined as differential reproduction of genetic types. That is, if people with blue eyes have more children on the average than those with brown eyes, natural selection is occurring. More genes for blue eyes will be passed on to the next generation than will genes for brown eyes. Should this continue, the population will have progressively larger and larger proportions of blue-eyed people. This differential reproduction of genetic types is the driving force of evolution; it has been driving evolution for billions of years. Whatever types produced more offspring became the common types. Virtually all populations contain very many different genetic types (for reasons that need not concern us), and some are always outreproducing others. As I said, reproduction is the key to winning the evolutionary game. Any structure, physiological process, or pattern of behavior that leads to greater reproductive success will tend to be perpetuated. The entire process by which man developed involves thousands of millenia of our ancestors being more successful breeders than their relatives. Facet number one of our bind—the urge to reproduce has been fixed in us by billions of years of evolution.

Of course through all those years of evolution, our ancestors were fighting a continual battle to keep the birth rate ahead of the death rate. That they were successful is attested to by our very existence, for, if the death rate had overtaken the birth rate for any substantial period of time, the evolutionary line leading to man would have gone extinct. Among our apelike ancestors, a few million years ago, it was still very difficult for a mother to rear her children successfully. Most of the offspring died before they reached reproductive age. The death rate was near the birth rate. Then another factor entered the picture—cultural evolution was added to biological evolution.

Culture can be loosely defined as the body of non-genetic information which people pass from generation to generation. It is the accumulated knowledge that, in the old days, was passed on entirely by word of mouth, painting, and demonstration. Several thousand years ago the written word was added to the means of cultural transmission. Today culture is passed on in these ways, and also through television, computer tapes, motion pictures, records, blueprints, and other media. Culture is all the information man possesses except for that which is stored in the chemical language of his genes.

The large size of the human brain evolved in response to the development of cultural information. A big brain is an advantage when dealing with such information. Big-brained individuals were able to deal more successfully with the culture of their group. They were thus more successful reproductively than their smaller-brained relatives. They passed on their genes for big brains to their numerous offspring. They also added to the accumulating store of cultural information, increasing slightly the premium placed on brain size in the next generation. A self-reinforcing selective trend developed—a trend toward increased brain size.[8]

But there was, quite literally, a rub. Babies had bigger and bigger heads. There were limits to how large a woman's pelvis could conveniently become. To make a long story short, the strategy of evolution was not to make a woman bell-shaped and relatively immobile, but to accept the problem of having babies who were helpless for a long period while their brains grew after birth.[9] How could the mother defend and care for her infant during its unusually long period of helplessness? She couldn't, unless Papa hung around. The girls are still working on that problem, but an essential step was to get rid of the short, well-defined breeding season characteristic of most mammals. The year-round sexuality of the human female, the long period of infant dependence on the female, the evolution of the family group, all are at the roots of our present problem. They are essential ingredients in the vast social phenomenon that we call sex. Sex is not simply an act leading to the production of offspring. It is a varied and complex cultural phenomenon penetrating into all aspects of our lives—one involving our self-esteem, our choice of friends, cars, and leaders. It is tightly interwoven with our mythologies and history. Sex in man is necessary for the production of young, but it also evolved to ensure their successful rearing. Facet number two of our bind—our urge to reproduce is hopelessly entwined with most of our other urges.

Of course, in the early days the whole system did not prevent a very high mortality among the young, as well as among the older members of the group. Hunting and food-gathering is a risky business. Cavemen had to throw very impressive cave bears out of their caves before the men could move in. Witch doctors and shamans had a less than perfect record at treating wounds and curing disease. Life was short, if not sweet. Man's total population size doubtless increased slowly but steadily as human populations expanded out of the African cradle of our species.

Then about 8,000 years ago a major change occurred —the agricultural revolution. People began to give up hunting food and settled down to grow it. Suddenly some of the risk was removed from life. The chances of dying of starvation diminished greatly in some human groups. Other threats associated with the nomadic life were also reduced, perhaps balanced by new threats of disease and large-scale warfare associated with the development of cities. But the overall result was a more secure existence than before, and the human population grew more rapidly. Around 1800, when the standard of living in what are today the DCs was dramatically increasing due to industrialization, population growth really began to accelerate. The development of medical science was the straw that broke the camel's back. While lowering death rates in the DCs was due in part to other factors, there is no question that "instant death control," exported by the DCs, has been responsible for the drastic lowering of death rates in the UDCs. Medical science, with its efficient public health programs, has been able to depress the death rate with astonishing rapidity and at the same time drastically increase the birth rate; healthier people have more babies.

The power of exported death control can best be

seen by an examination of the classic case of Ceylon's assault on malaria after World War II. Between 1933 and 1942 the death rate due directly to malaria was *reported* as almost two per thousand. This rate, however, represented only a portion of the malaria deaths, as many were reported as being due to "pyrexia."[10] Indeed, in 1934–1935 a malaria epidemic may have been directly responsible for fully half of the deaths on the island. In addition, malaria, which infected a large portion of the population, made people susceptible to many other diseases. It thus contributed to the death rate indirectly as well as directly.

The introduction of DDT in 1946 brought rapid control over the mosquitoes which carry malaria. As a result, the death rate on the island was halved in less than a decade. The death rate in Ceylon in 1945 was 22. It dropped 34% between 1946 and 1947 and moved down to ten in 1954. Since the sharp postwar drop it has continued to decline and now stands at eight. Although part of the drop is doubtless due to the killing of other insects which carry disease and to other public health measures, most of it can be accounted for by the control of malaria.

Victory over malaria, yellow fever, smallpox, cholera, and other infectious diseases has been responsible for similar plunges in death rate throughout most of the UDCs. In the decade 1940–1950 the death rate declined 46% in Puerto Rico, 43% in Formosa, and 23% in Jamaica. In a sample of 18 undeveloped areas the average decline in death rate between 1945 and 1950 was 24%.

It is, of course, socially very acceptable to reduce the death rate. Billions of years of evolution have given us all a powerful will to live. Intervening in the birth rate goes against our evolutionary values. During all those centuries of our evolutionary past, the individuals who had the most children passed on their genetic endowment in greater quantities than those who reproduced less. Their genes dominate our heredity today. All our biological urges are for more reproduction, and they are all too often reinforced by our culture. In brief, death control goes with the grain, birth control against it.

In summary, the world's population will continue to grow as long as the birth rate exceeds the death rate; it's as simple as that. When it stops growing or starts to shrink, it will mean that either the birth rate has gone down or the death rate has gone up or a combination of the two. Basically, then, there are only two kinds of solutions to the population problem. One is a "birth rate solution," in which we find ways to lower the birth rate. The other is a "death rate solution," in which ways to raise the death rate—war, famine, pestilence—*find us.* The problem could have been avoided by *population control,* in which mankind consciously adjusted the birth rate so that a "death rate solution" did not have to occur.

NOTES

1. Since this was written, 1968 figures have appeared, showing that the doubling time is now 35 years.
2. J. H. Fremlin, "How Many People Can the World Support?" *New Scientist,* October 29, 1964.
3. To understand this, simply consider what would happen if we held the population constant at three billion people by exporting all the surplus people. If this were done for 37 years (the time it now takes for one doubling) we would have exported three billion people—enough to populate a twin planet of the Earth to the same density. In two doubling times (74 years) we would reach a total human population for the solar system of 12 billion people, enough to populate the Earth and three similar planets to the density found on Earth today. Since the areas of the planets and moons mentioned above are not three times that of the Earth, they can be populated to equal density in much less than two doubling times.
4. "Interstellar Migration and the Population Problem." *Heredity* 50: 68–70, 1959.
5. I. J. Cook, *New Scientist,* September 8, 1966.
6. The birth rate is more precisely the total number of births in a country during a year, divided by the total population at the midpoint of the year, multiplied by 1,000. Suppose that there were 80 births in Lower Slobbovia during 1967, and that the population of Lower Slobbovia was 2,000 on July 1, 1967. Then the birth rate would be:

$$\text{Birth rate} = \frac{80 \text{ (total births in L. Slobbovia in 1967)}}{2,000 \text{ (total population, July 1, 1967)}} \times 1,000$$

$$= .04 \times 1,000 = 40$$

Similarly if there were 40 deaths in Lower Slobbovia during 1967, the death rate would be:

Death rate $= \dfrac{40 \text{ (total deaths in L. Slobbovia in 1967)}}{2{,}000 \text{ (total population, July 1, 1967)}} \times 1{,}000$

$= .02 \times 1{,}000 = 20$

Then the Lower Slobbovian birth rate would be 40 per thousand, and the death rate would be 20 per thousand. For every 1,000 Lower Slobbovians alive on July 1, 1967, 40 babies were born and 20 people died. Subtracting the death rate from the birth rate gives us the rate of natural increase of Lower Slobbovia for the year 1967. That is, $40 - 20 = 20$; during 1967 the population grew at a rate of 20 people per thousand per year. Dividing that rate by ten expresses the increase as a percent (the increase per hundred per year). The increase in 1967 in Lower Slobbovia was two percent. Remember that this rate of increase ignores any movement of people into and out of Lower Slobbovia.

7. McGraw-Hill Book Company, Inc., New York. 1965.
8. Human brain size increased from an apelike capacity of about 500 cubic centimeters (cc) in *Australopithecus* to about 1,500 cc in modern *Homo sapiens*. Among modern men small variations in brain size do not seem to be related to significant differences in the ability to use cultural information, and there is no particular reason to believe that our brain size will continue to increase. Further evolution may occur more readily in a direction of increased efficiency rather than increased size.
9. This is, of course, an oversimplified explanation. For more detail see Ehrlich and Holm, *The Process of Evolution*, McGraw-Hill Book Company, Inc., New York. 1963.
10. These data and those that follow on the decline of death rates are from Kingsley Davis's "The Amazing Decline of Mortality in Underdeveloped Areas," *The American Economic Review*, Vol. 46, pp. 305–318.

Mankind's Inalienable Rights

Paul R. Ehrlich

from The Population Bomb

1. The right to limit our families.
2. The right to eat.
3. The right to eat meat.
4. The right to drink pure water.
5. The right to live uncrowded.
6. The right to avoid regimentation.
7. The right to hunt and fish.
8. The right to view natural beauty.
9. The right to breathe clean air.
10. The right to silence.
11. The right to avoid pesticide poisoning.
12. The right to be free of thermonuclear war.
13. The right to educate our children.
14. The right to have grandchildren.
15. The right to have great-grandchildren.

The Recovery of Cities

Berkeley People's Architecture

CITIES: THE ARTIFACTS OF EMPIRE TECHNOLOGY

Pretechnical man was not a dominant species. He existed for millenia as a minor element in the biosphere. But he had a special brain and a special pair of appendages which allowed him to make and use artifacts— to create an extension of his will—to create technology.

With the growth of technology, territorial control became extended and more ritualized. Control became ownership, and ritual became law. Cities emerged and grew from centers of trade to centers of commercial and governmental control over the countryside. The related factors of automated farming and increasingly centralized production technology are now completing the rural to urban settlement.

Now men must live in cities in order to survive, to work, to feed off the interdependent energy networks that have replaced growing things. Today urban man is extending his synthesized environment towards total replacement of natural processes. Freedom is now viewed as independence from natural rhythms.

Downtown, the governmental and financial bureaucracy of centralized power and control is moving outwards and displacing the surrounding community life. Through political control, downtown is moving monolithic highrise developments out into the surrounding areas with the least political power—the old residential communities—the middle city ghettoes. For the past

234

several decades the affluent have been fleeing the downtown residential communities, leaving behind the old, the unemployed, the fatherless families, and the racial minorities. The suburbanites commute back to downtown on concrete umbilical cords that cut through the old urban communities. And the rapid expansion of the suburban perimeter is replacing vital farmland with wasteful monotonous noncommunities that derive their primary form from the movement of automobiles and standardized consumer centers.

What happens to the individual in a system of urban expansion where "progress" is an unquestioned premise and centralization is the method? The energy circuitry of production becomes more complex in the name of management efficiency (measured in centralized profits rather than in terms of human utility) and the "human switches" become simpler. We become passive consumer producers, common and predictable units to be plugged in to the energy grid. We are increasingly divorced from competence, unable to live self-reliantly:

Get born keep warm
short pants romance
learn to dance
get dressed get blessed
try to be a suck-cess
please her please him
buy gifts
don't steal don't lift
twenty years of schooling
and they put you on the day shift
look out kid
they keep it all hid . . .

There is a growing popular awareness of the most obvious symptoms of arrogant "progress." It's fashionable to talk of the urban crisis, pollution, suburban monotony, and the disappearance of individuality.

Powerful government and corporate interests are also becoming uneasy, but their approach to the crisis is opportunistic. They are capitalizing financially and politically on the public's anxiety about environmental doomsday predictions. The automobile industry's recent announcement of pollution control programs for the private automobile merely prolong the agony of the private transportation system; the net effect of urban renewal is to reduce the total amount of moderate and low-income housing; California's governor speaks out for ecology and simultaneously pushes a project for water diversion from the Central Valley to Southern California which will destroy the Los Angeles basin through overdevelopment and make the Sacramento River Delta a saline desert; industrial air pollution control measures cause industrial wastes to be washed out of factory exhausts into the sewer system, polluting our waterways in the name of clean air.

The problem which politicians and businessmen will not publicly acknowledge is the one which is at the root of the crisis: Whole-earth ecology dictates that Americans must reduce their consumption of resources, but corporate investment return requires expanding energy consumption. Government and corporate programs for urban recovery require massive consumption of energy and goods to treat only the *symptoms* of the urban crisis.

There is a broad difference between attempting to modify the most obviously harmful defects of centralized "progress", and taking the first of many revolutionary steps to re-establish a mutually beneficial steady-state relationship between our species and the whole earth. This second view takes a cautious attitude toward technology and recognizes that the urban complex of artifacts and energy networks is an ecosystem synthetic in its parts but organic in its whole. Changes which depend on massive centralized technology will be ecologically disastrous.

Pressuring central powers to relieve the crisis will not result in a voluntary dismantling of centralized systems of production: the problems *are the result* of greater centralization of power and profit. Environmental recovery means the recovery of community control, communities organizing to achieve their right to a rich and varied self-sufficiency.

It is important to make a sharp change in *direction* and to have a program for urban recovery that is an organic process for change, each step discreet and growing from the preceding one. This way energy is conserved; there is time for re-evaluation, to test the new thing against the old thing. Many different experiments by many people working together with a shared understanding of direction is much more likely to achieve its ends than any massive centrally imposed crash program. Precisely because there is a crisis in the urban environment, because we are at the edge of disaster, we must move carefully. The urban complex never will be completely understood, and waiting for "definitive" research in the face of obvious and predictable urban failure is absurd. Right now different urban areas must be freed to make different experiments for urban recovery based on community control.

The military is an appropriate model for describing the way that downtown expands. The corporate and government leaders meet. Needs are expressed, a territorial objective agreed upon. The program is turned over to the strategists—the architect is the executive general. He makes a detailed description, a design. His plans are reviewed by the leaders. The approved plans are turned over to the field officer for logistical implementation. The *general* contractor places various subcontractors under his command, and in turn these various subcontractors, or platoon leaders, carry out the directive with the deployment of troops—the building-trades union workers.

This whole process secures new territory for the corporate and government leaders. If the people who live in the path of the extension of government and corporate needs appear to have the ability to organize—to resist —to defend their territory—the downtown forces have many special weapons at their command to deploy, to soften up the territory before the troops move in. The zoning and assessors' departments are mobilized by downtown control. They work in tandem to rezone and selectively tax a desired territory. If necessary, the police department is deployed to make selective arrests for petty offenses. The press is notified and public opinion is directed against the territory as a high crime area. The property owners are bought off. If there is resistance at this point, the right of eminent domain and condemnation can be used for many building programs. Public renewal money in a building project guarantees this power. Nowhere in this process is there any effort taken by the experts to make an evaluation of the influence of the new product in terms of human ecology, and for obvious reasons.

But there is no legitimate reason why there should be any more downtown office space. Communications technology now permits a geographically decentralized association of people who are engaged in information processing. Even now most lessees of space in highrise downtown buildings don't share anything with their neighbors except the crowded elevators, inadequate sidewalk space, and the six-lane freeway on the way home.

The present form of downtown growth represents massive profits to the big building interests (banks, realtor-developers, insurance companies, big corporations). Clean monumental space, undefiled by noncommercial realities of the funky diversity of true community, is the jealously guarded status image of downtown territory. Highrise office buildings are designed more to advertise the prestige of large corporations, to announce their arrival in the world of downtown, than as a response to any real corporate need for ten thousand people working in the same building.

PROGRAM FOR DOWNTOWN RECOVERY

1. Freeze downtown highrise development. THERE IS NO NEED FOR ANY NEW HIGHRISE STRUCTURES.

2. Selectively dismantle whole buildings and parts of buildings; save materials for reuse.

3. Close off streets for orchards, vegetable gardens, parks, market places. Close the city center to private automobiles. Buses and other service transit only.

4. Rebuild southern exposures for hydroponic gardens.

5. Renovate office space for multiple use—housing, community marketing, meeting places, schools and other much needed things for the surrounding communities. DIVERSIFY AND DECENTRALIZE DOWNTOWN.

Cities don't work as highly centralized areas for specialized bureaucratic functions, but the highrise downtown structures would work very nicely with minor modifications as living places for diverse communities of people. The center city must reclaim its share of people from the suburbs and the suburbs must achieve their own integrity and viability as whole communities. The idea is not to flatten out the difference between the suburb and the city, but to develop diverse integrated activity within each local environment. Renaissance Florence had a population of less than 30,000. Neighborhoods are cultural entities; decentralized and integrated suburbs can be too. There is certainly no justification for modern urban giganticism on the grounds that centers of "cultural progress" must be big.

Of the three areas—downtown, the suburbs, and the middle city—it is the middle city which is the only matrix for new culture. Downtown does not create new culture; it merely markets it to the suburbs. The middle city will be the first to reclaim its environment, the suburbs second, and downtown last. The downtown environment will be reclaimed when the middle city defeats the bid of downtown for its territory and when suburbia becomes self-supporting communities.

Middle City: The Colonized Culture

In many ways ghettoes in America are the most together communities. The middle city has the longest history of unbroken social growth (there are a few exceptions, however); the street is still a meeting place for people not merely a transportation artery for somewhere else; neighborhood grocery stores still exist. Neighbors are often relatives and religious and social life is centered in the neighborhood. The middle city has been the source of most urban American culture.

A viable working community of people is the prerequisite for decentralization of production, integration of living space with cultural and work space, and community control of resources. Paradoxically, the oldest and poorest sections of the city have a head start. They will be the first areas to show the rest of the urban population the way to an ecologically sane environment. They will eliminate what they don't need and recover what they do need.

The problems of the ghetto are comparable to a colonized country. Middle city businesses and housing are owned and taxed by downtown and nothing is given in return except renewal programs that are determined by and serve "foreign interests" and the transportation network that feeds downtown. Police control is the only public service that is adequately funded. The job market is determined by the needs of "foreign business" geared to producing goods that middle city ghetto dwellers can't afford and often don't want. And automated industry demands skills which the "uneducated" don't have access to or necessarily want.

The problem with the poor and the minority populations is not that they consume too much nor that their style of living rapes the land.

We can't expect to continue to push the "American dream" through consumer advertising brainwash and programs to train minorities to become skilled commodity producer-consumers, and at the same time expect them to buy birth control programs for themselves along the way. The poor and minority populations feel that their children are just as deserving of the good life as anyone else's, and as long as "deserving" means free to move on up to Consumerville, minorities will justly demand economic security before birth control.

The answer to the problem of poverty is community control over resources. In the present urban system, *the* resource is money. More money to free the ghetto dweller from the pressure of having to seek work outside his community, more money to provide essential medical and day-care centers, more money to provide schools, more mony to bring housing up to standards (the dweller's standards, not F.H.A.'s), more money to take care of the old and disabled who can't work in the present system or in any future more humane one, more money for the ghetto community to own its land and its means of production. And more money so those who want to leave the ghetto can do so.

There must be a freeze on downtown building programs in the ghetto in order to allow neighborhoods to form cooperatives to renovate existing buildings with community labor. More relevant than trying to crack racial barriers in the building trades unions is to allow the organization of black builders' cooperatives to challenge the nature of building construction programs themselves. Who benefits from federal housing programs, the community or the outside labor force and investors? If emphasis were directed away from the construction of new buildings toward the reclamation of highrise buildings for middle city community use instead, there would be a reduction in expenditure of energy and materials. The money that could be freed could go towards providing needed neighborhood services and the relocation of commuters' working places back into the suburban community.

Ghetto communities are misled by programs to put new industry into their neighborhoods. In Berkeley, black leaders were sold the idea of a waterfront industrial park which will cut into a black neighborhood, on the grounds that it will provide initial construction jobs for black people and employment when the industries move in. In fact, the large majority of firms which will occupy the site are electronics and data-processing companies, the kind of thing that imports a white labor force rather than seeking employees among the "unskilled" unemployed.

The welfare system is another example of imperialism in the ghetto. The graduated income tax is a myth; low and middle income families, unable to take advantage of "loopholes," pay a higher proportion of their earnings than the rich. Middle city residents pay substantially more taxes to support welfare *machinery* than they get back in their communities as *services*. If the welfare machinery were dismantled, and the money given directly to the middle city community, welfare workers could be paid not to work, and the middle city would have the funds to obtain community control.

Community control of the police is another dimension of environmental recovery. Ghetto uprisings in recent years have demonstrated to the world just how much people there see their very environment as a source of their oppression; in Detroit and Watts they burned their "own" homes, and only the businesses of "soul brothers" escaped their full wrath. Crime in the ghetto is a matter of "redistributing" what slim resources remain there, after rent, taxes and outside-owned businesses have siphoned off their share. When the ghetto begins to feel a stake in its environment, law enforcement will come to mean protection of community resources and property, rather than pacification by downtown's domestic army.

If ghetto communities successfully resist the usurpation of their land for transportation corridors from suburbia to downtown, they will force the rest of society to rethink the pattern of downtown and suburban growth, with its increased separation of living and working areas. Middle city ghetto communities, although economically on the margin of society, are located on America's most valuable land. Their strategic geographical position around the downtown perimeter gives them a potential of tremendous leverage for assuring their own future and the future of urban recovery.

If you told the suburbanite that the way his house was built, the elimination of food-producing land that it caused, his long-distance drive to work, his work in the military-industrial-governmental structure, his use of power gadgets, his wife's consumption of clothing, his family's consumption of prepackaged synthetic foods, the daily pouring of thousands of food calories into the "garbage" disposal under his kitchen sink, and the birth of his third child are making the world unlivable, he wouldn't believe you. If you discussed it with him for a while, he would eventually insist that he was law-abiding and paid his taxes, not realizing that conformance to the great American Way is accelerating the process which is destroying the earth.

The youth of suburbia don't necessarily all go along with this vision. Though the new earth ethic has already begun to be commercialized and packaged for them, they are nevertheless uneasy about being suburbanites. They are open to the suggestion that the whole earth life style is more than the packaged artifacts pushed by media advertising . . . that the good "vibes" come from a total change in the way that people are relating to nature and to each other, that "dropping out" means less consumption, not more. The low-pressure, varied and spontaneous environment of underground culture at its best, represents a love of simple things—trees, handcrafts, old clothes, and sharing.

A "program" for suburban recovery might begin with high school kids taking a good look at their sterile home environment and deciding to get it together with what is available:

1. Groups should organize to take down fences separating yards to make truck gardens and neighborhood sheds for storing shared tools.

2. Efforts should be made to recycle car allowances from Daddy by amassing a fleet of used vehicles to be shared cooperatively by young people. (About one car per ten people should suffice.)

3. Experimental living groups should construct their shelters from used building materials (church windows, old car parts—hoods and trunks make beautiful domes

—and wood from the dismantled fences from number 2 above).

4. High school community action groups should attempt to stop the building of more housing tracts in the area. The "massive American housing shortage" is a myth. Right now the amount of shelter per capita in America is several times greater than that of the rest of the world. Several countries house their populations comfortably above the subsistence level with much less means than America. We don't need more shelter, rather we must learn to use our existing buildings more efficiently, to justly redistribute our shelter resources. No more new suburbs should be built until we are prepared to build semi-rural self-sufficient communities from reclaimed, rather than virgin building materials, integrated with food-producing open space, following the natural ecology of each particular area.

Factories: The Material of "Progress"

Developing neighborhood communities as ecologically balanced, self-managing entities appeals to underemployed ghetto dwellers, the "new earth" counterculture, and disillusioned school-age suburban youth as they are the least integrated into the centralized system of production. But for millions of Americans who are plugged in to the system through a forty-hour-a-week job and credit payments, the decentralized vision is seen as a threat to industrial workers.

The "community" to which industrial workers presently belong is the union, which is no longer a force for challenging the corporate system that has locked them into the earn more-pay more syndrome. Union structures have expanded into the same bureaucratic machines they once opposed.

The factory worker, whose life is tied completely to his job and who has no time to see his neighborhood as his "community," will be initially unreceptive to geographically-based community action for recovery of the environment. This means that the factory itself must be thought of as a potential community, from which working people can begin the job of dismantling centralized corporate control and reassembling geographically decentralized work places.

Young workers are already showing unrest in many places; they will take the lead in challenging the unions and educating their fellow workers to the alternatives. The following are both long-range ideas as well as immediate goals for industrial recovery:

Long-range ideas:

1. Production should serve, as much as possible, the immediate environment in which it is located, to scale down the need for wasteful long-distance transport of goods, and to fill the real needs of internally integrated communities.

2. Working people should regard the *kind* of goods they produce, and how much they cost in terms of environmental rape, as equal in importance to the size of their paychecks. Work will again regain its meaningfulness for many former production workers once the skills of the artisan and craftsman are favored by decentralized communities.

3. Work places should be scaled down in size, redesigned as multiple-use environments, and dispersed throughout communities so as to bring the job to the people, and not the other way around.

Short-term goals:

1. Industrial workers should insist on conversion to nonpolluting production methods. Along with all the other ecological reasons, a nonpolluting factor environment means that people can live near where they work.

2. Working people should insist on a reduction in working hours to give everybody more time to live in his community. People would then have more time to repair their own appliances, grow some of their own food, and mend their own clothes, rather than having to pay others for these services. They could spend less

money, and be able to get off the time-payment tread-mill; they would be *free* to consume less.

3. Work-connected facilities, such as day-care centers for the children of working mothers, should be located in the living neighborhood rather than at the central factory. Care should be taken not to strengthen corporate structures at the expense of the potential for community growth.

4. Certain entire trades should rethink their present role in the environment. For example, we do not need to harvest and process massive quantities of new building materials, nor build gigantic new housing and business complexes. The construction trades should modify their role to become expert dismantlers of unusable buildings and develop the art of *re*construction. Older union members could be retired, and the remaining members and new apprentices could go back to "school" (on-the-job training will work for this) to learn how to dismantle buildings efficiently, recombine the salvaged parts, and then go out into the community and teach building and dismantling skills to groups that want to build for themselves.

In the short run, a guaranteed annual income, new opportunities for cooperative work and individual craftsmanship within the community, less pressure to move up a salary scale in order to buy a second car to get to the faraway work place, or to buy a house outside of the middle city—all will mean a less desperate situation for the worker who feels threatened by talk of change.

But in the long run, it is questionable whether large factories can be scaled down and decentralized without dismantling the corporate investment and profit system. When working people begin to have a comprehensive vision of their lives as related to the environment, once they begin working for the short-range changes, they will figure out the answer to this question through their experience.

COMMUNITY LIBERATION: PROGRAM FOR SELF-SUFFICIENCY

We must now begin to integrate ecological reasoning into all community and political organizing for social change. What follows are suggestions for community recovery that necessarily start from where we are right now. Remember that education and action are one, for what is a tangible issue to a neighborhood and community becomes a bridge to people's understanding of whole earth ecology.

A. Make an ecological analysis of your city government. Compare how many vehicles are actually used to the number that are really needed. Find out how your city disposes of its garbage—how could it recycle its wastes? What kind of growth does your city's master plan indicate—how many people and cars *should* there be in your city? Analyze your city's budget. How much of it is being spent to destroy the environment?

B. Go over this list with your neighborhood groups (don't forget the PTA's, local churches, League of Women Voters, trades unions, Boy Scouts, student groups) and make your own list of things that people would like to do. To achieve many of these things it will be necessary to organize a nonprofit community development corporation. Such an organization will allow the community to consolidate its power in order to effectively challenge the downtown forces that will inevitably stand in the way of the community. We speak more about this process at the end of this chapter.

C. Mini-buses. By cooperatively operating a fleet of used vans and VW buses the notion of community carpools can be carried to its next logical extension. The amount of land and resources needed to move people around an urban area, by cooperative means is dramatically less than our present system uses.

D. Systematically close-off streets to plant growing things, fruit trees, vegetables; create play areas, day-care centers, and other community facilities.

E. Preserve the existing open space in your city for

community management and use. Unused urban land is our most valuable resource.

F. Lobby City Hall to freeze new downtown high-rises. "Progress" in the face of urban overload is no progress at all. Emphasize to the taxpayers that the claim by downtown that large numbers of highrise buildings will broaden the tax base is true but *misleading*. There is substantial historical evidence that as urban population increases, the amount of taxes that each home-dweller has to pay for city services (police, fire, utilities, schools) increases. At the same time the quality of these services decreases when they become overloaded by the new people crowded in.

G. Organize free marketplaces for exchange of locally produced food and new and used goods. Build them on interim-use vacant city land. Regular transitional use of land might mean that outdoor markets migrate from place to place in a community. Such a migrating market, combined with fixed neighborhood distribution points for items which can be stored for longer periods of time, might be integrated with neighborhood food-buying cooperatives. Neighbors on a block pool their money and make weekly orders for perishables and monthly orders for dry goods. The work of obtaining the goods and distributing them at the local distribution points is shared by the participants. Try to organize tool-sharing cooperatives on a neighborhood basis. Remodel old buildings or use recycled building materials for constructing day-care centers and housing for the elderly.

H. Reorganize educational facilities for multiple use. In many cases college students could recover classroom space for living space without disrupting the educational process. (Remember the original meaning of "college"?) The diversified use of classroom buildings might be one solution to the problem of student housing. Classes can also be held in living areas. Building occupations during campus rebellions have led in many cases to off-campus classes in apartments and freeform "counterclasses" in the buildings themselves—learning and living coexisted amicably.

I. Work for community control (and eventual ownership) of everything that isn't legitimately private property. The treatment of environment as a profit-making commodity is bad ecology. Form a tenants' union to work toward this goal, viewing housing as a basic material resource subject to community decision-making control.

Other business ventures by individuals and small groups might contribute to environmental recovery and control, turning over their profits beyond wages and overhead to the community-controlled corporation (see below for a full explanation):

1. Junk yard or "antique dealership."

2. Automobile wrecker: Try to recycle steel parts to something other than the automobile industry. Give customer preference to the guy who is trying to fix his own car rather than the parts department of an automobile dealer. Give special preference to old bus needs. New cars are bad ecology; used cars aren't quite as bad. New buses are better, old buses are best. We are thinking here, beyond the consideration of exhaust pollution, to the limiting of the production of new vehicles and reclaiming land from the automobile.

3. Garbage collection: You may be able to contract to the city to collect organic waste for slightly less than the going rate and then resell it after processing to organic growers or even to the city parks department. After explaining the benefits to city hall, try to set up a contract for one locality first, before taking on the whole city. If you are really clever, you may be able to get the city to fund the necessary neighborhood educational drive to separate organic and inorganic waste rather than having to do that without pay.

4. Small buildings wrecker and remodeling contractor: Contract to dismantle local buildings and stockpile recovered materials for resale or incorporation into your remodeling work. Get a drop-out architect and engineer on your staff.

5. Bicycle hospital and used-bike store. Call up your local police department. They find unclaimed stolen

bike parts all the time and could be persuaded to give them to this enterprise (especially if something with the moral purity of your local Y.M.C.A. or Boy's Club fronts this). The store can be set up in an old garage somewhere. One form is to get a bike repair freak and an artist to get it on together and paint big repair diagrams and instructions on the walls with the appropriate parts and tools hanging below each repair diagram. This way when somebody brings in a broken bicycle he can fix it himself.

6. Develop your own community development master planning department staffed by drop-out architects and ecologists.

There are several existing bureaucratic obstacles to community control of environment. The following is a check-list of powerful influences and institutions which will be obstacles.

1. Zoning: This is a tool used by downtown to protect its interests. It is designed to prevent neighborhood industry and multiple use of building space. To change the zoning laws in your city your community development corporation will have to have a broad base of political power.

2. Building Code: The Uniform Building Code is written and enforced by the International Conference of Building Officials. Building officials are usually retired building-trades union members and sometimes retired policemen who have special interests to protect. The Building Code has two general sets of criteria—performance and specifications. The specifications criteria are especially designed to protect the interests of the building industry.

3. Building Products Manufacturers: The building products manufacturers are protected by many specifications sections of the building code. Your community development corporation will have to pressure city hall to lift several of the specification requirements to allow community development of building space with recycled materials. Again, the C.D.C. will have to achieve considerable political strength to achieve this.

4. Building Contractors: When the local building contractors in your area discover your intentions to bypass them they will attempt to mobilize public sentiment against community development in the name of protecting the building trades unions.

5. City Planners and Traffic Engineers: City hall bureaucrats will resist the community development corporation's encroachment on the established decision making process. If a community has a strong and viable vision for their environment, there is no use for downtown planners.

6. Board of Realtors and Chamber of Commerce: City hall is under the influence of these interest groups which profit directly from the way that things are presently done.

To counter this strong exploitive process it is necessary to organize a body in the community that can effectively challenge downtown. Ad-hoc organizing will not have the strength to counter downtown interests for any length of time. This structure, which we have been calling the Community Development Corporation, will have to effectively confront—by power of numbers —city hall interests. This means citywide organization of the Community Development Corporation. If you live in a moderate or large city, greater than about 50,000 people, this will have to be a federation of neighborhoods—neighborhood communities which are geographically limited in size to allow direct participation in decision making.

The most effective mechanism for obtaining community control of the environment is to organize around specific issues in neighborhoods, getting media coverage of newsworthy events, and building energy to the point of an implicit threat of the possibility of direct action and confrontation in order to negotiate for community control. The community development corporation through its self-governing capability will be able to ritualize and maintain whatever control is taken from downtown.

Is America disposable? Cities, especially those parts

AMERICAN JUNK SCULPTURE

built since the Second World War, are junk. Ugly, dangerous, wasteful junk. So we might as well approach the junkpile creatively and experiment with the worst parts—the suburbs and downtown. Maybe some things will actually be carried out which will be so attractive that some healthy mutant form will grow out of and organically replace the junkpile.

If the suburban youth can attack their environment and their parents' values, if the established middle city neighborhoods and ghettoes can organize to take power away from downtown, if working people can replace wage-profit spiral unionism with decentralized co-operative control of production, if America can become conscious of her limits—then we can continue living our lives with some assurance that we are working towards recovery, rather than fear that the urban monster will continue eating up the delicate earth-life and finally die in overcrowding, self-pollution, and desolation.

As People's Architecture develops the community recovery program for Berkeley within the next year, and as the Community Development Corporation is formed from the city-wide coalition of PTA's, neighborhood lobbying groups, grass-roots political groups and other community-based organizations, we will most likely encounter many unforeseen conditions that will alter both the physical plan and the action program outlined in this chapter. We would welcome the opportunity to share our future successes and failures with people in other parts of the country who wish to attempt or who already have achieved the basis for similar programs.

If some of the more technical stuff in this article is wrong or if there are some other important things to add, let us know.

Write: People's Architecture, 1940 B Bonita, Berkeley, California 94704. Telephone: (415) 849-2577. (For God's sake don't call collect—we don't have any money.)

The Media and Environmental Awareness

Jerry Mander

It has occurred to me that I am employed in a dying industry.

Advertising is not dying out for any of the usually advocated reasons—immoral or distasteful behavior in the marketplace. Perhaps it should be killed for those reasons but it will not be necessary.

Advertising is a critical element encouraging an economic system committed to growth. Expanding technology is a by-word of political and economic rhetoric, and the country's economic health is judged by the rate at which Gross National Product increases, year by year.

The advertising business—based on a commission system—is particularly tied to the expanding economy. As long as expansion continues, ad revenues increase and so things would seem to be going along just fine for everyone. After all, as David Ogilvy, a well known ad man has pointed out, "Clients are hogs with all four feet in the trough."

However, there is only so much getting bigger possible.

That should have been evident, of course, the moment our astronauts flashed us pictures of the Earth and we noted it was round. The idea of an infinitely expanding Gross National Product on an isolated sphere, a finite system, an island in space, is complete nonsense, to put it as lightly as possible, or, to put it the way I personally perceive it, may be, together with population growth, the most dangerous tendency in the world today.

You simply may not have a continually expanding economy within a finite system: Earth. At least not if the economy is based upon anything approaching technological exploitation and production as we now know it. On a round ball, there is only so much of anything. Minerals. Food. Air. Water. Space . . . and things *they* need to stay in balance. An economy which feeds on itself can't keep on eating forever. Or, as Edward Abbey put it, "growth for the sake of growth is the ideology of the cancer cell."

Yet just the other day Mr. Nixon reaffirmed his faith in American industry's abilities to continue its "healthy" growth rate. And the president of U.S. Steel said he doesn't believe in "clean water for its own sake."

The first remark tells us that the patient hasn't yet noticed he's near collapse, and the second tells us that the cancer hasn't noticed it's running out of digestibles.

It will not of course be possible to ignore the disease much longer . . . not when whole bodies of water are dead, when species of fish and wildlife are disappearing, and now when forests are dying because of air pollution, with the oceans next on the list.

There *are* some hopeful stirrings in industry and we shouldn't be too surprised at that. After all, even a board chairman of a power company—no matter his politics and faith in the virtues of uncontrolled free enterprise—will feel some personal distress together with the rest of us when he finds that his weekend fishing isn't what it used to be. Dead fish.

So far, however, the response has remained very feeble and cynical at best, and destructive at worst. For the most part industry still sees pollution as primarily a public relations problem, duly assigned to P.R. and advertising men who are placed in charge of repairing the *image* rather than the cause. And so the company will contribute funds to conservation purposes

. . . a tenth of one percent of net profits, for example, which is to go towards fixing up the damage, one supposes, or else it's an incipient "stop me before I kill" phenomenon.

Or, the public is treated to the sort of ads that oil companies are now placing, explaining how their rigs in swamps actually preserve the wildlife and plantlife there by preventing other worse encroachment. Another oil company tells us in ads of research having to do with the throwing of old cars into the oceans. It does wonders for the fish, say the ads, who use the rusting hulks as new homes. No reefs necessary.

Well, even fish will make the best of a bad situation of course, as exemplified by the fact that in the dead waters of Lake Erie, there was recently discovered a new strange mutant of carp, which actually lives off the poisons in the water. Not good for eating by man yet, however.

We also see vast advertising expenditures for spectacular technological antidotes, appearing everywhere. The hottest growth industry is in the field of anti-pollutants, air cleaners, water cleaners . . . or high yield chemicals to get the soil to produce more than it naturally would . . . all of which in my own view, have the effect of reinforcing an already suicidal tendency in a society dazzled by technology's feats to believe that technology will itself cure its own self-invented sickness.

I am prepared to believe it can in some isolated cases, such as in capture of polluting wastes in some industries, but in general, I doubt that the answer lies with more technological innovation.

All this industrial hustle to fix things up by more and better gadgets and chemicals is just one more example of man forever bringing rabbits to Australia, as Dave Brower has described it.

The cure always causes a new scourge of its own.

Take antibiotics. According to some people, they will soon kill off enough of the weaker virus strains to leave us with only a killer virus.

Or high yield wheat strains. Though they do keep

some people fed for a bit, what else do they do? To the soil. To the wheat. To the people who eat it and to the plant life around it. We don't know, but I'm afraid we'll find out soon enough.

And now we find hundreds of thousands of advertising dollars being spent by companies girding themselves for the big gold rush in the oceans. The ads proclaim how everything in the world is just fine because of the "infinite" resources in the oceans . . . food and mineral wealth. They don't recognize, yet, that there is no such thing as infinity, and even if there were, industry's other hand is busily pulling infinity back in this direction by killing off the ocean's resources with DDT and garbage and a hundred other creations at a rate which is increasing faster than population.

I am prepared to bet that the ultimate answer to ecological problems is not cleverer technology. It will probably be less technology, at least of a certain sort, and I never would have thought five years ago that I'd be coming out on the side of the Luddites today.

Unlike them, however, I am not saying we should tear down factories, or that there should be no technology. Naturally. But I am saying there should probably be a lot less of it, and less people to be served by it of course, but most important, *less emphasis on increase, starting now*. Less emphasis on acquisition and material wealth as any measure of anything good.

Beginning now, national preparations toward a no-growth economy.

Not *no* cars. We are too far gone for that. But no new roads, say, starting today. And the beginnings of a national effort to de-glamorize automobiles and their so-called advantages. Eventually, I predict, we will have national control of auto manufacture . . . no *new* cars unless one is turned in simultaneously somewhere else. Like New York taxi medallions. Or liquor licenses. It seems as sure to me as that the Earth is round. And I believe we'll have a ban on auto company advertising, or at least that portion of it that encourages the sale of new cars or that has the effect of increasing production.

If I judge the developing public mood correctly, we are nearer to that necessity than most of us would have believed a few years ago. Maybe we will continue to have *some* legal auto advertising, but it will be strictly informative in nature—WE HAVE THESE FORDS HERE TODAY—or, if there is a God it will be something like the World War II slogan, IS THIS TRIP NECESSARY? It could happen, especially if auto companies purged themselves of all thoughts of annual style change—which encourages the more, more, more kind of thinking in society—and went for one high quality (expensive) very long lasting non-polluting model. And stabilized their production level. Either voluntarily, or because of government action.

The auto industry will of course not be the only industry to feel the bite when it finally gets through that Gross National Product is going to be stabilized, eventually, no matter what. All industry will feel it, but I believe the more polluting and exploiting industries will be the first to have their expansion curtailed.

It is not so important really that a computer manufacturer stabilize his production right now, but it does seem important that oil company expansion should be controlled, as well as power company expansion. Not no power, you understand, but no promotion of power and hopefully the beginnings of a mentality in the public mind of a stabilization of power levels towards a no-growth system. Even if power supply does not keep up with temporarily rising demand. The consequences of uncontrolled population growth and industrial expansion might then be brought home, literally; less power for everyone.

I think we will soon see public outcry against pushing of certain chemicals and detergents and certainly against all pesticides. I am already aware of movements to ban the ads of airlines and airplane companies. (It is certainly true that people who need to get from here to there will still manage to do so.) Similar movements are underway to ban ads of products which are sold in non-biodegradable containers, like glass; to ban the advertising of lumber company products and mining company products; and, in another vein, the advertising of furs of endangered species.

It seems to me that the trend got started with cigarette advertising, although cigarette advertising is demonstrably much less of a menace to society's survival and well being than lumber company advertising or chemical company ads. Cigarettes are only a menace to an individual person. Doubling of power, say, doubles pollution and thereby affects everyone, and we've no choice in the matter besides.

Lest it seem I am advocating the loss of a lot of good advertising talent, may I suggest that there may be *some* new growth industries to ease the strain. When power company ad dollars drop, perhaps the ad agency can keep going by a great big government subsidized campaign on behalf of the contraceptive industry. And the agency that had handled the Dow Chemical account could have the pornographic products campaign. And if the commercial media refuse to carry those sorts ads, despite the fact that promoting for pleasure in sex rather than procreation might just help the population crisis, then may I suggest that free air time be offered by NET for that sort of commercial.

Despite the inherent logic of all this to me, I do not expect many advertising people to come rallying round at the end of this panel to discuss how they might encourage a no-growth mentality. My late partner, Howard Gossage, in his last speech, put it this way: "Public service advertising as it is advocated and performed by the ad industry, is willing to innovate and alarm and cause controversy, but only within those elements of society who are *for* cancer or *against* safe driving."

Someone *will* come rallying round after this speech to tell me that my observations are idiotic, for the following reasons: 1) The economy will fall apart if we begin to slow down certain industries starting now, eventually striving towards a no-growth system, and 2) it is impractical, because the masses of people would never go for it. They "want" the fruits of technology even if it's poisoned fruit.

I have some answers, insufficient though they may be.

One. As I've said, I do not see the elimination of industry any more than one sees the elimination of North American Rockwell Corp. at the end of a wartime period. There may well be other things North American Rockwell can do besides making armaments but if not there are other companies which can.

Likewise, there are plenty of companies engaged profitably in non-polluting or exploiting industry, or at least not seriously so. Let *them* do the brunt of whatever growing is still left, until things finaly level off.

Also, it should be said, I am no economist and it will take an economist or a few thousand of them to figure out what this imminent no-growth system means— and I do mean it is imminent whether we like it or not, if you accept that the earth is round. While I don't know personally all the economic details, I do understand the consequences of *not* pulling back. You don't proceed over a bridge that will fall from your weight just for lack of another one in sight. The consequences of a short-run reduction in power, while population growth gets stabilized, which may mean that all of us will live with 20 percent dimmer light bulbs, strikes me as infinitely more desirable than no life in the rivers, or no oxygen in the air.

One more point in this area. I believe that the economic hardships which may accrue to society because U.S. Steel does not expand anymore, will only be hardships if, A) population and the work force continues to grow, and B) if society refuses to redistribute available capital and material to those who are currently deprived.

Two. Impracticality. These ideas are impractical only in the sense that it's impractical to remove one concerous kidney before it proceeds to the other. It's a painful and dangerous operation, but consider the alternatives.

Preparing the public for the changing facts of life is of course the major effort and requires every bit of media understanding and cooperation. And it requires every bit of professional advertising and public relations talent and a government commitment to use that talent for an effort on a par with, or greater than, the preparation of society to the end of a wartime economy, and I hereby volunteer my own office to undertake the ad campaign for the government, free, whether it's contraceptives or reduced power, if the government would only be willing to recognize the importance of both.

I don't think the communications problem is insurmountable. Great things were achieved during the Second World War when another sort of rationing became the absolute requirement. There are whole societies in the world who are very relaxed about enforced limits and it could be shown that they seem to be doing just fine.

I am speaking of people who have been born on and live on islands. I have just returned from the tiny islands in Micronesia and I can tell you that the natives there don't have any problem at all about understanding limits, or rationing of resources, or a no-growth system.

Micronesian "out-islander" in particular—that is, those who live across a hundred miles or more of sea from any neighboring islands, and whose contact with the rest of the world is limited to the few souls who arrive on the eighty foot government boat every six months—simply don't think about infinity, or to put it more accurately, the idea that everything is possible.

In order to survive out there by themselves, they've had to gain a pretty good feeling for pacing the breadfruit production and the coconut eating. In some of those places the highest crime is cutting down a coconut tree without communal permission.

And on the islands surrounding Yap—where a culture thrives that is as nearly untouched by non-island ideas as any in the world—there is a very rigid birth control which works this way: Everyone gets married very late—late twenties or early thirties. While there is no particular emphasis on virginity until then, there is plenty of emphasis and sanctions against illegitimate children.

No man will ever marry a woman who has given birth first, and consequently the ladies have devised an intra-uterine device made of hibiscus bark which works as well as the plastic ones and I'll bet doesn't cause cancer.

All the things we've been raised to worship—Man's limitless power, the ever-giving nature of Mother Earth —all those infinite possibilities are now beginning to seem less infinite. I'm suggesting that perhaps it's time to take as a model for our future survival-thinking and propaganda the way islanders have managed to do things, because that's what we're on, it's round, and there's only so much of everything and in general people haven't realized that.

At this moment we are totally unprepared emotion-ally, psychologically and technologically for the emerg-ing facts. We are very much in the position of two friends of mine who recently left their home in Chicago to move to the island of Oahu and who recently wrote me that they are suffering from a syndrome very com-mon to expatriate mainlanders. Island sickness. Every weekend they get in the car and drive clear around the island, maybe several times, hoping that some new direc-tion will appear, but it never does.

Our struggle is toward what the black studies demon-strators have called "reeducation." Develop an island psychology in everyone on Earth and if there are any young activist SDS hippie anarchist conspirators in the audience, I would urge you to go out and get your college to institute departments of green studies at once, and, while you're at it, put away the books on traditional economics.

If we can convey that notion, somehow, in a mass way, the islandness of things, we may have to live through some mass hysteria while people drive around (or fly, perhaps) aimlessly, but once they get the idea that it's all a big circle, the race may survive. (Nature will survive in any event, of course, since it is every-thing. If we all go under that won't stop the regenerative process, so let's be clear that it's people that are the endangered species.)

I never thought I'd be glad about the flight to the moon, but in spite of its absurdity, in my view, considering the other needs of the day, it may yet turn out to be the critically important thing from a conservationist's viewpoint, because *it* may accelerate the idea of Earth as an island; its finiteness.

It seems to me that if we can get enough pictures of earth taken from space, and the further away the better, the more the context will sink in. We are isolated in all that blackness. We can never, as a race, make it across that vast sea in time to find any new home. This is the only place we have and these people on this globe are our only possible friends and lovers.

We proposed once before in a Sierra Club ad the idea of an earth national park; a wildlife island in space, where *we* are the wildlife. It is our only possible home and perhaps we should practice thinking and talking about it in those terms and thinking of more ways to pass it along.

Eco-Pornography or How to Spot an Ecological Phony

Thomas Turner

Now that the environmental crisis is in the daily news and maturing in political sex appeal, panaceas are coming from curious sources—the ad agencies of the major industries that created the crisis. Advertising on television and in magazines reflects industrial awareness of the ecology crisis—and the urge to lull. So cover ads such as the following with grains of salt before reading.

Pacific Gas and Electric Company, the world's second largest electrifier (after Con Edison of New York), has advertised in four colors:

WE KEEP A SMILE ON MOTHER NATURE'S FACE

At the same time that it ran this ad the San Francisco-based utility was fighting conservationists who wanted to keep PG & E power lines out of nearby Briones Regional Park. PG & E alleged that the damage would be "merely visual." Concurrently, PG & E was digging a great hole in the ground at Diablo Canyon near Big Sur on the California coast to accommodate a pride of nuclear reactors. *That* smile suggests that Mother is having a miscarriage.

A few questions may help to defrock these advertising wolves.

1. Is (insert name of company) advertising in this voice to solve a problem or to prolong it?

Recent Reynolds Aluminum advertisements offer 200 dollars per ton of aluminum cans (40,000 cans) returned for recycling. Great! Far out! However, it is useful to reflect on the recent concern of some legislators on the nondegradable nature of aluminum cans, which do not rust as do tin cans. Was Reynolds backed into a corner by several states on the verge of outlawing use of aluminum cans altogether? One can be skeptical—or thank Reynolds for a good move and suggest still better approaches in recycling.

2. Does a press conference fog up what counts?

Recently both Ford and General Motors pledged (in press conferences) their best efforts to build automobiles that cause minimum smog. This naturally suggests that guilt about driving and poisoning the air is old hat, and all are free to use more and more of the present cars.

However, emissions from tank and tailpipe are only the tip of the pollution iceberg. To these must be added other ecological sins of the automobile—spread of highways and suburbia, carcinogenic particulate rubber from tires, asbestos pollution from brake linings, and tetraethyl lead. In the effort to diminish the identifiable pollutants not yet touched by smog-control devices, further poisons are already on hand as additives. No doubt additional poisons, as yet unidentified, will be introduced as time goes on. If the press conference has a high coefficient of haze, flunk the spokesman and his boss.

3. Does an ad obscure the issue?

A Shell Oil ad carried this legend:

LAST YEAR WE SAVED A LOT OF FISH FROM DROWNING AND MADE A LOT KIDS HAPPY

The ad went on to explain that Shell had removed the sudsing agent from some detergents. This, they said, improved the effluent discharged into streams and rivers.

Actually, suds don't pollute. Foam has always been easily handled by ecosystems. The soaping or detergent action is done by agents independent of the foam. So the removal of suds could amount only to elimination of the pollution indicator, while the pollutant itself is present as always.

Check it out. If the advertiser fails, tell him and your friends. The company can't pollute if nobody buys its products.

4. Does the ad sell pie before it is in the sky?

Atlantic Richfield (Arco) stated in an ad that they had sent agronomists to the tundra land in Alaska to find ways to heal damage done by the North Slope oil activities. But in a press release the same company revealed something not stated in this ad—that no one knew whether the exotic grasses would take. If they could grow there, it was possible that the alien plantings would do more harm than good. Even preliminary indications would not be forthcoming for months.

5. Is the ad really suggesting more dangerous alternatives?

Beautiful four-color ads by Atlantic Richfield have been running all over the place, saying that the automobile carcasses they dump into the oceans are providing wonderful new homes for fish. "Apartment houses," they say. In the same vein, the purveyors of nuclear power plants proudly point out that fish are drawn to the spots where their pipes return heated water to the oceans or rivers. Thermal pollution then becomes "thermal enrichment." Fishermen love it, they say. No more tramping all over the place to catch a limit.

What's really going on? No one can say for sure, but any artificial intrusion that upsets the life style of fish or any other creature surely has repercussions on the rest of the ecosystem. If perch can hide from their shark enemies in Atlantic Richfield's prefabs, what will the sharks do? Maybe they'll die of starvation, or maybe they'll regain their appetite for Southern California surfers. Similarly, so what if bass like warm water? What about water skaters and mosquitos and all the other folks who live and work and spawn in our waterways? We'd better be careful of all our citizens, not only the most visible, like fish—and men.

There are literally hundreds of ads these days, with approaches so varied that they are very hard to categorize. Some are frontal assaults that don't pull many punches, like recent full-page newspaper ads headlined:

A HANDFUL OF PEOPLE ARE PULLING THE PLUG ON AMERICA

A bunch of well-meaning but misguided conservationists, said the ad, have managed to block the construction of so many power plants in recent years that we face almost certain blackouts and brownouts in the near future. True, perhaps, but their solution is to override opposition and build the plants, when we insist and will continue to insist that the only viable answer is to use less power.

Somewhat more tricky are the gasoline company ads which claim that their motor oil is the least polluting of any available on the market. Fine, but a ten percent reduction in ten times too much poison doesn't make enough difference to matter.

One final question which applies to nearly every conceivable ad is "Should this problem really have been assigned to an adman, or should it have been sent to an engineer or an ecologist?"

It appears that these ads with which we are being bombarded are saying good things for the wrong reasons. O.K. Maybe the thing to do is just take them at face value, and force the companies to come across. PG & E claims to keep Ma Nature smiling—let's make them live up to that claim. Shell saves fish from drowning, they say—let's make sure they do.

Friends of the Earth is compiling a file of eco-obscenities, and if we're to have any effect, we need to know what's going on all over the country. Please clip bad ads and send them in along with your ideas for next year's book to:

FRIENDS OF THE EARTH
30 East 42nd St.
New York, New York 10017

In the meantime, here are words from a civilization that *did* keep a smile on Mother Nature's face:

CAVEAT EMPTOR

On How to Be a Constructive Nuisance

Harrison Wellford
(with assistance from James Turner and John Esposito)

Governments have been experimenting with solutions to environmental pollution for a long time. In the city of London in the fourteenth century men were put to death for violating a royal ordinance against the burning of coal in furnaces. In medieval Europe, in the American West of the nineteenth century, and in parts of India today, it has been a capital crime to foul local streams. In this country, it is safe to say that public sanctions against polluters are now somewhat less severe. In 1969 a Union Oil blowout covered the Santa Barbara Channel with three million gallons of oil and threatened an ecological disaster for the area. The blowout began in January; by June limited drilling in the channel resumed under authority of Walter J. Hickel, Secretary of Interior.

In July of 1969 this announcement was frequently heard on radio and TV in California: "The children of Los Angeles are not allowed to run, skip, or jump inside or outside on smog alert days by order of the Los Angeles Board of Education and the County Medical Association." These children were forced to observe this unique "rainy day" because photochemical smog, 85 percent of which is caused by automobile exhausts, had reached a critical level in the area.

Throughout 1969, the Department of Justice in Washington held a secret hearing to discuss with industry lawyers its charge that automobile manufacturers had conspired to stifle the introduction of smog-control devices on automobiles. On September 11, the department announced that it had entered into a consent decree, allowing the companies to escape federal sanctions by promising that they would not conspire any more. We have it on the best authority that no executions are expected in either case. Surely there are not many areas where governmental response to a technological peril reached its acme in the fourteenth century.

The failure of government and the intransigence of industry has made protection of the environment a cause where public concern about an impending crisis is matched only by public despair about what an individual can do to stop it. This feeling of helplessness carries with it the threat that, like the commuter on his daily freeway crawl, we will become indifferent through acclimatization, with pure water and clean air passing from the collective memory like a dream. Because Ralph Nader has a reputation as a man who gets things done in Washington, many people expect that he has some secret formula which can put an end to governmental paralysis and public helplessness in the environmental field. Nader has played a leading role in bringing new legislation for the protection of citizens from unsafe automobiles, exploding pipelines, impure meat and poultry, and gaseous coal mines, but there is nothing mystical or magic about his success. His pursuit of the public interest is a game everyone can play.

We shall summarize the chief characteristics of Nader's approach and then suggest some ways in which they can be applied to environmental problems.

WINNING CREDIBILITY THROUGH ACCURACY

First if you speak out for reform, you must remain free of special interests with axes to grind. Offers of support must be scrutinized to be sure there are no hidden ties. There must be no holds barred on the search for information or the use of it, even if personal financial sacrifice is required.

Second, you must do the tedious and unglamorous research which ensures that your reports are marked with the highest accuracy in the smallest details. Especially in technical areas, where established experts are quick to impute emotionalism to unestablished critics, all charges must be supported by a mountain of sifted evidence.

Third, you must amass the technical skills appropriate to the issue. Whether the problem is pesticides, auto safety, rural poverty, or air pollution, the vital issues are complex and technical. They demand the interdisciplinary expertise of doctors, lawyers, economists, scientists, engineers, and other people with special skills. Working together on task forces, such groups escape the narrow channels of graduate training and make sure that all sides of a problem are covered. The reign of the expert on environmental issues is one of the major defenses of polluters. The interdisciplinary task force concept gives credibility to research and allows the group to talk back to the expert in his own language.

Identifying the Equities

There are basic human rights at stake in environmental issues as well as social wrongs. The silent violence of pollution is an offense to moral values. Specifying the equities, the right and wrong of an issue, provides a yardstick for assessing blame and enforcing accountability of public and private officials.

Fuzzy judgments about the shared responsibility of government officials, the polluters and private citizens are simply inaccurate and encourge compromises which stultify reform. There is no natural law which gives companies the right to pollute. They assumed it and they should now bear the major burden of cleaning up after themselves. Moreover, insistence on the human rights at stake in the war on pollution helps bureaucrats get off the fence. The typical administrator sees himself as a man in the middle, an arbitrator between two competing interests. There is little incentive for him to seek out an abstract public interest on his own.

EMPIRICAL RESEARCH TO ISOLATE THE PRESSURE POINTS

The vital point of leverage in a policy arena is rarely apparent at first glance. It might be a government official or an entire agency; it might be a "recognized expert"; it might be a corporation president. Finding the point or points against which to apply pressure requires hard empirical research. Without this kind of effort, internal agency or corporate decisions which determine policy for millions will remain unrecorded history. Never has there been a greater gap between library research using printed documents and empirical research inside a decision-making body. The facts of vital decisions rest in the memories of participants, in interoffice memos which are never made public, in meetings at which no transcript is taken, and in telephone calls which go unrecorded. If one is investigating a public agency, it is essential to insist that one interview personnel all the way down the hierarchical chain. Exposure to the fresh air of citizenship has been known to make some bureaucrats hysterical, but it is the only way to break through the public relations curtain so carefully drawn by the top administrators.

We are convinced that the vital points of leverage in a policy area cannot be discovered at distance sitting in a library. For example, which public official has the greatest day-to-day impact on pesticide policy? Do we look for him in the Science Advisory Council in the White House? In the pesticide branch of the Food and Drug Administration? In the Pesticide Regulation Division of the Department of Agriculture? In the Fish and Wildlife Service of the Department of Interior? Or in some obscure congressional subcommittee? Even examining agency regulations setting jurisdictions is little help. There is an interdepartmental agreement which on its face gives the Food and Drug Administration, the Public Health Service, the Pesticide Regulation Division, and the Fish and Wildlife Service a shared role in seeing that pesticides are safe for people and their environment as well as effective in use. Only empirical observations of the agencies at work would reveal that Dr. Harry Hays, director of the Pesticide Regulations Division of USDA, routinely registers proposed pesticides over the objections of the Public Health Service and Fish and Wildlife Service. He has regarded the interdepartmental agreement as a dead letter. Still further research would reveal that none of the manifold agencies involved with pesticides feels directly responsible for testing proposed pesticides for long range effects, in order to prevent the introduction of new ecological time-bombs such as DDT and 245-T. For pesticides, PRD is the point of leverage on which environmental activists should focus. As a general principle, it is futile to rail against unpleasant outcomes if one will not take the effort to master the details of the policy process which yielded the outcome. You will always end up hitting the wrong target.

THE PROPER NAME APPROACH

A study of pollution which does not name the polluters and the public officials in their sway is destined for the archives before it has been read. While weakness in institutional structure may ultimately be the culprit, the temperament and values of individual personalities in the institutional slots have immediate impact on policy. Failure to hold individuals accountable allows them to substitute corporate irresponsibility for individual conscience. For example, Dr. Hays of the Pesticide Regulation Division of USDA must be made to realize that he will lose his comfortable obscurity if he continues to neglect evidence of environmental hazards in registering new pesticides. For the purpose of getting information from recalcitrant officials, the prospect of seeing their name in print and their actions exposed is more threatening than any law. How many environmental activists know the names of the chief polluters in their community: who is the head of the local plastics factory or public utility? On the national level, how many know the names of the men who run General Motors, U.S. Steel, or Union Oil? If pollution control is to come in time, the names of these men will have to become words not to be heard on the lips of children.

GETTING THE FACTS

On environmental problems, where there are so many *ex cathedra* claims to inside knowledge by putative experts, good information is absolutely essential. Environmental activists need reliable facts not only to inform themselves about where the problems are, but also to free public officials from specious information which convinces them that the problems do not exist. In challenging American intervention in the Vietnamese War, student critics were rebuked by their elders with the assertion that the American government must have secret information which justified its action. In the new war against environmental pollution, students now criticizing the *non*intervention of government are hushed by new claims of inside information, this time coming from scientists on industry payrolls, government officials with Ph.D.'s, and cost accountants adept at demonstrating (with appropriate graphs and charts) that pollution is an acceptable cost. The insiders were wrong on Vietnam and they should not go unchallenged on environmental issues. Charles Frankel, in a recent memoir on his service in the State Department, tells it like it is. "I used to imagine," he states, "when the government took actions I found inexplicable, that it had information I didn't have. But after I had served in the government for some months, I found that the issue was more complex: often the government does know something that people on the outside don't, but it's something that isn't so."

Pollution is a crime compounded of ignorance and avarice. Ignorance exists at the very top where men in high places daily make decisions about weapons, pesticides, and pollution tolerances with only a vague idea, if any, of their ecological implications. In his memoirs, the English Prime Minister Clement Attlee admitted that he concurred in President Truman's decision to drop the bomb without knowing anything about fallout or the genetic effects of an atomic explosion, even though the genetic effects of radiation were well known in the scientific community (and H. J. Muller had won a Nobel Prize for demonstrating war as far back as 1927). To paraphrase Clemenceau, war on pollution is too serious a matter to be left to the experts, whether they are prime ministers, presidents, or the head of PRD.

Environmental activists must get information, not only to arm themselves, but to disarm the experts. Like every act in the environmental field, however, this is easier said than done. After a summer spent investigating federal agencies we concluded that the "relationship between free access to information and responsible government is very direct. All of the agencies we have studied enjoy large discretionary power over the programs they administer. Under the agency's legal structure, they can go one way or another; they can delay action, decide what portions of the law to enforce or not to enforce, and even adamantly refuse to carry out programs mandated by Congress. These agencies are more agencies of discretion than of law . . ." (Quoted from *The People's Right to Know: A Status Report on the Responsiveness of Some Federal Agencies to the People's Right to Know about Their Government,* by Ralph Nader, Gary Sellers, Reuben Robertson, John Esposito, Harrison Wellford, James Turner, and Robert Fellmeth, published in the *Congressional Record,* September 3, 1969.) When the public doesn't have free and rapid access to information, the individual official exercising discretion often becomes progressively more attached to special interests. The reason is not far to seek. As Dean Landis pointed out in his *Report on the Regulatory Agencies to the President-elect in 1960,* "it is the daily machine-gun like impact on both agency and its staff of industry representation that makes for industry orientation on the part of many honest and capable members as well as staffs." If local and federal agencies are not to become simply service stations for pollution lobbyists, there must be countervailing pressure from environmental activists. The latent reformers in the agency must be given bargaining power with which to resist.

Unfortunately very little is yet known about the openness of pollution control agencies to public inquiry. At the federal level, citizens can invoke the Freedom of Information Act; but it has been our experience that this law, designed to provide citizens with tools for disclosure, has been regressively forged into a shield against access. Even after daily approaches with carefully reasoned requests, the Pesticide Regulation Division and the Federal Water Pollution Control Administration frequently denied us information, in blatant violation of the letter and spirit of the act. One can imagine the chances of a citizen writing in from Kansas or Oregon.

Examples of agency intransigence on access to information in the environmental field abound. Our water pollution study group asked the Defense Department for information about oil dumping. The Department of Defense has denied us access to information on the quantity of oil being pumped from the bilges of naval ships on the grounds that this data would be available only in a report containing operational data relative to military characteristics, which would therefore have to be classified. The Defense Department made no claim that the specific information requested was itself classified or in any way exempt from the Freedom of Information Act. The Defense Department is a past master of the "contamination technique"—take several doses of unclassified material that may prove embarrassing and mix them with other doses of classified information and, lo and behold, the sum is entirely classified. Civilian agencies have been quick to adopt this method.

The Federal Water Pollution Control Administration (FWPCA) has denied access to copies of research proposals that have been made to the agency but not yet accepted. The study group wanted this information in order to assess the research priorities at the agency, to determine whether there was any unfair preference by FWPCA and to see what reasons were given for turning proposals down. Frequently, information was denied on the ground that the information still had not been verfied or was in incomplete form. The FWPCA gave the latter as its reason for refusing permission to a student, after a ten-day delay, to see reports on the status of water pollution abatement programs at twenty federal installations.

This request for the status reports was made after FWPCA had denied more detailed information about the entire problem on the ground that this general data would give the researcher a "warped impression." At another time the same researcher was told that release of information would endanger Interior's relationship with the Department of Defense (DOD) "because DOD is finicky about releasing figures on total sewage." Presumably, if an enemy had that information he could rush to his abacus and calculate the manpower strength of a military base on the basis of its sewage. In any case, the FWPCA considers sewage from domestic military bases a national security matter. Perhaps it is coincidentally a national pollution matter that is the basis of the agency's reluctance.

More primitive responses come forth as an agency loses its last ready props for rationalizing the withholding of information. Relevant materials on pesticides in the Department of Agriculture disappeared, on the action of a high official, after students began researching them with permission at the Pesticides Regulation Library. The same materials had been routinely used by lobbyists for the pesticide industry before the students arrived on the scene.

We have tested these discretionary denials through negotiations with key agency officials, through talks with congressmen and reporters who take an interest in information policy, and through lawsuits in the federal courts. Generally the Freedom of Information Act has not been used by citizens to secure relief in the courts. Up to M rch, 1969, only three suits involving a clear claim by the public to information had been filed since the act became law on July 4, 1967. We now have six suits pending under the act. If they are successful, we hope to widen the scope of public access and set valuable precedents for groups who follow us into the federal agencies.

What advice do we have for environmental activists preparing to joust with public officials on information issues? First, remember that the citizen's right to know about his government is a frontier area of the law. Frequently public officials have a very vague idea of what the law allows them to do, but their motto, especially in the area of water pollution, is "when in doubt, deny." The only way citizens can check these discretionary denials is to challenge them in the courts. Often only the threat of a lawsuit will suffice.

Beware especially of denials based on assertions by public officials that trade secrets of private polluters are at stake. In the environmental field, the trade secret exemption, unless refined in the courts, is infinitely elastic in the hands of officialdom. A typical case recently occurred in South Carolina. A German chemical company, constructing a massive plastics and dyestuffs complex near Hilton Head, asked local conservation groups to accept on faith their claims that pollution would be controlled. To tell more, they said, would infringe on industry trade secrets. The state water pollution control authority concurred. With the ecological threat of pollution mounting daily, the courts may now be ready to balance the equities on the side of the public interest. Only challenges will tell.

Unfortunately, at the state and local levels, there is no Freedom of Information Act to invoke. Nevertheless there are several weapons you should employ. First, make "the citizen's right to know" a local issue, wrapping your rhetoric in the flag if necessary. Second, make clear to the resisting public official that you are in the anti-pollution movement for the long haul. This denies the bureaucrat his greatest defense—his ability to delay until his adversary gives up from exhaustion. Third, insist on interviewing public officials up and down the chain of command. Nothing is more unsettling to an administrator than the persistent anxiety that some unknown faceless subordinate is letting his conscience overcome his discretion.

Avoiding the Avenging Angel Syndrome

When national neglect of a vital issue stirs emotion, as environmental problems inevitably do, it is tempting to mount a high horse of moral indignation and approach all public officials with a "throw the rascals out" attitude. To do so is to squander opportunities for tapping the reservoirs of latent idealism which may exist in the agency. Many bureaucrats are secretly resentful at the compromises they feel forced to make. If not alienated at the outset, the prospect of outside support will give them strength to resist industry pressures. An ally, not an enemy, may result. No agency has a really solid front. There are always chinks in the mortar. It just takes time to find them.

Offering Constructive Alternatives

It is absolutely fundamental that if one criticizes an official for falling from grace, one ought to give him an opportunity to climb back. For example, it is pointless to call the director of the Pesticide Regulation Division to task because the Pentagon uses 245-T in Vietnam and deformed babies result. One must propose reasonable alternatives which are within the power of the official to implement. This keeps him from passing the buck, the occupational disease of all bureaucrats.

It is now time to make specific suggestions as to where environmental activists should focus their energies in the coming months. First let us consider the regulation of pesticides. The true federal government agencies most intimately involved with pesticide control are the Agricultural Research Service (of which the pesticide regulation division is a branch), and the Food and Drug Administration. Neither has even begun to do a creditable job in the field of pesticide control, though their legal mandate from Congress is clear and has been for years. In reports by the General Accounting Office and through investigation by Congressional committee, PRD and its director, Harry Hays, have now come under heavy attack. The Comptroller General of the United States in a September 10, 1968, report to Congress said that the pesticide regulation program of the Department of Agriculture was a virtual failure. These critical reports conclude that PRD is more concerned with protecting the chemical industry from the hazards of regulation than in protecting our health and environment from hazardous chemicals. If there is to be significant reform of pesticide regulation attention should be focused on the following areas:

ACCIDENT REPORTING

The first step in keeping pesticides from injuring people is finding out what pesticides are dangerous and for what reasons. PRD cannot take this step because it makes only a half-hearted effort to compile accidents reports on pesticides in use. An effective accident report would include environmental accidents, such as fish kills and the deaths of bald eagles and Perigrine falcons.

EVALUATION OF THE SAFETY
OF PROPOSED PESTICIDES

PRD's failure to insure the safety of marketed pesticides is primarily a failure of concept as far as the environment is concerned. PRD has an artificially narrow view of what factors constitute a pesticide hazard. Traditionally, it has focused on the immediate dangers to those people who come into contact with the pesticide. The long term dangers to the environment and wildlife from residual pesticides have been neglected. Long term impact on human beings through mutagenic carcinogenic and teratogenic effects have been referred to FDA or are ignored altogether

OVER-RELIANCE ON TEST DATA SUBMITTED BY INDUSTRY

At no point in the process of registering a proposed pesticide does PRD do any testing of its own. It accepts at face value data submitted by the manufacturer as to the safety and effectiveness of its product. As one PRD staffer recently told us, "the manufacturer runs the tests he wants to run, selects the results which are more favorable to him, and sends them to us. Rarely, if ever will PRD ask him to submit additional data." Ecologists are disturbed that industry tests the pesticide only for severely toxic effects on man and animals, ignoring the broader ecological consequences.

The Food and Drug Administration performance has been as ineffective as that of agriculture. FDA performs three functions in the pesticide field. First, it advises the Agriculture Department on the safety of pesticides being registered for use. Second, it sets tolerances for the use of registered pesticides; and third, it monitors the food supply to determine whether the tolerances are exceeded. It has failed in all three areas.

The FDA's advisory program on pesticide safety has not succeeded primarily because PRD has refused to cooperate. The FDA program for setting tolerances is caught in the middle of a scientific debate about excluding certain pesticides completely from food. The Mrak Commission on pesticides, which has presented a relatively conservative report on the control of pesticides to the Secretary of HEW argues that in some places, "carcinogenic response increases with increasing dose levels of the carcinogen." This view, which led to the recommendation that small amounts of cancer causing chemicals be permitted in the food supply, has been challenged by eminent scientists both inside and outside government. Such deep scientific controversy over so serious a problem can only make the consumer uneasy and ask for errors on the side of safety.

The FDA monitoring program is not only ineffective, but is scientifically controversial. The program has concluded that the amounts of pesticides in the American diet remain at safe levels. The methods used to reach this conclusion have been vigorously attacked by one FDA science advisor, who states that many widely used pesticides are left out of the testing altogether. The scientific insensitivity and regulatory failure of the FDA programs designed to ensure safe pesticide use, plus the total breakdown of standards in the Agriculture Department's pesticide registration program, explain how the silent spring is coming about and demonstrate that the public's reaction against pesticides has important basis

In the face of all this criticism there are now superficial signs that remedial action has been taken. In the pesticide area, the Department of Health, Education and Welfare has established an interim team to implement recommendations designed to ensure that only beneficial uses of pesticides are approved. The chairman of that team is Dr. Emil Mrak, Chancellor Emeritus of the University of California at Davis, and Dr. William J. Darby, head of the Division of Nutrition, School of Medicine at Vanderbilt University. We urge participants in the Environmental Teach-In who are concerned about pesticides and anxious to influence the industrialists who produce them to focus their attention on the Mrak-Darby temporary committee. It is important to study the background of Drs. Mrak and Darby in order to learn who they are likely to go to for advice, where they will seek support for their decisions, and the nature of the biases they may entertain. It may be important to know that Dr. Mrak took no action when members of his commission asked that the financial interests of all commission members be filed for review with the commission staff. This request was prompted by the belief of some commission subcommittee members that arguments were inspired not by science, but by thoughts of financial gain.

Dr. Darby is chairman of the food protection committee of the National Academy of Sciences. Dr Darby is on very close terms with what is called the industry committee of the industry liaison panel of the food protection committee. Recently his committee has been attacked for ignoring data linking cyclamates to deleterious effects on chromosomes. With these backgrounds Drs. Mrak and Darby may need a push from the concerned public if they are to be effective in clearing the environment of offensive pesticides.

In the fields of air and water pollution we strongly suggest that environmental activists experiment in a variety of forms to escalate the pressure for change. Using the methods which we have described, they should subject administrative agencies involved in pollution control to the most thorough scrutiny and monitoring.

There are also a number of additional roads which may open new fronts in the war on pollution. First, consider the courts. One of the country's leading environmental trial lawyers, Victor J. Yannacon recently said, "every piece of enlightened social legislation that has come down in the past fifty or sixty years has been preceded by a history of litigation in which lawyers around the country have focused forcibly the attention of the legislature on the inadequacies of the existing legislation." (*Christian Science Monitor,* October 2, 1969). The courts provide an arena in which industry lobbyists and indifferent bureaucrats are least able to exert their powers of dead center inertia. Because of this, the judicial approach to environmental issues may lead to immediate and surprisingly large-scale pollution abatement.

The class action is the most effective technique for demonstrating, by strength of sheer numbers, that the weight of the equities is on the side of environmental safety. A recent federal court decision held that the necessary "aggrieved parties" required by a class action may be environmental health groups such as conservation groups. Such groups may now become the vanguard for widespread courtroom attacks against environmental pollution. Some of the legal possibilities in this area are:

1. Product liability suits against automobile manufacturers—a manufacturer has a responsibility for injury resulting from the use of his product. This is a duty which extends to all persons who the maker should reasonably have expected to be endangered by its use. In the case of automobiles, that class of persons includes everyone who breathes the tons of carbon monoxide, hydrocarbons, oxides of nitrogen, lead and asbestos spewed out of automobiles annually. The medical evidence to develop cause-effect relationships is mounting. (For instance in a single year, doctors advised 10,000 people to move out of the Los Angeles area because of the smog problem.) Furthermore, there is mounting evidence that to put it as charitably as possible, the auto makers have not done all they could have to reduce the deadly emissions from their product.

2. Stockholders suits—stockholders could sue directors on the theory that the directors have breached a fiduciary duty to the corporation by using corporate profits in a manner which violates public policy. However, the pocketbook approach—namely that the corporation's failure to purchase and install pollution equipment may subject the company to large damage suits and possibly large fines—may have more force with the courts.

3. Actions against public officials—many public agencies with responsibility for pollution control are guilty of blatant non-feasance. The failure, either negligent or an outright violation of the law, are not difficult to uncover. In this area, investigation at any level will produce instances of statutory violations when unprosecuted—because of the whim or laziness of an official, or because of the political power of the scofflaws, or because of their superior access to agency personnel. When simple disclosure of a misdeed brings no reform, a taxpayer suit is eminently available and, on the basis of past experiences, highly effective.

4. Nuisance, trespass, and negligence suits on pol-

luters. These are the common law's rudimentary attempts to redress identifiable injuries caused by the external diseconomies of profit-seeking ventures. A more widespread use of these legal theories may prevent corporations from engaging in the calculus revealed in the statement of one Reynolds Metals Company executive that "it is cheaper to pay claims than it is to control fluorides."

In addition to pressure on the agencies and lawsuits, we urge activists to experiment with direct action: the pressure can be kept up on both government and industry by the use of dramatic devices designed to focus on responsible individuals. The following random list indicates a few of the techniques already being employed:

1. Polluter of the week award to local industry presidents

2. Picketing of automobile manufacturers, as was done with GM in New York

3. Returning food wrappings and empty cans to supermarkets

4. Handing out leaflets in traffic jams saying, 'Don't you feel stupid sitting here?"

5. Raising questions and offering resolutions at stockholder meetings regarding corporate policies on environmental questions

6. Regular training of spotlights on smokestacks belching noxious fumes in the darkness of night

7. Persuading citizens to sign thousands of petitions for intervention at public utility rates hearings

One recent example of this approach is the advertisement sponsored by the Campaign Against Environmental Violence in Chicago (see Appendix).

These are only a minute portion of the possibilities for direct action. As the Environmental Movement gains momentum, activists will develop many more effective techniques for dramatizing the crisis. They need be limited only by their imagination and their sense of outrage.

Eco-Tactics—Part I

Individual Action

As an ecologist at the Berkeley Ecology Center for the past six months I have had the chance to speak with hundreds of people. They all seemed to want to know three things . . . What is going wrong? Is there an alternative path? What can I do? This book is an attempt to provide some answers to those questions.

In the first part of the book we have tried to explore the nature of some of the causes and some of the possible solutions to the major problems in the environmental crisis. We have attempted to present a variety of suggestions that can serve as the basis for discussions during the Teach-In in April. We hope that active discussions will take place in hundreds of colleges and communities at that time and until the problems are dealt with.

In this section of the book we hope to provide some answers for the questions, "What can I do?" The last article in the preceding section serves as a good introduction to the section that follows. What can the individual do as a consumer, as a worker, and as a voter? It is clear that only a return to large scale citizen involvement at all levels can turn us from our destructive path. There are suggestions here for direct action, how to organize a group, what other organizations have done, addresses of major environmental groups, political platforms, and what services are available from the National Teach-In office.

Many land developers send out slick advertising which offers free trips to inspect their land-raping schemes. (For "land-raping schemes," you may insert "non-optimal land-use practices.") Take them up on it. Waste their money flying, wining and dining, you. Propagandize the uninitiated. If you are into media, film the whole scene and tape the sales pitch—it goes well with a light-show.

Mail in any prepaid envelopes you get in advertisements for ecologically undesirable products. Each one sent in costs the polluter about 7 cents of his profits.

Complain to the post office about any mail advertisements you receive that are ecologically obscene. The post office is required to have you taken off the mailing list, and this costs the mailer more than sending you the material in the first place.

When you go to the supermarket for milk, take an empty jug with you. At the check-out stand, pour milk from the disposable carton into your recycled jug, give the empty "disposable" carton to the checker, and explain your action to him. This type of action could be done with other goods packaged in nonrecycleable containers.

Conservation research organizations should be established to do research on the environmental effects of various products and practices. Such organizations could develop data on which companies produce the most pollution, so that pressure could be brought on offenders. They can encourage consumers to consider not only the quality of the product but also the total environmental effects of its production, distribution and disposal. How about an *Earth Housekeeping Seal of Approval* for products with no harmful side effects of production, use and disposal?

Convince nurseries in your town to provide information and sell publications on the control of pests without pesticides rather than selling pesticides. Encourage them to hire someone part-time to work as a pest-control consultant. (See Bibliography on pesticides and agriculture for references.) Boycott and picket uncooperative stores.

Service clubs such as PTA, Lions, Kiwanis, Rotary, AAUW and church groups can raise money to fund ecological jobs such as:

1. Gardening consultants to show people how to grow gardens without pesticides.

2. Advertising men to develop counteradvertising that shows the harmful effects of many products; advertise ways to free us from the grip of unnecessary products; and to seek free media time for public service advertising.

3. Environmental advocates or environmental defenders—lawyers to serve the public interest in a quality environment by prosecuting polluters and by seeking way to preserve environmental quality.

4. Ecologists to set up nature education centers, junior museums and community ecology centers to promote ecological reform.

5. Community-sponsored, ecologically oriented planners to design a transformation of the city by re-creating streams and parks where there are now concrete ditches, roads and parking lots.

Mechanized recreation, such as using snowmobiles, dune buggies, power boats, trail bikes and jeeps, is the epitome of a trend which is going in exactly the wrong direction. With our current population increase and the even greater increase in leisure time that people desire to spend in recreation, space should not be wasted. Mechanized forms of recreation use a much larger amount of space per person than do the simpler activities such as canoeing, hiking, cross-country skiing and snow-shoeing. On a given area of land, a large number of people can get high-quality recreation hiking or engaging in other nonmechanized activities; if they are replaced by people using mechanized recreational implements, the number of people that can be accommodated per square mile is much less. Ten hikers could share a mile of trail without getting in each other's hair. Nine hikers and one trail bike is a real bummer. Ten trail bikes on a mile of trail would be a noisy disaster.

Many organized groups are attempting to open up national forests and similar areas to mechanized recreation. Join with local conservation groups to keep land for people, not machines.

Press for the adoption of a responsible pesticide policy at local, state and federal levels, such as: "Since pesticides are poisons with many harmful ecological and medical side effects that are not yet fully understood, they should not be used except in the minimum amounts necessary for essential public health purposes and for the production of staple food crops needed to avert famine."

Many public officials will claim that this *is* the present policy. A few comments that can be made to them:

1. Why do we use pesticides on cotton when cotton is a surplus commodity and farmers are paid not to grow it?

2. Did our grandparents suffer more from eating an occasional wormy apple than we will suffer from pesticide residues on shiny, worm-free apples?

3. What possible justification is there for using pesti-

cides in the home garden where neither food supply nor disease is at issue?

4. Whereas it is clearly necessary to take some risks to avert famine and plague, is even the slightest risk acceptable for growing ornamental plants? The U.C.-Berkeley campus has one man employed full-time to spray the campus, which consequently reeks of chlordane and other poisons. Is this the case on your campus? Should it be tolerated?

5. You may hear that there is no evidence that a particular pesticide is harmful to humans. Ask if there is positive evidence that the chemical is not harmful to humans. If the answer is yes, ask what kind of experiments have proven that the chemical does not cause a one percent increase in the leukemia rate. If you get an answer, ask a statistics professor if he believes the figures shown by the experiment.

Now that DDT and some other chlorinated hydrocarbon pesticides are being banned, the homeowner is left with bottles of difficult-to-dispose-of chemicals. A good project for local ecology groups would be to arrange for the collection and disposal of unwanted poisons. The public should be cautioned not to put poisons down the toilet, in the garbage can, or into a home incinerator or fireplace. Each of these results in the release of the poison into the environment. The poisons should be disposed of by chemical oxidation or incineration at very high temperatures (at least 1300° F.) under competent supervision. Try to arrange with local industry, especially those that produce pesticides, or government agricultural or health organizations to use their incinerators (if adequate in design and temperature) for disposal. Get fire stations or other public offices to act as collection stations. Also make door-to-door drives. But sure the agencies are really disposing of the poison. In California, announcements were released asking people to take unwanted DDT to county agricultural agents, but investigation showed that they were just putting the stuff into garbage cans.

This sort of campaign can have great benefit beyond the safe destruction of the poison. People will become aware of the dangerous nature of pesticides and the need for extreme care with them. They may also start asking questions about the responsibility of industry to arrange facilities for the ultimate disposal of dangerous products, wasteproducts, and so on.

All detergents are now said to be biodegradeable, but they are still causing problems for two reasons. First they only truly degrade when plenty of oxygen is available which is not the case in many older types of treatment facilities. Second, the phosphorus from the detergents causes water pollution. The best thing to do is use soap like Ivory Flakes. It does an adequate job and even comes in biodegradeable cardboard boxes instead of plastic bottles. When we suggest this we often hear, "But my glasses will have soap-scum." It's time to start making some hard choices. Do we want sparkling rivers or sparkling glasses?

Christmas has become a materialistic environmental rip-off. In simpler times Christmas may have been fun, with Christmas trees decorated with popcorn and berries, sleigh rides, snowmen, mistletoe, stockings full of oranges, apples and chestnuts. Now, beginning before Thanksgiving, we are bombarded with advertising: "30 more buying days until Christmas." We must buy, we must consume. This materialism has made Christmas into a tranquilizer-salesman's dream.

This can be one of the many trends that the environmental revolution completely reverses. Let's start with the Christmas tree. Why should we rip off Christmas trees from acres and acres of land to sit in houses for a few days or weeks and then throw them into the trash heap to become part of our solid-waste problem? How about using live trees instead, if we use trees at all, and then planting them in some area reclaimed from the automobile?

If possible, use vegetation native to your area instead of exotic trees grown in some distant place. This makes a lot more ecological sense for three reasons. First, native plants are more resistant to pests because they've lived in the area all along and are adapted to the insects in the area; they won't require pesticides. Second, they are adapted to the climate of the area and won't require any special care or any watering. Third, the animals native to a given area are dependent upon the plants native to that area for their food and shelter. Exotic plants may not be suitable to the needs of the animals indigenous to your area.

About presents: it seems that most people spend a lot of time rushing around frantically trying to get a present for each person they feel obligated to. Instead of buying more and more possessions, why not donate money to organizations that are working actively for the kind of world your friends would like to live in? Donate money to Friends of the Earth, League of Conservation Voters, Zero Population Growth, the Wilderness Society, Nature Conservancy, Sierra Club, Planned Parenthood/World Population, Citizens Against the Sonic Boom and other groups working for a world that has the quality we would like for ourselves and our children.

Residential subdivisions are often a drain on a city's resources—they require more expenditures for schools, roads, police and fire protection, than they pay in taxes.

Have economics students check this out for specific existing or proposed developments in your area. Prepare alternate development plans such as cluster developments which have less need for services, waste far less land in roads and utilities, are cheaper to build for a given quality of dwelling, and provide a higher quality of living.

People for Open Space, 126 Post Street, San Francisco, California has done a detailed report of the economic benefits of preserving open space in the San Francisco Bay area and concludes that the direct *economic* benefits are so great that all available open space should be acquired as soon as possible. Write for their report to use as a model.

Fighting threats. The Apperson Ridge controversy illustrates many actions people can take. A permit was requested by the Utah Construction and Mining Co. to quarry basalt on Apperson Ranch in Alameda County. The ridge overlooks a good part of Sunol Valley Regional Park, a wilderness park typical of California coastal oak woodlands, little of which is available for public enjoyment. The park is easily accessible for camping and hiking from Oakland, San Jose, and other population centers.

Concerned individuals formed the Save Apperson Ridge Committee. With the East Bay Regional Park District, they lined up 102 city government, conservation, sportsmen, and civic groups and collected over 21,000 signatures in opposition to the quarry. The permit was fought before the County Planning Commission and the Board of Supervisors in terms of the necessity and benefits of undisturbed parkland; the effects of quarrying on visual quality, and ecology; and the destructive aspects of noise, dust, vibration, movement, lights, and gravel trucks on public roads. Also questioned were estimates of value and need for basalt, tax and job benefits, and trusting Utah Mining to meet conditions.

At the hearings, representatives of groups emphasized public opposition. Individual testimony was valuable when people spoke to specific points from their own experiences, or raised good questions. Testimony by acknowledged experts was mainly handled by the park district, but individuals giving proficient discussions on their own were also effective. In similar fights, people should try to round up experts for witnesses if no agency in opposition is providing them.

The committee tried getting the chairman of the board to disqualify himself because the applicant's lawyers had contributed to his past campaigns. This information was found researching election code statements—public records in the county courthouse. The chairman refused but was forced to be careful running the hearings. The public was watchful for dealings such as the unsuccessful negotiations between Utah Mining and the park district in which land exchange, cash settlement and percentages of profits were considered in exchange for the district dropping its opposition.

Actions for individuals and groups other than mentioned above included slide shows and talks before groups; letter-writing to commissioners, supervisors, and newspapers; sponsoring trips to the area; circulating literature; attending park district discussions; distributing bumper stickers; and getting articles published in local papers.

Last-ditch actions. When damaging permits are granted, one can attempt to prevent the operation in hopes that it will be dropped due to expense, adverse publicity, or some higher agency overturning the decision. Examples of such actions are the Santa Barbara fleet of private boats hovering over oil company drilling sites, and participation of the general community in stopping bulldozers to protest the paving of Tamalpais Creek in Marin County.

Ideas for eco-pornography displays: Pair ads for "modern conveniences" with pictures of the environmental destruction caused by the mines and power plants necessary for the existence of the "convenient" appliance.

Once ecologically sound households are established in your area, take a photograph of a week's garbage output by an ecologically sound versus a normal middle-class consumption household.

Keep a bulletin board of the month's best eco-obscenity or eco-pornography (see article on eco-pornography). Many advertisements by utilities, automobile manufacturers, oil industry, real estate speculators, and appliance manufacturers are gems.

Keep a chart of politicians' statements and actions, such as Nixon's statements on ending pollution and his go ahead on the SST. Give a prize to the most contradictory person of the month.

Ecological activities should be consistent with the points you are advocating. Make your ecology pins and posters out of biodegradable materials such as scrap wood; avoid the irony of metal buttons reading "Don't waste our natural resources" and bumper stickers that proclaim "Ban the automobile."

Make sure any ecology meetings, such as the teach-in, are internally consistent ecologically. Don't criticize Reynolds for making aluminum beer cans if you use them. Don't use plastic "disposable" cups and tons of paper "information." Serve food that represents a fair share of the world's food for each person.

During the teach-in, set up a book-stand selling paperback books on environmental problems to raise funds and get information out. See the Bibliography for suggestions. Persuade your campus bookstore to set up a year-round ecology book section. Some bookstores have set up a Survival Section displaying the books in the Bibliography.

Suggestions for the Schools

Gary C. Smith

First let me say that I think it would be desirable if some of the preliminary assignments could be started *well before* your teach-in. For instance, your art classes might hold a poster-design contest, starting very soon and climaxing during the April week with displays in every classroom. Your English classes could assign outside reading at once, with book reports to be read in class during the April week. Your manual training classes could start soon to construct some sort of central display (perhaps designed in an art class) for erection on campus in April. And so on.

Here are some thoughts for projects for various classes:

Art—See above. Also make charts to illustrate other classes' findings.

Biology—Compare elimination of predation and consequent overpopulation of animal species (e.g. deer) with health advances followed by overpopulation of human species. Investigate other examples of natural balance (perhaps with field trip). Discuss methods of contraception.

Chemistry—Catalog sources of pollution in your area. Discuss chemistry of chemical contraception.

Economics—Investigate key to affluence. (If it were mere numbers, China and India would be best-off countries. Obviously, instead, a free, able-to-save-and-buy citizenry is more important.) Compare rates of population. Growth of various countries with rate of GNP growth; where former exceeds latter, living standard declines.

English—Read (perhaps as outside reading, with book reviews given in class) Malthus, Ehrlich's *Population Bomb*, Paddocks' *Famine 1975*, Rienows' *Moment in the Sun*, any of the Sierra Club's Wilderness Conference books.

History (U.S.)—Consider changing attitudes toward birth control; compare statements on subject by Eisenhower, Kennedy, Johnson, Nixon. Consider changing attitudes toward wilderness: once it was something to be defeated or tamed, now becoming something of which remnants should be cherished.

History (World)—Trace population growth in various areas of world. How and when did Europe stabilize? Why are some nations losing the race? Which most serious?

Mathematics—Provide illustrations of geometric progressions *vs.* arithmetic progressions to illustrate Malthusian principle. (Perhaps two series of jars containing marbles.) Calculate some of the horrors that will take place if breeding isn't slowed (e.g. weight and volume of humanity in 3000 AD at present rate of increase).

Psychology—Study (perhaps experiment with) effects of overcrowding, noise, air pollution, etc. on laboratory animals.

And so on, for the other classes. Perhaps student clubs could be brought into the act too. If there's a photography club, it could photograph and display the sources of pollution in your town. If there's a school paper, it might run an ad or do a series of articles. If there's a dramatic group, it could put on a conservation play, like Maxwell Anderson's "High Tor." If there's a movie projector and auditorium available, films are available through Planned Parenthood, the Audubon Society, the Sierra Club and other sources listed in the Film Bibliography.

Curriculum for Cubberley High School— Curriculum for the Nation

This rather pretentious title supports the growing conviction of many that environmental survival over the next twenty-five years depends critically on the environmental awareness of the high-school students who graduate within the next five years. The response to this challenge of two particularly creative high-school seniors, Claire Boissevain and Jim Harding, both of Cubberley High School in Palo Alto, California, is presented in the following words, compiled from their notes and from conversations with them during the several weeks that it took them to prepare their ecological awareness program.

Why is it so important to develop environmental awareness in high school students? Because high school reaches all but the most disadvantaged youth, including those who do not go on to college; because the first years in college should not be wasted with introductory concepts that can easily be taught in high schools; because eighteen-year-olds will soon have the vote; and because we high school students *want* to know how we can contribute—*now*—to the quality of the world that we shall live in for the rest of our lives.

In response to these motives, we are preparing an "ecology awareness program" to be a workshop aimed at the April 22 Environmental Teach-In—the first national day of environmental concern. We hope that this can be a model for other high schools to consider, because we are calling for the second annual national day of environmental concern in 1971 to be oriented primarily toward the high schools. By including ourselves this year in what is mainly a college effort, perhaps we can show the value of high school participation next year.

Palo Alto High School, another in our city, recently held an antipollution forum, in which speakers representing both sides of several pollution issues presented their cases for student consideration. The organizers of the forum (Jack Daiss, Pam Pedersen, and others) worked extremely hard to present a balanced program. They wanted to introduce their classmates to some of the primary forces that cause pollution, to help them see areas in which solutions can be found, and to motivate them to seek these solutions.

But the Palo Alto High School program was voluntary, and barely 200 out of senior-high student body of 1,500 felt it worth their while to attend. Only those who were already concerned were reached, leaving 1,300 students who were untouched by this excellent program. Further, there was no follow-up to the forum—no continuity to the efforts resulting from the forum.

We chose to make our ecology awareness program mandatory. With a senior high enrollment of 1,200, this challenged us to offer considerable variety. And we wanted to frame our program so that it would be a beginning, leading to efforts that would extend through the rest of our school year, hopefully producing some useful results.

Here is why national environmental day of concern, or an environmental teach-in day, is of such value. Our environmental program, slated for January, becomes a workshop, focused on developing ideas and activities that will grow and carry on, culminating in April on the teach-in day. Instead of just listening to speakers for the educational values of what they have to say, we shall be evaluating what they say, and participating in debates and seminars, in order to define what we can do and what programs and changes we should call for. And the cooperation of our teachers in all of this, certainly to the extent that large portions of the class work after the ecology awareness program are devoted to pursuing ideas introduced during the program, will assure the continuity of our efforts.

Although any program should be developed by the students from their own ideas, let us describe ours as an example. The program will be three days long, from January 26 to 28. Each day there will be a principal speaker to help focus attention on some of the issues. David Brower, president of Friends of the Earth, will open the conference Monday morning. Stephanie Mills will highlight the population discussions in her talk on Tuesday. And Dr. Donald Aitken, Stanford University physicist and a director of Friends of the Earth, will sumarize the three-day program in a talk on Wednesday afternoon on "Where do we go from here?" Dr. Aitken's talk will be based on his appraisal of our performance over the three day program.

These talks will be to assemblies for the entire student body. For the rest of the time there will be forty seminars, field trips, and movies, all repeated on an almost continuous basis for the entire three days. Although attendance during the three days is compulsory, the students will select which seminars they wish to attend, and work out their own time schedules in advance of the program. Each student must think of what he wants to do, or what he might want to learn, ahead of time. For example, does he want to learn all aspects of a single issue, such as the San Francisco Bay, or does he want to learn something of several issues, to see how different ecological problems are related? This is his choice.

Here are some specific examples from our agenda. A population debate will be offered, featuring a woman with thirteen children who opposes population control. A pesticide debate will be offered, featuring a defendant of DDT. Oil companies and electric utility companies will be on hand to defend their policies.

The field trips will include a Bay-walk ecology tour; a trip to Half-Moon Bay to pick up trash from the shore and to analyze the types of containers and other articles that contribute to the greatest amount of litter; and a trip to the DuPont factory in Antioch, to inspect their recent installations of antipollution devices, as well as to ask questions about their general program.

The seminars will cover fields represented by the discussion leaders. Among these will be our own teachers, outside conservationists, and county officials. Subjects covered will include ecology programs for high schools; high-school student participation in local political decision-making and in community conservation activities; technical aspects of certain types of pollution control; legal aspects of environmental defense; and other subjects along these general lines.

The program will be closed by a pantomime presented by the Ecology Action Theater group from the University of California at Berkeley. In pantomime, this group traces the entire cycle of ecological destruction from plants to fish to animals to man. At the end, a human machine is formed which is about to destroy the last life on earth. The students themselves must run from the audience to stop the machine, symbolic of the urgent need for our own participation in the global environmental battle.

Our goal in this program is fivefold: 1. we want to set a precedent for future workshops of this type, especially for the high-school teach-in for 1971; 2. we want to impart an awareness of the dependence of man on his environment to every student in the school; 3. we want to motivate our classmates to involve themselves in the preservation of the environment; 4. we want to make legislative recommendations to our legislators for action; and 5. we want to offer curriculum additions to our own school, to provide a long-term benefit resulting from our first efforts this year.

Material resulting from our studies initiated by the program will be assembled, along with photographs from the program and from the field trips, into a book for action. This book will be released on April 22, when we will send it to all who might be affected by our suggestions.

The only missing ingredient is the assurance that *you*, the high-school student reading this, will join with us this year, on April 22, in calling for the second annual day of environmental concern in 1971 to be directed at an environmental teach-in for high schools, and to join with us next year in developing programs that focus the national attention on what we can do in the high schools to help keep the earth a nice place to live on.

Applied Eco—Tactics

Boston Ecology Action distributes this leaflet at supermarkets and large department stores.

Packaging=Trash

The packaging you take home today becomes trash tomorrow. This is costing you in terms of dollars and health. Packaging can be deceptive, disguising product contents. Packaging increases the cost of the products you buy. By converting trees to paper, it upsets the forest life-cycle. You must pay high municipal taxes for trash disposal. When packaging is burned in building incinerators and city dumps, it contributes to air pollution. Burning paper gives off carbon monoxide and particulates. The new polyvinyl chloride (plastic) packaging materials, which have just been cleared by the FDA for food packaging, are even more dangerous as their incineration produces hydrochloric acid, a very toxic substance. All of these pollutants irritate your eyes, nose, throat, and lungs.

Fight Trash and Pollution

Carry a bag or basket with you. Don't accept unnecessary paper bags. Remove excess packaging (like boxes around bottles and toothpaste tubes) at the store and ask the sales personnel to return it to the manufacturer. PASS THIS ALONG TO A FRIEND.
Ecology Action 925 Mass. Ave., Camb.

(For more militant action, take your own containers to the supermarket, empty the products into them, and leave all commercial packaging at the counter.)

Subway Action

The following is a mini-leaflet that is handed out to passengers on subway cars. It stimulates discussions and generally raises the spirit of an otherwise dull subway ride.

Go ahead. Read this. You don't have to watch the road the way you do when you drive the car.

CONGRATULATIONS!

By riding public transportation, you are helping to solve some of the major pollution problems plaguing Boston.

1. *AIR POLLUTION.* Motor vehicles powered by internal combustion engines are responsible for over 80 percent of the deadly carbon monoxides as well as the cancer-causing benzpyrene and nitrates in the air. Eighty-nine percent of the vehicles on the road in Massachusetts are privately owned and are often operated with only one person in the car. If people would use public transportation instead of their cars, air pollution levels could be significantly lowered.

2. *SPACE POLLUTION.* Thirty percent of the land in downtown Boston is devoted to cars. Where there are garages, there could be gardens. Where there are highways, there should be homes and places to work and play.

3. *NOISE POLLUTION.* Studies show that people today show a greater hearing loss with age than ever before. Much of this is due to honking horns, loud engines and general traffic noise.

The cost of a personal car is high to the individual. The average person pays about $2000 per car per year in depreciation, gasoline, insurance, taxes, and maintenance. *But for society as a whole, personal cars are a luxury we cannot afford.* We pay in death from auto accidents, in poor health from air pollution, in loss of hearing from noise pollution, and in the destruction of our cities by the ever increasing number of highways.

HOW YOU CAN HELP:
1. DO NOT DRIVE IN THE CITY.
2. Walk, whenever possible, or ride a bike.
3. Use public transportation.
4. Oppose legislation calling for more highways in the cities.
5. *Support legislation for improving public transportation facilities.*

For further information, contact Boston Area Ecology Action, 925 Mass. Ave., Cambridge, 876-7085. Please pass this on to a friend. RECYCLE THIS PAPER.

Environment Hot Line

This is an example of a 3″x5″ card which is useful for turning in polluters whenever you see them.

Most people don't know the channels that exist in the system to control polluters. Boston Ecology Action hands out a card with numbers to call for each type of antiecological action. Try it in your community.

Air Pollution—General (smoke, odors, burning dumps). Mass. Dept. of Public Health, Metropolitan Air Pollution Control, Frank Reinardt *727-5194*
From motor vehicles. Registry of Motor Vehicles, Joseph Hourihan *727-3185*
Noise Pollution—From airplanes. Mass. Port Authority, Thomas P. Callaghan. *482-2930*
From motor vehicles. *Write* to Registry of Motor Vehicles, Dept. of Selective Enforcement, 100 Nashua St., Boston and *give registration number* of vehicle.
Water and/or Oil Pollution—Mass. Dept. of Natural Resources, Water Pollution Control, Thomas McMahon *727-3855*

Environmental Law Societies

Students from ten law schools across the country recently formed the National Environmental Law Society. The purpose of this national organization is to coordinate the efforts of local environmental law societies which have recently been established at several law schools, and are presently being organized at many more.

Environmental law societies on law campuses provide students with an opportunity to aid attorneys who are bringing suits concerning environmental issues, and to assist groups working for needed legislation. For example, students at George Washington Law School in Washington, D.C., prepared the suit brought by G.A.S.P., Inc. against pollution by municipal buses. Stanford ELS members helped attorneys prepare a suit which was recently filed against Stanford University to halt industrial development in the Coyote Hill area. These extracurricular activities are closely linked with the establishment of new courses in environmental law which are fast becoming a regular part of law school study.

Initially, the National ELS will publish a regular report on the activities of the member societies. It will also coordinate local efforts on problems of national interest such as a concerted legislative and constitutional attack on antiabortion laws.

Address: National Environmental Law Society, Stanford, California 94305.

Furs Look Better on Their Original Owners

Would you please help lead a fashion revolution by taking a simple pledge that you will no longer buy furs and other *wild animal* products?

In the past many of us have purchased and enjoyed wild furs. However, what was once innocent is now ecologically inappropriate. In today's changed circumstances, the survival of many wild creatures requires that we change to fit the times.

At stake is the survival of many species of wild animals. At least 861 species and races of mammals, birds and reptiles are now in danger of extinction. All wild creatures are subject to increasing pressures from different sources: the loss of space to live; the loss of life itself through pollution, direct poisoning and hunting; the taking of specimens for zoos, the pet market and large scale research. If you add into this already unbalanced equation the incredible demand for skins, fur and feathers, prompted by the fashion and interior decorating market, then the outlook for wild creatures is very grim indeed.

We hope you will sign the following pledge and mail it to Friends of the Earth, 30 East 42nd St., New York, New York 10017.

Because of the mortal threat to the wildlife species of the world posed by the exploitation of wild creatures for their skin, fur and feathers; I pledge that I will not in the future purchase these products or promote this use of wild animals.

A rough tabulation of some of the pelts offered for sale for ten months during 1968-69, as reported by *Women's Wear Daily,* yield the following figures:

178,656	Red Foxes
43,931	White Foxes
107,381	Raccoons
881,614	Squirrels
4 to 5 million	Muskrats
774,287	Beavers
17,915	Otters (The ban on hunting sea otters was just lifted —they have been protected since 1911 to save the species from extinction. The Alaskan population is estimated at 50,000 animals.)
540,000	Seals were taken from the Gulf of St. Lawrence alone
85,782	Wild Mink were killed
64,481	Lynx
23,702	Prairie Wolves
4,350	Timber Wolves (The total timber wolf population of the Canadian Northwest is estimated at less than 3,000 animals. Timber wolves are considered an endangered species by the U.S. Department of the Interior.)
7,104	Fishers
2,490	Badgers
2,996	Black and Brown Bears
79	Polar Bears (Polar bears are listed as an endangered species.)
28,700	Martin (Pine martin are becoming scarce)
94,488	Opossums

510   Leopards (5 species of leopards are listed as rare
       and endangered. An estimated 7,000 skins a year
       are illegally shipped from Tanzania, Uganda and
       Kenya.)

Ecology Food Store

The impact of the "supermarket" on the ecosystem is
in large part destructive. Most of the garbage from our
households is packaging, containers, nonreturnable bottles, and cans that come from supermarkets. Virtually all
food sold in supermarkets contains combinations of
pesticides, preservatives, additives, stabilizers, etc. Most
cleaning agents sold in supermarkets are not biodegradable and contain phosphates that pollute the water.

An *Ecology Food Store* is an ecologically sound alternative to the supermarket. One is scheduled to open
in Cambridge, Massachusetts, in early 1970, sponsored
by Boston Ecology Action. It will follow these guidelines:

1. It will be a nonprofit store staffed by volunteers who
   will live on free food from the store.
2. It will sell organically grown foods, free of pesticides
   and preservatives.
3. All packaging and containers will be recyclable. Returnable bags and containers will be available at the
   store.
4. It will sell biodegradable soaps.
5. It will distribute the *Household Ecology Handbook*—
   a guide for running a household in a way least destructive of the environment.
6. It will sell handmade products or products that are
   made of recycled materials that are useful in the
   home.
7. Books—such as the *Whole Earth Catalog,* natural
   foods cookbooks, etc.—will be sold.
8. The staff will always be available for household
   ecology counseling.

The overall effect of the *Ecology Food Store* should be:

A. To support local organic farmers and bakers and to encourage more people to use organic methods by providing a market for organic products.

B. To provide an opportunity for people to actually use an alternative store based on recycling principles.

C. To counsel people on how to apply in their own homes the recycling principles they find in the store.

D. To provide an effective means for boycotting and eventually transforming existing "supermarkets."

Survival Walk

Cliff and Mary Humphrey

We have found in the closing moments of the sixties that many people are willing to make a strong commitment to new values and priorities once these values are made accessible to them. There has been enough gloom and doom, and expression of pessimism about our ability to survive the ecological crisis. However, a sinking ship can not be abandoned without great anxiety unless everyone is confident the rescue vessel can be reached in safety, its crew friendly, and its quarters at least adequate. We want to help people get together, to help each other deal with the difficult period just ahead.

On March 21, 1970, several hundred people will begin a journey to Los Angeles, some five hundred miles to the south. We will walk all the way. We will have a few relatively smog-free vehicles with us. They will be powered by propane, electricity, and muscles. Converging walks are being planned from Santa Barbara and Irvine. Others may come from San Diego and San Bernardino. We will all gather in Los Angeles the first weekend in May to celebrate the coming of a new era— the 1970's—the Survival Decade.

We consider our passage through the towns of

others a discovery process, that those individuals who share our concern, commitment and knowledge might meet one another, as well as learn of those who desire and need more information. At each town we will set up exhibits, have short plays and puppet shows, answer questions, circulate petitions. Environmental fairs will be held in at least six of the San Joaquin Valley's major cities. We plan to work closely with many people along the route of the walk—county supervisors to high school students.

We also hope to plant wildflowers along our route as well as some oak trees, to establish study plots of native grasses close to schools and colleges. We will emphasize several issues of specific interest to people living in California. Many serious problems have been created by the simplification of the Valley's diverse native ecosystems into one of the largest commercial agricultural regions on the planet.

This walk will enable all Californians, and perhaps the entire nation, to share a common experience that will address all the diverse ingredients of the survival crisis. We believe the magnitude and imminence of this crisis to be so great as to warrant a formal declaration of an international state of environmental emergency. We suggest that the first six months after calling such an emergency be devoted to *intensive* public education concerning the crisis. After that, a series of town meetings across the country should be held to accept proposals for programs, and statements of changed values and priorities. These activities would serve to develop a new consensus that would assure the emergence of values and institutions to promote environmental health. It appears that nothing short of a major cultural transformation can assure our survival.

Let us not forget our position in the world. Over three billion people are affected a little more each day by our actions. No one wants to breathe foul air, drink poisoned water or digest empty foods. We believe that no one has ever purposely decided to force this upon others. But, through our cultural practices we have given our consent to those who procure the goods and services that we feel our needs and aspirations require. When we gave this consent we were as ignorant of ecological principles as the industrialists, politicians, and businessmen. Our naive trust has resulted in widespread destruction of our life-support system. We are now withdrawing our cultural consent from them and their institutions. To do this holds uncertainties for all of us. Your personal anxiety can be reduced by facing this environmental crisis, becoming involved with the solutions and taking action rather than complaining about what someone else is or isn't doing. We must give ourselves, each other, and our surroundings the tender care we all need so much.

For further information and details concerning this Survival Walk contact: Ecology Action Educational Institute, Box 9334, Berkeley, California 94709, 843-1820 (415).

Air Pollution Hearings

The following describes activities organized by Boston Area Ecology Action around public hearings on air pollution standards for Massachusetts. These activities might be used as a model for activities around other government hearings.

1. Picketing—Spirit was important. The picket in front of the state house included lots of balloons with "Clean Air" written on them, posters ("The Air is a Gas," "If You're not Part of the Solution, You're Part of the Pollution"), and people parading in surgical masks and gas masks (available cheaply at war surplus stores). Advance publicity was released for several weeks prior to the hearings, involving mostly leafletting on street corners and getting signatures for the petition.

2. Petition—Took the position that debate over how many parts per million of poison to put in the air was irresponsible, and demanded an immediate end to air pollution. Petitions signed by 2,500 people were sub-

mitted as testimony along with Boston Area Ecology Action statement.

3. Testimony—Made an oral and written statement at the hearings which challenged the view that man has the right to muck up the air, water, and living space of the planet in order to produce power for electric toothbrushes, electric can openers and electric vacuum cleaners (which are used to clean up dirt produced by the electric utilities and other industries themselves). We demanded a new ethic which puts first priority on care and respect and love for our friends and surroundings.

We tried to focus on implicit and unchallenged assumptions (such as "Power 'demands' must rise; therefore, the only question is how to best produce the power") and broke through euphemistic language. (We called "sulfur oxides" by the more descriptive name "sulfuric acid-producing gases"; "suspended particulates" we called "airborne dirt.") We tried to avoid the number-bargaining game and asked simply for sulfur dioxide levels "as close to zero as humanly and technically possible; particulates should be held to naturally occurring background levels and types and size of materials." We said the polluters, not the consumers or taxpayers, must pay to clean up their own pollution. We warned that nuclear power plants must not be considered as a "clean" alternative to present power sources. We tried to make people aware of the ecological nature of all pollution—that simply to deal with air pollution without simultaneously considering needed restrictions on water pollution was self-defeating, and that it is not acceptable to say that on windy days air pollution is taken care of because it is blown over the Atlantic or "dissipated" in the upper atmosphere (as the electric utilities maintained).

In general, we tried to get people out of the rut etched for them by industrialists and bureaucrats who seek "solutions" which are not "unduly burdensome" on business interests.

4. Air Pollution Prize—This was a huge blue ribbon and a citation presented to the vice president of Boston

Edison at their offices. The presentation of the award, accompanied by much ceremony, drum rolls and fanfares, was the conclusion of a spirited parade from the state house, where the hearings were being held. (Boston Edison electric power generating plants are a major single source of sulfur dioxide pollution in Boston.)

All of the above actions were coordinated and preceded by news releases and notification of the media. We got tremendous local and national press and TV coverage, almost all of it very favorable.

Eco-Tactics—Part II

Political Action

Eco-Politics and The League of Conservation Voters

Marion Edey

I will never forget a conversation I once had on a plane. The girl sitting next to me had very strong feeling about moral rightness and purity, and she was also very intelligent.

She had read somewhere about the population explosion, and it had terrified her. She didn't know much about ecology, but she did understand that man could not survive in a dead world. We talked about this for a while, surprised at the depth of our agreement.

Then I remarked that the only way to solve the population problem was to make it a political issue. Instantly she recoiled. "But this is for the benefit of *everyone*. You can't mix it up with power politics like that—politics is dirty!"

Yes. A healthy environment, a balanced ecology—is for the benefit of everyone. Why is it that a cause which is approved by the majority is so blindly neglected in government policy decisions?

Mainly because the passive support of a majority will have no real power until conservation becomes a major election issue. And the majority can only express itself on a few such issues at a time. People don't get a chance to vote directly on the issues. They can only vote for a candidate and all his platform at once. Thus it is not enough for people to want clean air and water. They must demand it with such intensity that they refuse to vote for a man who would deny it to them, no matter what else he has to offer. Until this happens, pollution will continue to get worse.

The environment has never been a major voting issue in the past, partly because there has never been an organization designed to make it so. The traditional conservation groups are afraid to be openly political, because they have a tax exempt status to protect. Their official purpose is educational. They are forced to rely almost entirely upon persuasion. They have never really aroused their sleeping majority, because they never take sides where the numbers count the most—in elections. Because they are not active in campaigns, they have no political muscle when they do try to influence legislators who are not inherently receptive to their ideas.

They are acting almost like a small special interest, but cannot compete with the real special interests because they can't lobby openly, and they have far less money.

We must stop acting like a small pressure group, and become more like an unofficial political party that brings people together to elect better legislators. This is the path to better legislation.

That is why we started Friends of the Earth. We are *not* tax deductible. We are therefore free to take sides and to channel the growing concern about the environment into a unified political force. Our acronym, F.O.E., is very appropriate. Because we are friends of the earth, we must be the foe of whatever and whoever degrades the earth.

A branch of F.O.E. called the League of Conservation Voters will actively support candidates who are working hardest to protect the environment. In every election year the league will pick a slate of outstanding candidates who face an especially close race. Not only will we endorse them, but we will raise money and manpower for their campaigns. Thus we can protect our allies in Congress and possibly succeed in defeating legislators whose policies are especially destructive to the environment.

Our goal is to prove that issues like ecology and population can decide the outcome of an election. This will greatly enhance the bargaining power of all groups working on these problems. If we can gain a reputation for being able to "swing" a close election, legislators will begin changing their policies to gain our endorsement.

The League of Conservation Voters will be strictly nonpartisan. It will support a man from any political party if he is a true Friend of the Earth. The urgency of saving our environment and our species from ecological chaos should become obvious to liberals and conservatives alike. We must convince them both that this issue transcends the old ideological squabbles of the left and right.

We will solicit campaign funds nationwide, through advertisements and direct mailings. By asking people to channel their contributions through Friends of the Earth, we can compile them and impress upon the candidate that he received this money because of his support for conservation, and not for any other reason. Thus we will identify conservation sentiment in the nation and advertise its growing strength. When conservationists as individuals support or oppose a candidate, he may never know the reason why.

Ecological values have been neglected partly because support for them is so spread out and diffuse. Conservationists are not concentrated in any special region or economic group, and so there are seldom enough in one district to dominate the election. Friends of the Earth can overcome this by forming a national movement which will concentrate its strength on a few key local elections.

Some people seem to think it beneath them to contribute money to a "dirty politician." But the oil industry has no such scruples. Neither does the highway lobby or the AMA. We desperately need a lobby that can work to counteract their influence and power.

Yet more important than the financial contributions will be the effort and commitment of thousands of people across the country. In every target state or electoral district, F.O.E. will have local representatives to mobilize support for the candidate. Hundreds of volunteers will canvass door to door, to alert the voters to the candidate's record in conservation. The candidate's own campaign office can organize the details of this canvassing operation.

Wherever possible, our representatives will be known in the community. They will give and arrange speeches to universities, outdoor clubs, garden clubs and any other concerned groups, to raise money and volunteers.

Our success will depend very largely on the young. No other group is so important. For we are the people who have to inherit the nightmare ecology our parents have made. Moreover the young are not yet trapped in a system of vested interests which prevents them from seeing a way out of the crisis. We have the time and the freedom to give ourselves to this struggle.

Students who think only of demonstrations and confrontations, who despair of finding any friends within the system, are making the same old mistake of ignoring their potential majority. They spend all their time trying to influence the powers that be, but make no organized effort to determine who remains in power.

The ecology movement can do much better than that. It is very different from civil rights or Vietnam, where young people on both sides of the issue already have rigid ideas and have hardened their minds against each other's arguments. We can approach conservation with a new outlook. No one can say that a man trying to save the American environment does not love his country.

Because Friends of the Earth is nonpartisan, members and volunteers who connect themselves with us must campaign only on conservation issues. We must emphasize that the importance of saving the environment transcends the other issues. When the survival of the species is at stake, the question of how we divide up our frantic, last-minute spoils is trivial.

We must not let other people get hung-up on some trivial difference between us, such as our clothes or hair. When you face someone from across a chasm, you don't ask him to leap over to where you are. To build a bridge you must first come to where he is, then lead him back where you came. This is especially so when the chasm is only apparent, created by ignorance rather than a real conflict of interest.

Basically, the people are already on our side. They want to feel in harmony with their surroundings. Yet every year they will suffer more drastically and directly from abuse of the environment. We must make them see the connection between this suffering and rampant technology and compulsive growth. We cannot let them get distracted by mere symptoms like crime in the streets and the shortage of social services.

The key struggle is to make ecology the campaign issue of the future, so that people are forced to take sides. He who defines the battlefield can win the battle.

Friends of the Earth will also expose the differences between a congressman's rhetoric and his real policies. This gap between rhetoric and reality is widest in conflicts between public interests like conservation and the private economic interests that want no restrictions on their treatment of the environment. The public official shapes the actual effect of his actions around the needs of economic groups, while announcing words that agree with the public. Usually this technique works very well; the economic interests are far more aware of the real impact of his actions, since they are more obviously and directly affected.

Congress provides endless opportunities for nice symbolic gestures that have nothing to do with the legislation that results. A Congressman can give a speech warmly endorsing a bill, then turn around and vote for an amendment that cripples it entirely. On many such amendments his vote is never recorded. The vast majority of bills are introduced for the sole purpose of impressing constituents. They are immediately buried in a committee file and forgotten by everyone, while the real work of the legislator is done behind committee doors that are closed to the public.

Thus to make conservation speeches and introduce conservation bills does not necessarily mean anything. The unaided voter will become quickly confused in his efforts to find out what his representatives really do. We must have an organization that studies the various legislators as carefully and as critically as the special interest groups have always done. Traditional conservation groups already study this, but again their tax status inhibits them from publishing their findings or their recommendations to a very wide audience. But F.O.E. has no such inhibitions, and will do all it can to alert the public to the real friends and foes of the earth.

One of the most common smokescreen devices is extreme generality which is used to create a deliberate ambiguity. Department officials will issue new guidelines urging the industries they regulate to "take environmental values into consideration." They will appoint new commissions to study problems have have already been studied to death.

Conservationists should make their demands as concrete and precise as possible, not only pointing out the specific causes of the problem, but pointing to a specific solution. To urge a public official merely to "do something" about a problem is to leave it up to him to find the most impressive way of doing nothing. We must find out for ourselves what should be done and push for action.

Suggestions Toward an Ecological Platform

Keith Murray

POPULATION

Stabilizing the U.S. population should be declared a national policy. Immediate steps should be taken to:

1. Legalize voluntary abortion and sterilization and provide these services free.

2. Remove all restrictions on the provision of birth control information and devices; provide these services free to all, including minors.

3. Make sex education available at all appropriate levels, stressing birth control practices and the need to stabilize the population.

4. Launch a government-sponsored campaign for population control in the media comparable to the present antismoking campaign.

5. Offer annual bonuses for couples remaining childless and eliminate tax deductions for more than two children.

Control of world population growth is simply a matter of survival of the human race. Federal priorities must be made to reflect this fact. We propose:

1. Massive federal aid to supply birth control information, planning and materials to all countries that will accept it.

2. Foreign aid only to countries with major programs to curb population growth.

3. Increased research on birth control methods and on attitudes toward limiting births.

GROWTH

The runaway U.S. growth economy must be stabilized to halt the destruction of the world resource base before we choke in the waste products of our affluence. There should be a thorough reassessment and reversal of unlimited economic growth as a national goal. The first and most crucial step is a guaranteed annual income, to break the compulsory link between jobs and income that has been a principal stimulus to growthsmanship.

LAND USE

An entirely new framework of land-use policies is required. It must embody a land ethic that fulfills human needs and preserves natural values. Elements should be:

1. Massive use of revolving land purchase funds by government entities to (a) purchase and resell key lands with development rights retained and (b) purchase and hold for scenic, recreation or open-space purposes or to compel rational development. Employ these methods on a large scale to preserve prime agricultural lands.

2. Create ocean shoreline development commissions to plan and control development so as to preserve natural values and provide public access.

3. Drastically curb tax loopholes that favor land speculation and quick-buck development, such as favored capital gains treatment and fast depreciation schedules.

4. Institute state zoning of certain categories of land such as flood plains, shorelines, earthquake hazard zones, designated open-space lands and prime agricultural lands.

5. Rebuff the drive to relax cutting restrictions in national forests and to extend logging to wilderness-value lands; defeat National Timber Supply Act H.R. 12025; strengthen forest practices laws to protect forest lands from degradation.

Regional and basin-wide development programs should be created, funded by low-interest federal loans that would be available only to carry out an entire, comprehensive plan. Each program would include responsibility for land and water conservation, water supply, waste disposal, urban planning, agricultural aid, new cities, model cities, open space, pollution control. Existing programs would continue to function within this structure wherever possible.

OTHER

We propose the creation of a survival corps—payment of a living income to individuals who will devote full time to projects for population control, preserving the environment and environmental education of the public.

We favor massive investment in environmental and ecological education—with emphasis on creating purposeful generalists equipped to understand and solve the problems before us.

RESOURCES AND WASTE

Ways must be found to curb the U.S. appetite for goods, and to create pathways for recycling waste materials into reuse that would eliminate the "dump" as we know it. We propose:

1. A severance tax on all mineral extractions (Metcalf bill).
2. A combination of tax incentives, prohibitions and public education, designed to promote reclamation of salvageable materials; reuse of containers; reduction in the quantity of nondegradable materials (such as plastics and aluminum) loosend on the environment; large-scale composting of organic wastes.

POLLUTION

Industrial polluters should be required to pay effluent charges equivalent to the cost to society of polluting the environment.

Diverters of water for any purpose should be charged a fee for returning waste water of lower quality than when it was diverted.

There should be provision for payment of triple damages for pollution that violates laws and established standards of environmental quality.

The human race is being employed as an experimental population for unleashing new chemicals or massive technological undertakings. We call for:

1. Creation of a new federal center for testing the safety and efficacy of drugs, pesticides and food additives, and assessing their impact on the environment. This center should be absolutely protected from the political and industrial pressures that now characterize such evaluations.
2. An absolute moratorium on large-scale technological escapades such as Project Sanguine and a sea-level Panama Canal until controls are devised and their

potential hazards and prospective benefits are measured objectively.

3. A total ban on the use of persistent pesticides, especially DDT, in the U.S., and immediate steps to phase out their use worldwide; a crash program to substitute acceptable methods for control of malaria and other serious diseases.

4. Replacement of the present laissez-faire methods of promoting pesticide and herbicide use by objective and professional practices, with emphasis on integrated control.

5. Intensified research on integrated and biological control and environmental management of pests.

TRANSPORTATION

The cycle of ever increasing reliance on the automobile must be broken. Mobility should be recognized as a public right, and integrated means for long and short distance travel that do not pollute, eat up land or kill people must be widely available. Immediate steps should be:

1. Outlaw the sale of reciprocating internal combustion engines by 1975.

2. Massively shift gas taxes and other sources of revenue for freeways to urban and interurban mass transit, rational bus systems, and free or low-cost shuttle transport.

3. Progressively tax higher automobile weights and engine displacements according to a sharply rising scale.

The proposed supersonic transport plane would be wasteful, uneconomic, and would create intolerable sonic booms. No further federal funds should be appropriated for its development. United States airlines should be forbidden to use SSTs on any route; no SST from any nation should be permitted over U.S. airspace.

AGRICULTURE

Many urban and agricultural ills can be traced to the expansion of vast corporate farms which drive people off the land, destroy soil productivity and promote excessive use of harmful chemicals. We call for policies to reverse this trend and reject its false pretenses of efficiency.

1. There should be rigorous enforcement of the federal 160-acre limitation whereby an owner who contracts for the heavily subsidized water from a federal project must sell his holdings in excess of 160 acres (320 for a family). The federal government should be enabled to purchase and resell the excess lands on terms that will permit family farmers to return to the soil.
2. There should be a $10,000 limit on subsidies to any one farm owner.
3. Unless the heavily subsidized western reclamatic program returns to its aims of benefiting the many instead of the few, it should promptly be terminated.
4. The approach to agricultural subsidies should be overhauled so that they promote desirable land-use practices and curb the long-term harmful effects of factories-in-the-field.

WATER

Plans to transfer water from one basin to another should be drastically curtailed. Water should be priced according to its true value—to make waste costly and to force industry to employ conservation and recirculation methods.

Fully employ the alternatives of reclaiming water, converting seawater, reducing evaporation, and purchasing excessive agricultural water rights such as in Imperial Valley.

The California Water Plan should be halted, with no peripheral canal and no dams on north coast rivers. Comparable schemes elsewhere, such as in Texas, should be opposed.

POWER

Power can be generated only at serious cost to the environment—radiation hazard, thermal or air pollution, despoiling of rivers, or depletion of fossil fuels. The present goal of unrestricted increase of power consumption should be reversed. Advertising and promotion to increase consumption of electricity should be forbidden. Electricity should be supplied at moderate cost for normal household needs, but additional increments should rise sharply in price. A larger share of electricity should be publicly distributed to re-establish the yardstick principle and curb profiteering by private utilities. Utility users' counsels should be established at all government levels to argue the public's case for fair rates and environment protection before regulatory commissioners (Metcalf bill). A high-level review body should be created to evaluate the location of steam generating plants.

Four "Changes"

POPULATION

The Condition

Position. Man is but a part of the fabric of life—dependent on the whole fabric for his very existence. As the most highly developed tool-using animal, he must recognize that the unknown evolutionary destinies of other life forms are to be respected, and act as gentle steward of the earth's community of being.

Situation. There are now too many human beings, and the problem is growing rapidly worse. It is potentially disastrous not only for the human race but for most other life forms.

Goal. The goal would be half of the present world population, or less.

Action

Social / political: First, a massive effort to convince the governments and leaders of the world that the problem is severe. And that all talk about raising food-production—well intentioned as it is—simply puts off the only real solution: reduce population. Demand immediate participation by all countries in programs to legalize abortion, encourage vasectomy and sterilization (provided by free clinics)—free insertion of intrauterine loops—try to correct traditional cultural attitudes that tend to force women into childbearing—remove income tax deductions for more than two children above a specified income level, and scale it so that lower income families are forced to be careful too—or pay families to limit their number. Take a vigorous stand against the policy of the right-wing in the Catholic hierarchy and any other institutions that exercise an irresponsible social force in regard to this question; oppose and correct simple-minded boosterism that equates population growth with continuing prosperity. Work ceaselessly to have all political questions be seen in the light of this prime problem.

The community: Explore other social structures and marriage forms, such as group marriage and polyandrous marriage, which provide family life but may produce less children. Share the pleasure of raising children widely, so that all need not directly reproduce to enter into this basic human experience. We must hope that no one woman would give birth to more than one child, during this period of crisis. Adopt children. Let reverence for life and reverence for the feminine mean also a reverence for other species, and future human lives, most of which are threatened.

Our own heads: "I am a child of all life, and all living beings are my brothers and sisters, my children and grandchildren. And there is a child within me waiting to be brought to birth, the baby of a new and wiser self." Love, lovemaking, a man and woman together, seen as the vehicle of mutual realization, where the creation of new selves and a new world of being is as important as reproducing our kind.

II. POLLUTION

The Condition

Position: Pollution is of two types. One sort results from an excess of some fairly ordinary substance—

smoke, or solid waste—which cannot be absorbed or transmuted rapidly enough to offset its introduction into the environment, thus causing changes the great cycle is not prepared for. (All organisms haves wastes and by-products, and these are indeed part of the total biosphere: energy is passed along the line and refracted in various ways, "the rainbow body." This is cycling, not pollution.) The other sort is powerful modern chemicals and poisons, products of recent technology, which the biosphere is totally unprepared for. Such is DDT and similar chlorinated hydrocarbons—nuclear testing fallout and nuclear waste—poison gas, germ and virus storage and leakage by the military; and chemicals which are put into food, whose long-range effects on human beings have not been properly tested.

Situation: The human race in the last century has allowed its production and scattering of wastes, by-products, and various chemicals to become excessive. Pollution is directly harming life on the planet: which is to say, ruining the environment for humanity itself. We are fouling our air and water, and living in noise and filth that no "animal" would tolerate, while advertising and politicians try to tell us "we've never had it so good." The dependence of the modern governments on this kind of untruth leads to shameful mind-pollution: mass media and most school education.

Goal: Clean air, clean clear-running rivers, the presence of pelican and osprey and gray whale in our lives; salmon and trout in our streams; unmuddied language and good dreams.

Action

Social / political: Effective international legislation banning DDT and related poisons—with no fooling around. The collusion of certain scientists with the pesticide industry and agri-business in trying to block this legislation must be brought out in the open. Strong penalties for water and air pollution by industries— "Pollution is somebody's profit." Phase out the internal combustion engine and fossil fuel use in general—more research into nonpolluting energy sources; solar energy;

the tides. No more kidding the public about atomic waste disposal: it's impossible to do it safely, and nuclear-power generated electricity cannot be seriously planned for as it stands now. Stop all germ and chemical warfare research and experimentation; work toward a hopefully safe disposal of the present staggering and stupid stock-piles of H-bombs, cobalt gunk, germ and poison tanks and cans. Laws and sanctions against wasteful use of paper etc. which adds to the solid waste of cities—develop methods of recycling solid urban waste. Re-cycling should be the basic principle behind all waste-disposal thinking. Thus, all bottles should be reusable; old cans should make more cans; old newspapers back into newsprint again. Stronger controls and research on chemicals in foods. A shift toward a more varied and sensitive type of agriculture (more small scale and sub-sistence farming) would eliminate much of the call for blanket use of pesticides.

The community: DDT and such: don't use them: Air pollution: use less cars. Cars pollute the air, and one or two people riding lonely in a huge car is an insult to intelligence and the earth. Share rides, legalize hitch-hiking, and build hitch-hiker waiting stations along the highways. Also—a step toward the new world—walk more; look for the best routes through beautiful country-side for long-distance walking trips: San Francisco to Los Angeles down the coast range, for example. Learn how to use your own manure as fertilizer if you're in the country—as the Far East has done for centuries. There's a way, and it's safe. Solid waste: boycott bulky wasteful Sunday papers which use up trees. It's all just advertis-ing anyway, which is artificially inducing more mindless consumption. Refuse paper bags at the store. Organize park and street clean-up festivals. Don't work in any way for or with an industry which pollutes, and don't be drafted into the military. Don't waste. (A monk and an old master were once walking in the mountains. They noticed a little hut upstream. The monk said, "A wise hermit must live there"—the master said, "That's no wise hermit, you see that lettuce leaf floating down the stream, he's a waster." Just then an old man came running down the hill with his beard flying and caught the floating lettuce leaf.) Carry your own jug to the winery and have it filled from the barrel.

Our own heads: Part of the trouble with talking about DDT is that the use of it is not just a practical device, it's almost an establishment religion. There is something in western culture that wants to totally wipe out creepy-crawlies, and feels repugnance for toadstools and snakes. This is fear of one's own deepest natural inner-self wilderness areas, and the answer is, relax. Relax around bugs, snakes, and your own hairy dreams. Again, farmers can and should share their crop with a certain percentage of buglife as "paying their dues"—Thoreau says "How then can the harvest fail? Shall I not rejoice also at the abundance of the weeds whose seeds are the granary of the birds? It matters little comparatively whether the fields fill the farmer's barns. The true husbandman will cease from anxiety, as the squirrels manifest no concern whether the woods will bear chestnuts this year or not, and finish his labor with every day, relinquish all claim to the produce of his fields, and sacrificing in his mind not only his first but his last fruits also." In the realm of thought, inner experience, consciousness, as in the outward realm of interconnection, there is a difference between balanced cycle, and the excess which cannot be handled. When the balance is right, the mind recycles from highest illuminations to the stillness of dreamless sleep; the alchemical "transmutation."

III. Consumption

The Condition

Position: Everything that lives eats food, and is food in turn. This complicated animal, man, rests on a vast and delicate pyramid of energy-transformations. To grossly use more than you need to destroy, is biologically unsound. Most of the production and consumption of modern societies is not necessary or conducive to spiritual and cultural growth, let alone survival; and is behind much greed and envy, age-old causes of social and international discord.

Situation: Man's careless use of "resources" and his total dependence on certain substances such as fossil fuels, (which are being exhausted, slowly but certainly) are having harmful effects on all the other members of the life-network. The complexity of modern technology renders whole populations vulnerable to the deadly consequences of the loss of any one key resource. Instead of independence we have over-dependence on life-giving substances such as water, which we squander. Many species of animals and birds have become extinct in the service of fashion fads—or fertilizer—or industrial oil—the soil is being used up; in fact mankind has become a locust-like blight on the planet that will leave a bare cupboard for its own children—all the while in a kind of addict's dream of affluence, comfort, eternal progress—using the great achievements of science to produce software and swill.

Goal: Balance, harmony, humility, growth which is a mutual growth with redwood and quail (would you want your child to grow up without ever hearing a wild bird?)—to be a good member of the great community of living creatures. True affluence is not *needing* anything.

Action

Social/political: It must be demonstrated ceaselessly that a continually "growing economy" is no longer healthy, but a cancer. And that the criminal waste which is allowed in the name of competition—especially that ultimate in wasteful needless competition, hot wars and cold wars with "communism" (or "capitalism")—must be halted totally with ferocious energy and decision. Economics must be seen as a small sub-branch of ecology, and production/distribution/consumption handled by companies or unions with the same elegance and spareness one sees in nature. Soil banks; open space; phase out logging in most areas. "Lightweight dome and honeycomb structures in line with the architectural principles of nature." "We shouldn't use wood for housing because trees are too important." Protection for all predators and varmints, "Support your right to arm bears." Damn the International Whaling Commission which is selling out the last of our precious, wise whales! Absolutely no further development of roads and concessions in national parks and wilderness areas; build auto campgrounds in the least desirable areas. Plan consumer boycotts in response to dishonest and unnecessary products. Radical co-ops. Politically, blast both "Communist" and "Capitalist" myths of progress, and all crude notions of conquering or controlling nature.

The community: Sharing and creating. The inherent aptness of communal life—where large tools are owned jointly and used efficiently. The power of renunciation: If enough Americans refused to buy a new car for one given year it would permanently alter the American economy. Recycling clothes and equipment. Support handicrafts—gardening, home skills, midwifery, herbs —all the things that can make us independent, beautiful and whole. Learn to break the habit of unnecessary possessions—a monkey on everybody's back—but avoid a self-abnegating anti-joyous self-righteousness. Simplicity is light, carefree, neat, and loving—not a self-punishing ascetic trip. (The great Chinese poet Tu Fu said "The ideas of a poet should be noble and simple.") Don't shoot a deer if you don't know how to use all the meat and preserve that which you can't eat, to tan the hide and use the leather—use it all, with gratitude, right down to the sinew and hooves. Simplicity and mindfulness in diet is a starting point for many people.

Our own heads: It is hard to even begin to gauge how much a complication of possessions, the notions of "my and mine," stand between us and a true, clear, liberated way of seeing the world. To live lightly on the earth, to be aware and alive, to be free of egotism, to be in contact with plants and animals, starts with simple concrete acts. The inner principle is the insight that we are inter-dependent energy-fields of great potential wisdom and compassion—expressed in each person as a superb mind, a handsome and complex body, and the almost magical capacity of language. To these potentials and capacities, "owning things" can add nothing of authenticity. "Clad in the sky, with the earth for a pillow."

IV. TRANSFORMATION

The Condition

Position: Everyone is the result of four forces—the conditions of this known-universe (matter/energy forms, and ceaseless change); the biology of his species; his individual genetic heritage; and the culture he's born into. Within this web of forces there are certain spaces and loops which allow total freedom and illumination. The gradual exploration of some of these spaces is "evolution" and, for human cultures, what "history" could be. We have it within our deepest powers not only to change our "selves" but to change our culture. If a man is to remain on earth he must transform the five-millenia long urbanizing civilization tradition into a new ecologically-sensitive harmony-oriented wild-minded scientific/spiritual culture. "Wildness is the state of complete awareness. That's why we need it."

Situation: civilization, which has made us so successful a species, has overshot itself and now threatens us with its inertia. There is some evidence that civilized life isn't good for the human gene pool. To achieve the changes we must change the very foundations of our society and our minds.

Goal: nothing short of total transformation will do much good. What we envision is a planet on which the human population lives harmoniously and dynamically by employing a sophisticated and unobtrusive technology in a world environment which is "left natural." Specific points in this vision:

- A healthy and spare population of all races, much less in number than today.
- Cultural and individual pluralism, unified by a type of world tribal council. Division by natural and cul-

tural boundaries rather than arbitrary political boundaries.

- A technology of communication, education, and quiet transportation, land-use being sensitive to the properties of each region. Allowing, thus, the bison to return to much of the high plains. Careful but intensive agriculture in the great alluvial valleys; deserts left wild for those who would trot in them. Computer technicians who run the plant part of the year and walk along with the Elk in their migrations during the rest.

- A basic cultural outlook and social organization that inhibits power and property-seeking while encouraging exploration and challenge in things like music, meditation, mathematics, mountaineering, magic, and all other ways of authentic being-in-the-world. Women totally free and equal. A new kind of family —responsible, but more festive and relaxed—is implicit.

Action

Social/political: It seems evident that there are throughout the world certain social and religious forces which have worked through history toward an ecologically and culturally enlightened state of affairs. Let these be encouraged: Gnostics, hip Marxists, Teilhard de Chardin Catholics, Druids, Taoists, Biologists, Witches, Yogins, Bhikkus, Quakers, Sufis, Tibetans, Zens, Shamans, Bushmen, American Indians, Polynesians, Anarchists, Alchemists . . . the list is long. All primitive cultures, all communal and ashram movements. Since it doesn't seem practical or even desirable to think that direct bloody force will achieve much, it would be best to consider this a continuing "revolution of consciousness" which will be won not by guns but by seizing the key images, myths, archetypes, eschatologies, and ectasies so that life won't seem worth living unless one's on the transforming energy's side. By taking over "science and technology" and releasing its real possibilities and powers in the service of this planet —which, after all, produced us and it.

Our community: New schools, new classes, walking in the woods and cleaning up the streets. Find psychological techniques for creating an awareness of "self" which includes the social and natural environment. "Consideration of what specific language forms—symbolic systems—and social institutions constitute obstacles to ecological awareness." Without falling into a facile interpretation of McLuhan, we can hope to use the media. Let no one be ignorant of the facts of biology and related disciplines; bring up our children as part of the wild-life. Some communities can establish themselves in backwater rural areas and flourish—others maintain themselves in urban centers, and the two types work together—a two-way flow of experience, people, money, and home-grown vegetables. Ultimately cities will exist only as joyous tribal gatherings and fairs, to dissolve after a few weeks. Investigating new life-styles is our work, as is the exploration of Ways to explore our inner realms—with the known dangers of crashing that go with such. We should work with political-minded people where it helps, hoping to enlarge their vision, and with people of all varieties of politics or thought at whatever point they become aware of environmental urgencies. Master the archaic and the primitive as models of basic nature-related cultures—as well as the most imaginative extensions of science—and build a community where these two vectors cross.

Our own heads: is where it starts. Knowing that we are the first human beings in history to have all of man's culture and previous experience available to our study; and being free enough of the weight of traditional cultures to seek out a larger identity.—The first members of a civilized society since the early neolithic to wish to look clearly into the eyes of the wild and see our selfhood, our family, there. We have these advantages to set off the obvious disadvantages of being as screwed up as we are—which gives us a fair chance to penetrate into some of the riddles of ourselves and the universe, and to go beyond the idea of "man's survival" or "the survival of the biosphere" and to draw our strength from the realization that at the heart of things is some kind of serene and ecstatic process which is actually beyond qualities and certainly beyond birth-and-death. "No need to survive!" "In the fires that destroy the universe at the end of the kalpa, what survives?"—"The iron tree blooms in the void!"

Knowing that nothing need be done, is where we begin to move from.

Conservation Organizations

There are many organizations active in the fight for a decent environment. Many of these groups were active for many years before ecology became a glamorous issue and they deserve support for their efforts. Many groups such as the Sierra Club, the Audubon Society, the Wilderness Society, the National Parks Association, and Planned-Parenthood have the environment as their prime concern. Others such as the American Association of University Women, the League of Women Voters, AFL-CIO, and UAW have conservation interests as part of their broader programs. The 1969 Conservation Directory of the National Wildlife Federation lists hundreds of groups, so it is clearly impossible for us to cover them all here. We suggest that you refer to the four directories listed below before you start a new group, so that you don't unnecessarily duplicate work already done or in progress.

We strongly suggest that members of existing groups make a concerted effort to make themselves known to student organizers of the teach-in at local schools and colleges. It is very important to stress the activities of your organization in which students could have a meaningful role.

Students seeking help should not overlook organizations that are not primarily environmental, but that have active programs in this area, such as the AFL-CIO,

HAUW, and the League of Women Voters. The League of Women Voters, for instance, has been very active in the fight for a reasonable water policy and water pollution control. They have many regional studies available, and a lot of experience in practical politics.

Several organizations have been formed recently to devote themselves to a wholehearted effort to solve ecological problems. These organizations are not tax-deductible because they feel that many of the solutions to our environmental crisis are political, and the kind of activity needed to solve them is forbidden to organizations that are tax-exempt under Internal Revenue Service rules. These groups complement the activities of the more informational-educational groups that are tax-exempt. Because these new groups depend on a large number of individual supporters to be effective, we feel it is appropriate to push them here, with statements of their goals and tactics. Policy statements from ZPG and FOE appear elsewhere, and membership applications are printed on the last pages.

Catalogs of Conservation Groups

1. *State and Regional Conservation Councils* prepared by the Conservation Foundation: Lists clearinghouse, shared-service and joint action organizations formed by diverse environmental planning and conservation groups in states and regions of the U.S. Write: The Conservation Foundation, 1250 Connecticut Avenue, N.W., Washington, D.C. 20036.

2. *Community Action Agency Atlas* prepared by the Office of Economic Opportunity. Lists regionally funded Community Action Agencies (CAA's) and those funded by the Community Action Program Office of Special Field Programs (Indian, Commonwealth, Territory, and Trust Territory CAA's). Includes state county outline maps. Write: O.E.O., Executive Office of the President, Washington, D.C. 20506.

3. *Conservation Directory 1969* prepared by the National Wildlife Federation. Lists organizations, agencies and officials concerned with natural resource use and management. Write: National Wildlife Federation, 1412 16th Street, N.W., Washington, D.C. 20036.

4. *Grass Roots—Directory of Environmental Conservation Organizations* prepared by the Ecology Center and Planned Parenthood. Covers groups in the greater San Francisco Bay area. Write: Ecology Center, 2179 Allston Way, Berkeley, California 94704.

Some National Conservation Groups

Scientists' Institute for Public Information
    30 E. 68th Street
    New York, New York 10021
    (212)249-2886

The Nature Conservancy
    1522 K Street, N.W.
    Washington, D.C. 20005
    (202)223-4710

The National Wildlife Federation
    1412 16th Street, N.W.
    Washington, D.C. 20036
    (202)232-8004

National Audubon Society
    1130 5th Avenue
    New York, New York 10028
    (212)369-2100

The Sierra Club
    1050 Mills Tower
    San Francisco, California 94104

The Conservation Foundation
    1250 Connecticut Avenue, N.W.
    Washington, D.C. 20036
    (202)659-2180

The Wilderness Society
    729 15th Street, N.W.
    Washington, D.C. 20005
    (202)347-4132

National Parks Association
    1701 18th Street, N.W.
    Washington, D.C. 20009
    (202)667-3352

International Union for Conservation of Nature and
        Natural Resources
    2000 P Street, N.W.
    Washington, D.C. 20006

The Izaak Walton League of America
    1326 Waukegan Road
    Glenview, Illinois 60025
    (312)724-3880

John Muir Institute for Environmental Studies
    451 Pacific Avenue
    San Francisco, California 94133
    or, P.O. Box 11
    Cedar Crest, New Mexico 87008

Citizens League Against the Sonic Boom
    19 Appleton Street
    Cowbridge, Massachusetts 02138

Planned Parenthood/World Population
    515 Madison Avenue
    New York, New York 10022

Friends of the Earth (FOE)
30 East 42nd Street
New York, New York 10017

Zero Population Growth (ZPG)
367 State Street
Los Altos, California 94022

Suggestions for Organizations

Barbara Parker

Legitimize your teach-in. Seek endorsement from local, state, and federal authorities. This reassures the public and gives momentum to a total community involvement. Such involvement may be as small a thing as donating a ream of paper or as big a thing as committing the major portion of some group's resources. Perhaps your community could have a week committed to the environment including such things as: sermons and other programs in churches; a community-wide recycling project or clean-up with Boy Scouts, YMCAs, or men's groups; ecology fairs and projects in the schools (work with science teachers, PTAs and student teachers from your school); photographic exhibits through museums and schools.

In all cases, what kind of materials can you provide to get the individuals started? Can you provide speakers from your group? Do you have other programs you might be able to put on? Try putting together some local fact sheets for the community's benefit, and develop some people who can help other groups get started. Do not do everything yourselves. Get the community involved doing and managing their own institution's program for the teach-in as rapidly as possible so you can move on to helping someone else.

ENVIRONMENTAL INVENTORY

After generally educating yourselves on the problems, currently proposed solutions, and barriers to achieving any of these solutions, the most important task is to take an inventory of your region. Know something about the natural topography and resource-use patterns—climate patterns, water drainage. Who are the major pollutors in your area? Get the data on quantity and quality of pollutants. Graduate students and professionals may be able to help you with this aspect particularly when lab work is required. Such information and methods used to research it should be sent to the National Teach-In Office, 2000 P Street, N.W., Room 200, Washington, D. C. 20036. The national office is functioning as a communications and information office and, for the benefit of everyone, will be publishing news and ideas from all over the country.

Research the regulations on local, state and federal levels which might be applied to the problems. Know which agency, if any, has jurisdiction over specific aspects of a problem. Find out where useful sympathy and expertise lie within your community and legislature.

List and canvas the activities of all the colleges in your area. You may discover several lesser known colleges by using the phone book and zip code catalogue. Don't overlook institutions such as seminaries. Consider integrating your activities on the regional level if that seems profitable to all concerned.

Develop a list of resource people and experts on campus and off; ask them what problems they see as most important. Be sure to follow up on names of other interested parties they may suggest to you.

Compile lists of all kinds of talent—legal, musical, literary, press, theatrical, carpentry—as well as having people note their own talents at meetings on volunteer forms.

Know all of your local groups off campus and the members of them who are interested in these problems. Often, you will find one person involved in five or six groups who can help you reach organizations such as Kiwanis, League of Women Voters, PTA, Teachers groups, Council of Churches, and professional societies.

Media

When writing press releases or dealing with reporters, remember the media are always looking for new metaphors and good ideas. Questions such as: What is ecology? Why are you involved in it? What do you hope to accomplish by holding a teach-in? are going to be asked again and again. Be prepared to answer very broad questions like these in one or two sentences which are concise and interesting. The person doing PR should not only be informed and able to handle a variety of rhetoric but should also be interesting or unusual in his own right. Put yourself in the reporter's shoes: what is it about you, your group, and your activities that would make a good story?

When being interviewed, avoid verbal pitfalls. First, be wary about making statements which, if quoted out of context, might be misleading. Second, you may find a biased reporter approaching you for quotes and descriptions which he can use to fill in the blanks in a prepackaged, hostile story. In such a case, it is the job of the PR person to convince the reporter to revise his story. Ask him some questions. Get him personally interested in the problems you are dealing with. Excite him about your work. Involve him as you would any other busy member of your community. However, be forewarned: even should you succeed in changing his point of view, his article or report may not be all you could desire. Much of what a reporter brings in ends up edited out by others in control. Third, avoid sloppy language. Radical rhetoric and vernacular (groovy, hip, straight) are dead languages which say nothing. Be creative.

Press releases should:

Be written in active rather than passive language
Be brief and newsworthy
Have the major point or grabby phrase close to the top
Be usable just as written
Be out 5 to 7 days before the date of release

Have the date for release clearly marked at the top
List contact person(s) and their phone number(s)
Go to more than one department or person in big papers

A press release should be followed up with a phone call because releases often are misplaced. Also a phone call is one of the best ways to gain personal contact and develop credit, that is, become a person the press comes to for news.

FINANCING

Money is always a problem. First, learn to save it. See if a businessman will give discounts or even donate paper and such. Use the equipment of other groups when you can. Try to find free places, both large and small, for meetings. Also, when you request this kind of financial help from someone, it gives you a chance to talk to him about the importance of the teach-in. Never miss an opportunity to involve someone.

Secondly, small amounts of money can be raised from selling posters, bumper stickers, buttons, and two-penny fact sheets. Don't overlook plain old donations from groups on and off the campus. When seeking a donation be specific if you can. ("We need two hundred dollars to print five hundred posters.") People are reassured when they know how the money is to be spent.

Thirdly, benefits can be good ways to raise lumps of money. Organize events such as poetry readings, rock concerts, flea markets, auctions, and film showings. Aside from getting the talent, articles or films together, the most important item is the kind, amount and timing of the publicity for the event. Many times, a very fine event is not well attended because the publicity was poor or too late. Make use of school bulletin boards, local papers, public service announcements on radio, posters both on the campus and in store windows, and a few days before, handbills at the entrance to campus. Use the best graphics and catchiest designs you can find; design radio ads as more than mere announcements.

CHECK LIST FOR A BENEFIT:

1. Line up talent and location
2. Begin publicity campaign—design ads, produce posters, read press releases where appropriate. (Ads should be out a good two weeks before event.)
3. Arrange for equipment: microphones, tables, or whatever.
4. Check everything a day or two before to be sure everything will come off as planned.
5. Be sure to have change at the door and enough people to manage traffic and cover for someone who doesn't show up.

WHAT IS ECOLOGY ACTION?

Ecology Action is people actively trying to reverse the massive destruction of our environment, our earth household. We are beginning to realize that our life styles, our industries, and our population growth are leading to the extinction of more and more species, to the poisoning of our air, water and food, and to the exhaustion of resources on earth. This growing destruction already threatens the continued existence of the human species. We must face this problem, try to understand its causes, and inform others. Simultaneously, we are trying to find ways to transform our own personal values, our life styles, and our "economics" (ways of managing our household) that will insure our survival and the healthy continuance of our earth's life support systems.

WHAT IS THE ECOLOGY ACTION CENTER?

The Ecology Action Center is a self-supporting, community education and action resource, sustained by contributions and donations. (We have applied for nonprofit, tax-exempt status.) The center is a storefront on Massachusetts Avenue, a well-walked street in Cambridge, so every day many passers-by come in to ask questions, talk, read our walls, books, magazines. In addition to maintaining the center, we are also trying to aid communication between existing ecology-related groups in New England, encourage and assist the formation of local ecology groups in towns, high schools and colleges, and to organize ecology action projects in the Boston area. This involves a lot of energy, time and learning, but we are off to a good start. We already have people who will speak at high schools, grade schools, garden clubs, PTA's, college groups, radio stations, *etc.*, on ecology or specific problems. We are building a tape library and have access to movies and a scientist speaker service.

Other action programs include a guerilla theatre group, a Christmas craft workshop, campaigns to fight excess packaging and non-returnable containers, garbage dump-ins, direct action open space and tree protection programs, a cooperative food store with organic foods, bio-degradable goods and minimal packaging, high school ecology curriculum, and so forth. We can use help on all of these and more. Forthcoming programs which can use organizational help involve leafletting of supermarkets, a campaign to promote bicycles and other non-polluting vehicles, recycling campaign, campaign to improve garbage collection in poor areas, instant picketing and leafletting squads to work at obvious pollution areas such as traffic jams, *etc.*

We are a small but important beginning toward meeting the crisis.

Boston Area Ecology Action
925 Massachusetts Avenue
Cambridge, Massachusetts 02139
(617) 876-7085
Berkeley Ecology Action
Box 9334
Berkeley, California 94709
(415) 843-1820

A Fable for Our Time

Michael Perelman of Berkeley Ecology Action

Captain Cook visited a Polynesian island that no European had ever seen before. The good captain saw a native artisan working with a chisel made of the bone of a human forearm. Captain Cook bestowed to this primitive the benefits of civilization by giving him a steel chisel. The next time the artisan saw the captain he returned the steel chisel. The would-be Promethian captain was dumbfounded. "The chisel is a gift and it is yours; furthermore, I have even more of them for you." The poor native remained steadfast. "Your chisel is much better than mine. I do not know where it comes from or how to make a new one. If I became dependent on steel chisels, you could make me do things I would not want to do."

The primitive must have seen that the bone chisel was readily available to him and his family. So long as they relied only on the gifts nature laid out for them in their immediate eco-region, they could survive in harmony with nature. The people from Captain Cook's civilization saw the steel chisel as a more powerful gift with which to manipulate nature. The more power a society had, the more goodies they would squeeze out of nature. But coal and steel were not everywhere available. So the price they would have to pay for their steel chisel was membership in a vast interlocking system of trade. This system lost all human dimensions and men became objects. While society developed more power to manipulate nature, in truth, much of the power was used to manipulate men. The Polynesian artisan knew the consequences of the steel chisel.

The Polynesian society was simple enough to keep in contact with nature. Our enormous industrial system was too complex for us to read the feedback nature gave us. The destruction produced by our quest of wealth and power has caused cataclysmic damage to nature and the dehumanization of man. In spite of the obvious consequences of our greed, many people today are anxiously holding on to their wealth and power. Some of them say that those best equipped for power should exercise it, and those who presently are exercising it are best equipped. Others say only more or only better use of power can save us from the destruction caused by the use of power today.

We say that we want no part of their kind of power. Only by following the example of the Polynesian can we survive. We must assert ourselves as individuals while submitting to nature. Indeed, only by following his example do we deserve to survive.

Appendix

Bibliography

THE CRISIS

Ehrlich, P., *The Population Bomb*. New York: Ballantine, 1968. 95¢.

Ehrlich, Paul R., and Anne H. Ehrlich, *Population, Resources, Environment: Issues in Human Ecology,* San Francisco, published by W. H. Freeman and Company, 1970.

Galbraith, J., *The New Industrial State*. New York: Houghton-Mifflin, 1969. $6.95.

Commoner, B., *Science and Survival*. New York: Viking, 1966. $4.50.

Carson, R., *Silent Spring*. New York: Crest, 1969. 95¢.

Rienow, R. and Rienow, L., *Moment in the Sun*. New York: Ballantine, 1969. 95¢.

Marx, W., *The Frail Ocean*. New York: Ballantine, 1969. 95¢.

Dasmann, R., *The Destruction of California*. New York: Macmillan, $1.50.

Marine, G., *America the Raped*. New York: Simon and Schuster, 1969. $5.95.

ECOLOGY TEXTS

Storer, J., *Man in the Web of Life*. New York: Signet, 1968. 95¢.

Odum, E., *Ecology*. New York: Holt, Rinehart, 1969. $3.25.

Kormondy, E., *Concepts of Ecology*. New York: Prentice-Hall, 1969. $2.95.

ANTHOLOGIES

Kostelanetz, R., ed., *Beyond Left & Right.* Apollo, 1968. $2.95.

Hardin, G., ed., *Population, Evolution and Birth Control.* San Francisco: Freeman, 1969. $6.00.

Cox, G., ed., *Readings in Conservation Ecology.* New York: Appleton, 1969. $4.95.

Shepard, McKinley, eds., *The Subversive Science.* New York: Houghton-Mifflin, 1968. $5.95.

Hardin, G., ed., *Thirty-Nine Steps to Biology, Readings from Scientific American.* San Francisco: Freeman, 1968. $4.95.

Hardin, G., ed., *Science, Conflict & Society, Readings from Scientific American.* San Francisco: Freeman, 1969. $5.75.

Schwartz, William, ed., *Voices for the Wilderness,* from the Sierra Club Wilderness Conferences, New York, published by Ballantine Books, Inc., 1969.

AGRICULTURE AND PESTICIDES

Rudd, R., *Pesticides and the Living Landscape.* Madison, Wisconsin: University of Wisconsin Press, 1964. $1.95.

Borgstrom, G., *The Hungry Planet.* New York: Collier, 1965. $2.95.

Borgstrom, G., *Too Many, A Study of Earth's Biological Limitations.* New York: Macmillan, 1969. $7.95.

Miller, M. and Berg, G., eds., *Chemical Fallout.* Charles C. Thomas, $22.50.

Rodale, J., *How to Grow Vegetables and Fruits by the Organic Method.* Rodale, $9.95.

Rodale, J., ed., *Encyclopedia of Organic Gardening.* Rodale, $9.95.

Rodale, J., *Complete Book of Composting.* Rodale, $8.95.

Hunter, B., *Gardening Without Poisons.* New York: Houghton-Mifflin, 1964. $5.00.

Paddock, W., *Famine Nineteen Seventy-five.* Boston: Little, Brown, 1968. $2.35.

Jensen, M., *Observations of Continental European Solid Waste Management Practices*. Consumer Protection and Environmental Health Service, Bureau of Solid Waste Management, U.S.H.E.W. Public Health Service Publications, 55¢.

THE HUMAN ANIMAL

Vayda, A., *Environment and Cultural Behavior*. The Natural History Press, 1969. $2.95.

Morris, D., *The Naked Ape*. New York: Dell, 1969. 95¢.

Hall, E., *The Hidden Dimension*. New York: Anchor, 1966. $1.45.

Ardrey, R., *The Terratorial Imperative*. New York: Delta-Dell, 1968. $2.95.

Kroeber, T., *Ishi: Last of His Tribe*. Parnassus, 1964. $4.25.

Thomas, W., *Man's Role in Changing the Face of the Earth*. University of Chicago Press, 1956. $15.00.

Dubos, R., *So Human an Animal*. New York: Charles Scribner's Sons, 1970. $2.25.

ECOLOGICAL AWARENESS

Whole Earth Catalog. Portola Institute, $4.00.

Leopold, A., *A Sand County Almanac*. Oxford University Press, 1966. $1.95.

Thoreau, H., *Walden*. Mentor, 50¢.

Snyder, G., *Earth House Hold*. San Francisco: New Directions, 1969. $1.95.

De Saint-Exupéry, *The Little Prince*. New York: Harcourt Brace and World, 75¢.

WILDERNESS, OPEN SPACE AND THE CITY

Eldredge, H., *Taming Megalopolis*. 2 Vols. New York: Anchor, 1967. $2.45 each.

Muir, J. and Kauffman, R., *Gentle Wilderness*. New York: Sierra Club-Ballantine, 1968. $3.95.

Jeffers, R., *Not Man Apart*. New York: Sierra Club-Ballantine, 1969. $3.95.

Porter, E., *In Wildness Is the Preservation of the World*. New York: Sierra Club-Ballantine, 1967. $3.95.

Whyte, W., *Last Landscape*. New York: Doubleday, 1968. $6.95.

McHarg, I., *Design with Nature*. Natural History Press, 1969. $19.95.

Douglas, W., *Wilderness Bill of Rights*. Boston: Little, Brown, 1965. $1.95.

Cities, A Scientific American Book. New York: Alfred A. Knopf, 1965. $2.45.

ECONOMICS

Theobald, R., *Challenge of Abundance*. New York: Mentor, 60¢.

Galbraith, J., *Affluent Society*. New York: Mentor, 1969. 95¢.

Domhoff, G. W., *Who Rules America*. New York: Prentice-Hall, 1967. $2.45.

Murphy, E., *Governing Nature*. Quadrangle, 1967. $7.50.

Jarrett, H., ed., *Environmental Quality in a Growing Economy*. Johns Hopkins, 1966. $5.00.

Boulding, K., *Economic Analysis*. 2 Vols. New York: Harper: Vol. 1, *Microeconomics,* $10.95; Vol. 2, *Macroeconomics,* 1966. $7.95.

Mishan, *Costs of Economic Growth*. Praeger, $2.45.

Ciriacy-Wantrup, *Resource Conservation*. University of California Press, $6.50.

Annual Reports of Resources for the Future, Inc. list all their publications, which are very useful. Resources for the Future, Inc., 1755 Massachusetts Ave., N.W., Washington, D. C. 20036.

AN ALTERNATE FUTURE

Faltermayer, E., *Redoing America*. New York: Collier, 1969. $1.95.

Committee on Resources and Man, *Resources and Man*. San Francisco: Freeman, 1969. $2.95.

The Environmental Pollution Panel, President's Science Advisory Committee, *Restoring the Quality of Our*

Environment. U.S. Government Printing Office, $1.25.

Goodman, P. and P., *Communitas: Means of Livelihood & Ways of Life.* New York: Vintage, $1.65.

The Citizens' Advisory Committee on Recreation and Natural Beauty, *Community Action for Natural Beauty.* U.S. Government Printing Office.

Rudofsky, B., *Architecture Without Architects.* New York: Doubleday, 1969. $3.95.

EDUCATION

Hesse, H., *Beneath the Wheel.* New York: Farrar, Straus and Giroux, 1969. $1.95.

Steinhart, J. and Cherniack, S., *The Universities and Environmental Quality—Commitment to Problem Focused Education.* U.S. Government Printing Office, 70¢.

Hutchins, R., *University of Utopia.* University of Chicago Press, 1953. $1.50.

Goodman, P., *Compulsory Mis-Education: Community of Scholars.* New York: Vintage. $1.95.

Goodman, P., *Growing Up Absurd.* New York: Vintage, $1.45.

Jencks, C. and Riesman, D., "Where Graduate Schools Fail" *The Atlantic Monthly,* 1969.

Hapgood, D., "Degrees: The Case for Abolition" *The Washington Monthly,* August 1969.

Lichtman, R., "The Ideological Function of the University" *International Socialist Journal,* December 24, 1967.

FURTHER BIBLIOGRAPHIES

A Selected Bibliography: Family Planning, Population, Related Subjects. Planned Parenthood-World Population, 516 Madison Avenue, New York, New York 10022, 25¢.

1969 Publications About Planned Parenthood. Planned Parenthood-World Population, 515 Madison Avenue, New York, New York 10022, 25¢.

Carvajal, J. and Munzer, M., *Conservation Education: A Selected Bibliography*. Danville, Illinois: The Interstate Printers & Publishers, Inc., 1968. $2.50.

A PARTIAL LISTING OF THE OUTSTANDING WILDERNESS PICTURE BOOKS FROM THE SIERRA CLUB EXHIBIT FORMAT SERIES

"In Wildness Is the Preservation of the World, selections from Henry David Thoreau, photographs by Eliot Porter.

The Wild Cascades, by Harvey Manning, photographs by Ansel Adams, Philip Hyde, David Simons, Bob and Ira Spring, Clyde Thomas, and others.

Not Man Apart, lines from Robinson Jeffers, photographs of the Big Sur Coast by Ansel Adams, Morley Baer, Wynn Bullock, and others.

The Place No One Knew: Glen Canyon on the Colorado, photographs by Eliot Porter.

Summer Island: Penobscot Country, text and photographs by Eliot Porter.

Everest: The West Ridge, by Thomas F. Hornbein, photographs from the American Mount Everest Expedition and by its leader, Norman G. Dyhrenfurth.

Baja California and the Geography of Hope, text by Joseph Wood Krutch, photographs by Eliot Porter.

Kauai and the Park Country of Hawaii, by Robert Wenkam.

The Last Redwoods and the Parkland of Redwood Creek, text by Francois Leydet, photographs by James Rose and others.

Navajo Wildlands "as long as the rivers shall run," text by Stephen C. Jett, with selections from Willa Cather, Oliver La Farge and others, photographs by Philip Hyde.

Gentle Wilderness: The Sierra Nevada, text from John Muir, photographs by Richard Kauffman.

This is the American Earth, by Ansel Adams and Nancy Newhall.

Film Bibliography

Kenneth P. Cantor

There are literally thousands of films on topics related to ecology, population, city environments, and resources. Most of them aren't worth seeing. This list contains a few of the films we consider worthwhile. There are many more. Before showing a film to an audience, be sure to preview it, or check with someone you trust who has seen it. Films are available from university, college, and local libraries, commercial distributors, private organizations, and federal and state governmental agencies. A list of distributors following the films is meant to be suggestive only. Most of them charge a rental fee. There are sources of free films (including those on this list) such as local libraries, university departments, and so on. Check them out before renting films. Letters before a film title indicate one of several possible rental sources for that film. See the list of distributors following the film titles.

FILMS

The Automobile
CF	*The City—Cars or People?*	27 min. b/w
CF	*The Cars in Your Life*	30 min. color

The City
	How to Live in a City	30 min. b/w
	How to Look at a City	30 min. b/w
CF	*Heart of the City*	27 min. b/w
	City of Necessity	30 min. color
	How Things Get Done	30 min. b/w
	What Will You Tear Down Next?	30 min. b/w

Man and Nature Out of Balance

EB	*Strands Grow, A Strand Breaks*	two films, 15 min. each color
EB	*House of Man—Our Changing Environment*	17 min. color
SC	*Two Yosemites*	14 min. color
AVC	*Multiply and Subdue the Earth*	60 min. color or b/w
EB	*Age of the Buffalo*	14 min. color

Man in Harmony with Nature (Cultural Anthropology)

	Buckeyes: Food of the California Indians	13 min. color
	Acorns: Staple Food of California Indians	28 min. color
McG-H	*Dead Birds*	83 min. color

Nature Strikes Back

	Disaster at Dawn (the 1906 San Francisco earthquake)	27 min. b/w
	Though the Earth be Moved	45 min. b/w

Pesticides and Chemical Warfare

	Silent Spring of Rachel Carson	54 min. b/w
	Germ and Chemical Warfare	30 min. b/w
BBC	*A Plague on Your Children*	72 min. b/w
OCA	*By Land, Sea, and Air*	31 min. color

Pollution

	The Poisoned Air	50 min. b/w
	Noise: New Pollutant	30 min. b/w
ADF	*Spirit of '76* (Santa Barbara oil slick)	

Population

McG-H	*Population Ecology*	19 min. color
	Brazil: The Gathering Millions	60 min. b/w

Undisturbed Natural Environments

	Polar Ecology	22 min. color
McG-H	*Above the Timberline*	15 min. color
McG-H	*The Changing Forest*	19 min. color
	Environment and Survival: Life in a Trout Stream	10 min. color
	Sea Otters of Amchitka	45 min. color
SC	*Glen Canyon*	29 min. color
EB	*Succession from Sand Dune to Forest*	16 min. b/w

FILM DISTRIBUTORS

Most of these films are distributed by EMC, AVC, and others in addition to the listed distributors. The list which follows is far from exhaustive.

AVC   Audio-Visual Center
             Indiana University
             Bloomington, Indiana 47401
BBC   British Broadcasting Corp.
                 Films available in U.S. from:
                     Peter M. Robeck & Co.
                     230 Park Avenue
                     New York, New York 10017
EB   Encyclopedia Britannica Educational Corp.
                 They have 12 district offices serving differ-
                 ent regions of the U.S. The home office is:
                     425 N. Michigan Avenue
                     Chicago, Illinois 60611
                     (312)321-6800
EMC   Extension Media Center
             University of California
             Berkeley, California 94720
             (415)642-0460
McG-H   McGraw-Hill Films/Contemporary Films
CF   East: Princeton Road
                     Hightstown, New Jersey 08520
                     (609)448-1700
                 Midwest: 828 Custer Avenue
                     Evanston, Illinois 60202
                     (312)869-5010

West: 1714 Stockton St.
San Francisco California 94133
National Audubon Society
Film Department
1130 Fifth Avenue
New York, New York 10028
National Film Board of Canada
Suite 819
680 Fifth Avenue
New York, New York 10019

SC   Sierra Club Films
Available from:
Association Films
25358 Cypress Avenue
Hayward, California 94544
Stuart Finley, Inc. (Films on water pollution)
3428 Mansfield Road
Falls Church, Virginia, 22041
Citizenship-Legislative Department

OCA   Oil, Chemical and Atomic Workers
International Union
1126 16th Street, N.W.
Washington, D.C. 20036

ADF   American Documentary Films
East: 336 W. 84th Street
New York, New York 10024
West: 379 Bay Street
San Francisco, California 94133

Membership Application
for Zero Population Growth

ZERO POPULATION GROWTH is a political action organization whose purpose is to bring about population stability in the United States by 1980 through public education and political action.

ZPG has chapters throughout the United States. These local units are an effective and independent force working toward the common goal on national and local fronts. ZPG's effort will be concentrated in political lobbying and campaigning. To back the Washington activities, there must be a large and vital grassroots structure. A Congressman will listen more carefully to ZPG lobbyists if he is getting mail from home on the population issue. To join ZPG and receive the monthy Newsletter, fill out this form and return to:

Zero Population Growth
367 State Street
Los Altos, California 94022

Name_____

Address_____
                Street   City   State   Zip

General $10 annually
Student· $4
Donor· $20
Patron: $120

FRIENDS OF THE EARTH organized for the survival of life on Earth. We see the entire Earth as one ecosphere, to restore and preserve: restore the major portion misused by man; preserve the remaining wilderness where the life force continues to flow freely.

We are a non-profit membership organization streamlined for aggressive political and legislative activity. We have chosen to be neither tax-deductible nor tax-exempt in order to fight without restrictions.

Your participation is essential! Yes, we need your financial and moral support. But more than that, we need you to wage your own fight within your own ecosystem, and to discover and implement local solutions to the environmental crisis. We'll help you in your efforts and rely on your assistance in our national and regional projects, but we're counting on you to be self-generating and self-sustaining.

For our part, we have organized a League of Conservation Voters as our political arm. Task forces and committees will be organized around specific issues and functioning with your manpower. Believing that an informed public is the best defense against environmental outrages, we are developing means to get the word out, like our arrangement with the John Muir Institute, McCall Publishing Company and Ballantine Books to publish books on environmental problems.

Why not have a hand in shaping the world you'll inherit? The choice exists. Make it.

F.O.E. Membership: Regular, $15; Spouse, $5; Student, $5; Supporting, $25. Contributing, $50; Life, $250.

Name ....Street.................

City ....State........ZIP.......Date.......

☐ Please send me more information on FRIENDS OF THE EARTH.

☐ Can't wait for more information. My check or money order for $........ is enclosed; sign me up as a member of F.O.E.

Friends of the Earth
30 East 42nd St.
New York, N. Y. 10017
Contributions to Friends of the Earth are *not* tax-deductible.

Eco-Notes

from Chicago Sun Times, *Oct. 20, 1969, p. 67*

Happy Cleaner Air Week to Mayor Daley and His Friends

Happy Cleaner Air Week, Mayor Daley! Four months ago the Mayor personally sponsored the extension of a fuel conversion deadline, thereby guaranteeing Chicago at least one more year of highly polluted air.

Happy Cleaner Air Week, Robert Lundberg! Mr. Lundberg has been appointed Chairman of Cleaner Air Week. He also happens to be an executive with Commonwealth Edison, perhaps the worst polluter of Chicago's air.

Happy Cleaner Air Week, James O'Donohue! Mr. O'Donohue is Chairman of the Air Pollution Control Appeal Board, the group responsible for granting time extensions for compliance with anti-pollution laws. Mr. O'Donohue was appointed to this position by his wife's uncle, Richard J. Daley.

Happy Cleaner Air Week, Morgan O'Connell! Mr. O'Connell, an obstetrician, is the medical expert on pollution on the Air Pollution Control Appeal Board. He was appointed to this position by the husband of one of his former obstetrical patients. Her name: Mrs. Richard J. Daley.

Happy Cleaner Air Week, Paul Angle! Mr. Angle, third member of the Appeal Board, is a fine, upstanding citizen with no known conflict of interest in the area of pollution. Too bad he hasn't had more influence on his brother, the Vice President in charge of Operations for U.S. Steel, one of the worst polluters of Chicago's air and water.

Happy Cleaner Air Week, H. William Campbell! Mr. Campbell, the fourth member of the Appeal Board, is Manager of Witco Chemical Company. Not only is Witco a significant contributor to Chicago's air pollution, they happen to manufacture a line of industrial cleaners, necessary to clean up the results of the pollution they and others help cause.

Happy Cleaner Air Week, John Brady! Mr. Brady, the fifth member of the Appeal Board, is First Vice President of the International Union of Operating Engineers—the men in charge of maintaining and operating boilers and heating plants. A major breakthrough in pollution technology might reduce the number of operating engineers.

Happy Cleaner Air Week, Arthur Schoenstadt! Mr. Schoenstadt is an elderly retired millionaire. Wouldn't it be nice if the sixth and final place on the Appeal Board were filled by someone who wasn't an elderly retired millionaire?

Happy Cleaner Air Week, Tom Ward! Mr. Ward is handling public relations for Cleaner Air Week. He also handles public relations for U.S. Steel, one of the major polluters of Chicago's air and water.

Happy Cleaner Air Week, People of Chicago! Perhaps unbeknownst to the above gentlemen, we have the 2nd worst air pollution of any city in the United States. So they're having a Cleaner Air Rally at the Civic Center Plaza tomorrow morning at 10, complete with Jackie Chuckro (Miss Cleaner Air Week) and fifteen neighborhood tots, who will release dozens of symbolic balloons into our lovely air.

Mr. Nixon:

You have called for an all out attack on the pollution problems facing us. We urge you to act now to stop the SST. At a time when our money is needed to pay for cleaning up the environment we don't need to spend millions to create the biggest noise polluter yet devised by man.

If the British-French Concorde or the Russian TU-144 go into comemrcial use, it is they, and not us who will be considered the destroyers of peace and quiet for the convenience of a few.

	Signatures of five friends:
Send to: President Nixon	_____
c/o Friends of the Earth	_____
30 East 42nd St.	_____
New York, N.Y. 10017	_____
	_____

We urge you to take action immediately.

Stop the U.S. SST program now and shift the talent and funds to something useful like urban transit.

Press for legislation forbidding the use of the airports and airspace of the United States by the SST's of any nation.

Mr. Nixon:

Population

In order to maintain the quality of life in the developed countries, prevent famine and plague in the underdeveloped nations, and avoid ecocatastrophe, the world's population must be stabilized.

We insist that:

You declare a "state of environmental emergency" and proclaim a national policy of immediately stabilizing this nation's population as an example to the rest of the world.

1. The Federal Government must provide sufficient funds for all necessary research and the facilities to insure that birth control and abortions are available to all who want them.

2. The population problem is more serious than any other problem, therefore, at least 10% of the defense budget must be allocated to birth control and abortion in the U.S. and abroad.

Send to: President Nixon
c/o Friends of the Earth
30 East 42nd Street
New York, N.Y. 10017

_____

(Signature)

Contributors

KENNETH E. BOULDING was professor of Economics at the University of Michigan. Presently, he is with the Institute for the Behavioral Sciences at the University of Colorado at Boulder. He is author of *The Meaning of the Twentieth Century*.

JON BRESLAW is a graduate student in the department of Economics at the University of California, Berkeley.

DAVID BROWER has been active in conservation work since 1933. He is a member and director of many organizations devoted to conservation and preservation. He was the Sierra Club's first Executive Director; he conceived and edited The Sierra Club Exhibit Format Series of books. Mr. Brower is President of the Friends of the Earth, which he founded in 1969, and is Director of the John Muir Institute.

KENNETH BROWER is a free lance writer who recently edited *Galapagos*, a two-volume book in the Sierra Club Exhibit Format Series.

KENNETH P. CANTOR holds a doctoral degree in Biophysics from the University of California, Berkeley. He is presently devoting full time to writing, speaking and co-ordinating activities related to the ecological crisis.

GARRETT DE BELL received a B.S. in Biology from Stanford University in 1966. He was a candidate for the doctoral degree in Zoology at the University of California, Berkeley, but dropped out to devote full time to ecological problems, which he feels are too important to be left to overspecialized and irrelevant universities.

RENÉ DUBOS is a professor at the Rockefeller University in New York City. He has done research in microbiology and pathology for many years, and has published many noteworthy books, including his most recent, *So Human an Animal*.

MARION EDEY is with the League of Conservation Voters, Washington, D.C.

PAUL R. EHRLICH is professor and Director of Graduate Study in the department of Biological Sciences at Stanford University. Widely known for his studies and publications in the field of biology, he is one of the leading advocates of population control. His controversial and bestselling book, *The Popu-*

lation Bomb, has lead to hundreds of requests for lectures and two appearances on "The Tonight Show."

JOHN FISCHER is a contributing editor for *Harper's* Magazine. He does the regular feature. *The Easy Chair,* and is the author of several books.

JOHN W. GARDNER, former Secretary of Health, Education and Welfare, is author of numerous books. He now heads the Urban Coalition in Washington, D.C.

GARRETT HARDIN is professor of Biology at the University of California, Santa Barbara, and is author of *Population, Evolution and Birth Control.*

JERRY MANDER is President of Freeman, Mander & Gossage advertising agency in San Francisco. He wrote the Sierra Club advertisements, which are credited with saving the Grand Canyon, and also the widely-praised "Earth National Park" advertisement.

WESLEY MARX is a free-lance writer. His articles on conservation, natural history and public affairs have appeared in various national magazines. Mr. Marx's book, *The Frail Ocean,* provides a powerful statement of the need to protect our planet.

LEWIS MUMFORD, noted architectural and social critic, is author of numerous, widely-read books. He received the National Book Award for *The City in History*. Currently, he is writing a book which deals with the myth of the machine.

BARBARA PARKER is active with the Berkeley Ecology Center in a number of capacities. She speaks to groups, helps neighborhood action groups get organized, and works on programs with the news media.

MICHAEL PERELMAN is a doctoral candidate in Agricultural Economics at the University of California, Berkeley, and works with Berkeley Ecology Action.

PEOPLE'S ARCHITECTURE is an association of drop-out architects and environmentalists who sponsor youth club paper drives, better landlord relations, city ordinance enforcement of leash laws and other clean-up campaigns.

ROBERT RIENOW is professor of Political Science at the Graduate School of Public Affairs, State University of New York. Through long associations with conservation movements, he has brought an ecological orientation to his writings and work in the field of government and public affairs. His wife, Leona, has collaborated with him on several books, and is an author in her own right. The Rienows live on a 138-acre farm. The farm had been exploited almost beyond repair, but due to the Rienows' conscientious reclamation program, it is today an ecological showplace.

MAUREEN SHELTON is with the Ecology Information Group, Berkeley, California.

BRENN STILLEY is a writer and editor for the Berkeley Ecology Center.

THOMAS TURNER received a B.A. in Political Science from the University of California, Berkeley. After two years in the Peace Corps in Turkey, and a year with the Sierra Club, he joined David Brower at Friends of the Earth.

HARRISON WELLFORD works with Ralph Nader in the field of consumer affairs, and with the Center for Study of Responsive Law in Washington.

LYNN WHITE, JR. is professor of History a the University of California, Los Angeles. He was formerly the President of Mills College. He has received the Guggenheim Fellowship, among other awards, for his work in History. He is the author of numerous books; the most recent is *Machina Ex Deo*.

STEVEN WODKA is a student at Antioch College, Yellow Springs, Ohio, and is currently researching the occupational health problems of the members of the Oil. Chemical and Atomic Workers International Union. In the past year he has worked for the United Farm Workers Organizing Committee in Delano, California.

Many short pieces are included in the Chapter on Eco-tactics. Authors include: Cliff Humphrey, of Berkeley Ecology Action; Allan Berube and others, of Boston Ecology Action; Ruthann Corwin, of Berkeley Active Conservation Tactics; Claire Boissevain and Jim Harding, of Cubberley High School, Palo Alto, California; Joan McIntyre of Friends of the Earth; Keith Murray, an Ecologist with Berkeley Ecology Center, and Gary C. Smith.

Index

364

A powerful, provocative book
for those who care about
what tomorrow might bring . . .

Moment in
the Sun

Robert and Leona Train Rienow

A report on the Deteriorating Quality
of the American Environment

"A VERY IMPORTANT BOOK . . . We've been
told for some years now that the wide open spaces are
getting narrower all the time, and quicker than some of
us might think. The authors of this book lay it right on
the line . . . after reading this sane and humane book,
one wants to plead with everybody to keep aware, and
not regard these things as part of some inevitable black
comedy."

—*Harper's Magazine*

A Sierra Club-Ballantine Book   95¢

To order by mail, enclose price of book plus 5¢ a copy
for handling and send to Dept. CS, Ballantine Books,
36 West 20th Street, New York, N.Y. 10003.